YOUNG ADULT MINISTRY

By Terry Hershey

Group®
Books

Loveland, Colorado

Young Adult Ministry

Edited by Cindy S. Hansen
Designed by Jean Bruns
Cover design by RoseAnne Buerge

Scripture quotations are from the Revised Standard Version of the Bible, copyrighted 1946, 1952, © 1971, 1973. Used with permission.

Library of Congress Cataloging-in-Publication Data

Hershey, Terry.
  Young adult ministry.
  Bibliography: p.
  1. Church work with young adults. I. Title

BV4446.H47 1986   259'.2   86-3103
ISBN 0-931529-08-5

19 18 17 16 15 14 13 12 11
04 03 02 01 00 99 98 97 96

Printed in the United States of America.

To Rev. Robert Baker, pastor, friend and encourager.

SPECIAL THANKS TO

Norva, my wife, for her typing assistance and patience; for Group Books and their vision to begin a project aimed at young adult ministry; to Lee Sparks and Cindy Hansen for their careful editorial attention; to Rich Hurst and John Westfall for their collaboration on some principle concepts; and to young adults and young adult directors around the United States whose input proved invaluable for the book.

Contents

Why a Book on Young Adults?

You are about to embark on a challenging and rewarding journey: young adult ministry.

But let's be honest. It also will be sometimes frustrating, confusing and less than desirable. You may wonder if your commitment is worth the effort. You may wonder if the seeds you plant will ever see a harvest. And hopefully ... you will wonder how you were so fortunate to get involved in such a cutting-edge ministry for today's church.

Whatever your thoughts may be as you begin to read this book, welcome to young adult ministry. And for those of you who have been involved in young adult ministry for several years, thank you for paving the way.

Young adult ministry is nothing new—there always have been young adults. But until now, they have never been such a significant percentage of the adult population. The "baby-boomers" (those born between 1950 and 1960) have become adults. We're talking about almost 40 percent of the adult population. Combine that fact with the reality that most of the baby-boomers do not go to church. This is not to say young adults are not religious. On the contrary, statistics tell us that most hold traditional beliefs about God's existence. But church involvement—that is another story.

Why young adult ministry? Why a book on the subject? Is there such an "animal" as young adult ministry? It would help to begin with a definition. *Young adult ministry initially defines itself by one obvious distinction: its target population, namely adults between the ages of 18 and 35.* Some expand those parameters; others narrow the parameters. Nonetheless, we begin by defining young adult ministry as an age grouping.

The difficulty in young adult ministry as a category arises when we look at the different life settings that exist in that one age grouping:

- •single, career-oriented persons
- •college and graduate students
- •newlyweds
- •parents with young children
- •divorced persons
- •single parents

Where do we even begin to develop a young adult ministry or enhance a struggling one? With so many differences in the age grouping, it's hard to know what to do or where to turn. We'll take "first things first" and begin with some assumptions:

1. Young adult ministry cannot be contained in one central young adult program. Because young adults have a variety of social needs, any young adult program can only touch a portion of those needs. That fact must be understood as we begin to build a ministry. Not all young adults will be ministered to through a group or a specific young adult program. *Young adult ministry must include "target programs" aimed at specific needs in the young adult population of your church.*

2. Not all churches are called to create a young adult group or program, but all churches are called to minister with young adults. This is a vital distinction. No church is exempt from ministry with young adults. The question is not, "Do we want to minister to young adults?" But, "In what ways can we *best* minister to young adults?" and "How well are we meeting the young adults' needs?" Programs are born out of congregations where there is a foundational heart for ministry.

I hope this book helps shape a philosophy of ministry that touches the real needs of the baby-boomers in your congregation. Although you may not have the "biggest" or "best" young adult group of any church in your city, a solid philosophy will motivate your church to see lives changed and molded and used by God.

3. Young adult ministry is not synonymous with youth ministry. We're not building an extension to the high school and college group. Granted, many churches program for college or career adults by forming a group for people ages 17 to 25. While it is true that such a group is ministering to young adults as defined earlier, there are some differences.

Sometimes the church incorrectly perceives that youth programming is to "occupy teenagers' growing-up years until they become adults and settle down." Youth ministry is building relationships with young people to help them with the *unique* needs of their age. Young adults have entirely different needs. If we program for young adults the same way we program for teenagers, we miss the target. We would not build maturity—we would perpetuate youth.

Young adult ministry assumes that we are working with adults. That will have definite implications in giving away responsibility, in our view of leadership, and in our focus of programming.

4. Young adult ministry is not synonymous with single adult ministry. Granted, many adults between the ages of 18 and 35 are single. And many churches who have a young adult ministry often structure it under the single adult ministry. I will not argue with that. But there are some observations that need to be made. First, when a church starts a "singles group" (for ages 20 to 60), the average age of adults that will come will be 42 to 45. The church wonders why single young adults do not attend. The reason is simple: There are significant differences between single adults under age 35 and single adults over age 35. There's nothing magical about 35, but the differences begin to show at about that age. Groups with older single adults will have a greater focus on "emergency room" ministry—divorce recovery, widow support groups, etc.

Second, most young single adults do not like to be called "single." Their preference is to focus on their careers or the development of their relationships. One young woman informed me, "You don't deserve the title 'single' until you pass the age of eligibility." Whether she's right is not the issue. The issue is that you cannot program effectively by perceiving young adults to be something they don't perceive themselves to be.

Third, the focus of developmental needs between young single adults and older single adults is significantly different. It is true that they carry the common factor of "singleness," but that is not a strong enough tie upon which to build an "all-age" singles group. This type of group has a tendency to focus on singleness and can become a pep rally for persons depressed by their "singleness"—attempting to declare the virtues of "one as a whole number.'

There's nothing wrong with that message; but it is not for young adults. They are not at a developmental stage where they need to recover some positive perspective on single life. For young adults, singleness is almost irrelevant. Building a healthy life is relevant.

Building healthy relationships is relevant. Becoming whole persons is relevant. Making wise choices is relevant. And finding a faith that works is relevant.

Whether you call a young adult group "young singles" or "young adults" is not the primary issue. Either name can work. The issue is the focus of your ministry and the needs at which you are aiming.

5. Young adult ministry can be an integrated ministry of single and married persons; but, it is not easy or likely. For the most part, young adults who marry begin the journey away from the young adult group toward a group consisting primarily of married persons. Many will remain in a young adult group for up to an average of 12 to 18 months and then move on. If a baby enters the picture, the departure is almost immediate. Their primary concern is for an environment that will help them become effective parents. "Successfully" integrated young adult groups find that 10 to 15 percent is a significant percentage of married persons.

Without question, I am in favor of integrated young adult groups, but the bottom line is that one need not feel ineffective if complete integration is not possible. There are other effective means of programming that create opportunities for integration; for example, couples' fellowship or premarital groups linked to the young adult group. Program ideas such as these will be discussed later in the book.

I hope this book pushes you in areas where you never have been pushed before. I hope you ask more questions than you have answers. I hope it opens you to a God who is able to do immeasurably more than you could ask, think or imagine.

I want us to be "ministering" in the true sense, not just directing programs. I want us to call forth potential in people who don't see it, set captives free, develop latent leadership and give people permission to receive Jesus' abundant life.

Read this book with an open mind. Be willing to see young adults for who *they* are. Be willing to ask hard questions about your motivation and focus. Be willing to look honestly at your church and ask about areas that need change and revision. Be willing to risk and try new ideas.

Don't feel overwhelmed by the changes necessary for your church; know that small change is growth. Jess Laird's humorous addage is apropos, "We're not well, but we're not as sick as we used to be." The secret is to begin where you are. Don't pretend your situation is better or worse than it really is. Begin slow, small and solid.

And see every *small step* as essential to growth.

The book is divided into three sections. To help you focus, let's walk through a general overview.

SECTION ONE: YOUNG ADULTS AND THE CHURCH

Young adults—who are we talking about? Never go hunting until you're sure you can recognize your target. *Effective ministry begins with effective homework.*

Where do we begin to understand the young adults of today? How has our culture influenced our young adults? Where are the pressure points? What does it take to create an effective ministry?

If we don't begin with these questions, we begin on the wrong road. Why? Because Jesus touched people the way they really were, not the way he hoped they would be or thought they should be. Let's let young adults speak for themselves and let's be willing to listen.

SECTION TWO: CREATING AN EFFECTIVE MODEL OF MINISTRY WITH YOUNG ADULTS

This section discusses the development of an "intentional ministry." Once we've done our homework, what are the preparations—both personal and congregational—that are necessary to minister effectively to young adults?

As we said earlier, all churches are not called to create a "group" for young adults, but all churches are called to minister to them. What is the foundation for that ministry? What are the preliminary questions? What are the steps that lead to effectiveness?

This section is essential. And it will be necessary to walk through it with others. (See How to Use This Book for further instructions.)

Section Two describes the tools necessary to make our theology practical. You cannot do ministry by assumption. It is necessary to know why you do what you do. Section Two teaches you how to develop a strategy, build leaders, target needs, and create an effective structure for ministry.

SECTION THREE: EFFECTIVE PROGRAMS

Based on the work of the first part of the book, Section Three fleshes out program ideas. What do effective programs look like?

As discussed later in the book, not all programs are created equal.

And, not all programs are transferable. But it is also true that the wheel doesn't need to be reinvented, just adjusted. Where have effective programs worked? Why have they worked? We'll look at some "field-tested" models. What about those that begin with a flurry and then die in 18 months to three years? Why burnout? How can we minister effectively so that our time and resources are most efficiently used?

I cannot guarantee that this book will be the cure-all for an ailing ministry or the magic elixir for a start-up ministry. But I will say: If your heart is in the right place, and if you're willing to learn; you will be surprised at the possibilities God has in store for you.

KEY POINTS

1. Young adult ministry cannot be contained in one central young adult program. It must include "target programs" aimed at specific needs in the young adult population.
2. Not all churches are called to create a young adult group or program, but all churches are called to minister with young adults.
3. Young adult ministry is not synonymous with youth ministry.
4. Young adult ministry is not synonymous with single adult ministry.
5. Young adult ministry can be an integrated ministry of single and married persons; but, it is not easy or likely.

How to Use
This Book

This book is designed to be a catalyst for discussion, a challenge to the status quo, an encouragement for the discouraged, and a stimulus for churches to dream bigger dreams for ministry with young adults. To get maximum benefit from this book, you must do more than read it. I recommend one (or all) of the following ideas:

FORM A MINISTRY DEVELOPMENT GROUP

This group of three to seven people will walk through the book with you. They can be your young adult ministry leadership team; they can be interested lay people in your church; they can be some of your young adults who want to see more happen with young adult ministry in your church. Most important, it is a group of people who are committed to brainstorming and implementing principles for effective young adult ministry in your church.

A group is important because it gives ownership of the ministry to many rather than just one or two. As a group, you commit to meeting for eight to 12 weeks. At each meeting, brainstorm the book material by going over the questions at the end of each chapter. Use the worksheets in Sections Two and Three to dream and develop ministry direction for your particular situation. Following is a sample eight-week agenda:

MINISTRY DEVELOPMENT GROUP

Week 1   Review through Chapter 2
Week 2   Review Chapters 3-4

Week 3	Review Chapters 5-6
Week 4	Review Chapters 7-8
Week 5	Review Chapters 9-10
Week 6	Review Chapters 11-12
Week 7	Review Chapters 13-14
Week 8	Review Chapters 15-16

PLAN A MINISTRY DEVELOPMENT RETREAT

Set aside two full days (Friday evening through Sunday noon) to walk through the book material. The retreat can work with anywhere from eight to 35 people. The agenda requires five 45-minute presentations from the book's material, followed by five 45-minute brainstorming group times. The retreat concludes with a "Dream Session." The purpose of the retreat is to bring as many people as feasible into the development process, and to walk away from the weekend with projections for implementation. Ideas. Goals. Direction.

Who do you take? Interested and committed young adults, young adult ministry leaders, committed lay persons. Following is a sample agenda for this retreat:

RETREAT AGENDA

Friday	6:00 p.m.	Registration
	7:45 p.m.	Session 1: "Overview and Purpose of Retreat"
	8:30 p.m.	Discussion:
		1. Image Inventory (see the following pages)
		2. Why are you here?
		3. What do you hope we accomplish?
	9:00 p.m.	Refreshments and Free Time
Saturday	9:00 a.m.	Session 2: "Young Adults: Who Are They?" (use Chapters 1-5)
	9:45 a.m.	Break
	10:00 a.m.	Discussion (use questions at end of Chapters 1-5)
	10:45 a.m.	Session 3: "Intentional Ministry: Building the Arrow" (use Chapters 6-8)

	11:30 a.m	Discussion (use questions at end of Chapters 6-8)

11:30 a.m Discussion (use questions at end of
                             Chapters 6-8)

12:15 p.m. Lunch

 1:30 p.m. Session 4: "Effective Leadership" (use Chapters 9-10)

 2:15 p.m. Discussion (use questions at end of Chapters 9-10)

 3:00 p.m. Free Time

 5:00 p.m. Dinner

 6:30 p.m. Session 5: "Making Our Ministry Work" (use Chapters 11-16)

 7:15 p.m. Discussion (use questions at end of Chapters 11-14)

 7:45 p.m. Dream Session (see pages 140-141)

 9:15 p.m. Refreshments

Sunday   9:30 a.m. Sunday Morning Service of Commitment

10:30 a.m. Communion

11:00 a.m. Brunch

HOST A STAFF BRAINSTORMING TIME

Walk through the material with the staff members of your church. If the senior pastor is involved, the process is enhanced.

Arrange to use part of the time during the regular staff meetings or specifically set aside a separate time for brainstorming. I recommend one lunch a week to brainstorm and plan. The purpose is to create a unified philosophy of ministry that will be reflected by the staff—and not just one "department" or one person.

TAKE AN "IMAGE INVENTORY"

The following inventory is most helpful when used with a ministry development team, a planning retreat or staff brainstorming session. Before moving into Section One, it is important for everyone to take the following inventory and discover our tendencies toward stereotypes and myths.

IMAGE INVENTORY

What one-word descriptions come to your mind when you hear the phrase "young adult"?

List them below:

_____   _____
_____   _____
_____   _____
_____   _____
_____   _____

IMAGE INVENTORY ASSESSMENT

When you have finished your inventory, look back over the word list. Eliminate the status-tied characteristics; for example, single, married, etc. How many of the remaining descriptions are negative? How many are positive?

What does that say about the foundation upon which we intend to build a ministry? Does our attitude affect ministry? In what ways? _____

It has been my experience that most churches and groups who complete this inventory have found 80 percent of their responses to be negative; for example, lonely, busy, apathetic, selfish, afraid, too much free time, over-sexed, non-committed, ingrown, materialistic.

Only 20 percent of responses include positive words such as potential, involved, opportunities, energy, leadership, hopeful, less anxiety, available.

What's the lesson? *An effective minister is a lifelong learner.* We must begin this book with an awareness of our tendencies toward stereotypes, myths and closemindedness. We must make a commitment to be willing to learn. To learn about young adults; to learn about ourselves and our call to ministry; and to learn about the "open doors" of ministry God is making available to those who say *yes* to his call to be a reflector of grace and Good News.

KEY POINTS

1. Form a ministry development group. Three to seven people to walk through the book with you.
2. Plan a ministry development retreat. Set aside two full days to go over the material.
3. Host a staff brainstorming time.

4. Take an "Image Inventory." Discover tendencies toward stereotypes and myths.
5. An effective minister is a lifelong learner.

Young
Adults
and the
Church

CHAPTER 1

Changing America

Thirty-three percent. That's the approximate percentage of the American population between the ages of 20 and 35 in the mid-1980s. That translates to 77 million people. By 1990 the number will increase to 37 percent.[1]

How has the church reacted to the "baby-boom" generation now that they've all grown up? At no other time in our history has the young adult population affected the culture so dramatically. Much of that effect can be directly attributed to sheer numbers. Each of us, after all, is a consumer. And there is no doubt that young adults comprise the most influential block of consumers.

Young adults. Who are they? What makes this generation so different? And where is the church positioned in relationship to such a large block of people? To understand young adults, it first is necessary to study adult development. Let's walk through an overview of the research provided by **The Seasons of a Man's Life** by Daniel Levinson and **Passages** by Gail Sheehy.

Building on the work of Erik Erikson, Levinson and Sheehy argue that human development does not end at age 18. In fact, Sheehy argues for "a new concept of adulthood, one that embraces the total life cycle .. If one sees the personality not as an apparatus that is essentially constructed by the time childhood is over, but as always in its essence developing, then life at 25 or 30 or at the gateway to middle age will stimulate its own intrigue, surprise, and exhilaration of discovery."[2]

If she's right (and I believe she is) then the young adult years hold particular intrigue in view of their vital foundation for our later adult years. This insight has definite impact on the church. We can no longer conveniently ignore the underlying issues young adults face, consciously or subconsciously biding time until they become "mature, contributing" church members.

Adult development can be divided into fairly predictable stages. And both Levinson and Sheehy refer to the stages between ages 18 and 35 as the "young adult years." In the next chapter, particular attention is given to the key issues, concerns, and tasks of those stages and how they relate to ministry needs. At this point, however, our concern is overview. To simplify our task, we will use Sheehy's terminology.

Why are we going to the trouble of beginning a ministry book from the context of development? Because it is necessary that we understand young adults, not as a generic term for "young people," but as a description for a range of persons sharing significant development issues. Here are Sheehy's descriptions:

AGES 18 TO 22: PULLING UP ROOTS

This age is characterized by the need to test authority, to launch out on the journey toward independence. We begin to seek for something significant on which we can build our identity—an identity "away from home." That something may be a peer group, a hero or role model, an ideology, or a cause (including rebellion). It is usually a stormy time, though not necessarily volatile.[3]

AGES 22 TO 28: TRYING TWENTIES

Erik Erikson says that the key, most-important issue here is the development of intimacy. "I'm at the age where I'm realizing that I am an adult—or am expected to be. Now what do I do? Where do I go? What should I be?" These are the questions these people must answer.

In the Trying Twenties the tasks are "to shape a dream, the vision of ourselves which will generate energy, aliveness and hope. To prepare for a lifework. To find a mentor if possible. And to form the capacity for intimacy, without losing in the process whatever consistency of self we have thus far mustered."[4]

Consequently, the twenties give way to an inevitable tension. On the one hand, I am almost driven by what I "should" do to be okay, or successful or a tribute to my family name. On the other hand, I want to resist the sense of being "locked in"—sensing that my course is set before I ever turn 30. Sheehy observes, "Although the choices of our twenties are not inevitable, they do set in motion a life pattern."[5]

The Trying Twenties are the time for us to erect a "life structure," a foundation from which our values about life, relationships, work, God and play are formed. Such a structure is not indelibly imprinted as Sheehy noted. But now is the time for making commitments and testing relationships. Will we avoid relationships? Will we choose hostility in order to be secure? Will we risk? Where will we turn for our authority structure? What role will the church play in our Trying Twenties?

AGES 28 TO 32: CATCH 30

About age 27 or 28 we begin to walk through a transition—not dissimilar to the mid-life transition faced at age 40. It is a time of questioning. Life is upon us. "Age 30 is here. Where am I? Have my choices been good ones? Am I stuck?"

As Sheehy points out, "Important new choices must be made, and commitments altered or deepened. The work involves great change, turmoil, and often crisis—a simultaneous feeling of rock bottom and the urge to burst out."[6]

Those who are still single feel the pressure of the inevitable questions: "Is marriage ever 'in the cards' for me?" "Am I too old yet?" And there are also the nagging questions regarding career development, "Should I give up my career and work on relationships or can I possibly do both?" Those who were married young are facing a not-so-small crisis regarding their own future. Major questions about the satisfaction of the relationship keep lingering. There's a feeling of discontent. "Is this all there is?" "Is the grass greener for my friends who waited to marry?" And with the "biological time clock" ticking away, the questions about children automatically surface. Although the questions are more related to those married, it is growing more common to find single persons pursuing options for parenting—especially when they see no significant marital hopefuls on their horizon.

Catch 30. Is the church providing an environment of encouragement, or discouragement, for the pursuit of such questions?

AGES 32-PLUS: ROOTING AND EXTENDING

By the time one reaches age 35, fundamental life commitments have been made. It is now time to work on developing those commitments. In Levinson's words, "The young adult years have ended, the adult years have begun, and mid-life is upon us."[7] While it is true that many people attempt to extend their youth as long as possible, the reality is undeniable: It is time to begin to make good on the commitments I made during my young adult years.

Young adults—from 18-year-old coeds to 33-year-old single parents ... from a 31-year-old career single woman to a 23-year-old newlywed ... from a 28-year-old, well-adjusted, single-by-choice young man to a 26-year-old discouraged, anxious, single-by-default young woman ... from a 27-year-old couple with two children to a 31-year-old couple with no children by choice. Young adults—the challenge for the church in this decade.

There is no doubt that the young adults of today have a much different look than the young adults of even 12 to 15 years ago. The changes in many cases are dramatic and make a significant social commentary—of necessity affecting the way we as the Christian church should relate to these unfolding developments and needs. In order to better understand, let's look at some of the areas of dramatic change.

MARITAL STATUS

There is no doubt that marriage is not on the decline. But the age for marriage has seen a sharp rise. In 1950, 24.8 percent of people age 20 to 34 were single. In 1983, however, 38.2 percent were single. The impact can be seen on our culture as a whole. We now live in a nation where almost 48 percent of all adults are single. And 54 percent of the single adults have never been married. The age of first marriages has increased by 2.5 years since 1970.[8]

As a corollary, married couples are having fewer children. For women age 30 to 34, the rate of birth per 1,000 women dropped from 152.5 in 1950 to 96.7 in the early '80s.[9]

EDUCATION

Twenty-five percent of Americans between 25 and 35 have college degrees. That compares to nine percent of people over 65.[10] Young adults of this generation have the highest levels of education of any generation in the history of this country, with an average of 12.8 years of school completed. That compares to 11.5 in 1950.

The educational surge is especially felt among women. College enrollment among women age 25 to 34 tripled between 1970 and 1982. The number of completed degrees among the same group doubled. The outcome is a new educational sophistication. We will have to ask the question whether that affects the way we teach young adults in our churches.

AFFLUENCE

I have more, make more, and spend more money than my parents did at my age. In 1985, the average household income for people between 25 and 34 was $22,776 compared with only $15,850 in 1983 dollars for households in that age group in 1953.[11]

Is it any wonder that Madison Avenue aims its media guns at the young adult target? Is there any question that the young adult is the new consumer? The issue has, or course, been fueled by all the media concern over the "yuppie generation." In Newsweek's opinion, "The young urban professionals have arrived. They're making lots of money, spending it conspicuously and switching political candidates like they test cuisines."[12]

It is, of course, very unfair to stereotype all young adults as yuppies. For by definition a yuppie is a young adult who makes at least $40,000. This only comprises about 4 million Americans; a far cry from the majority of young adults. One wonders whether "yuppies" actually exist. But the presence of yuppie values is a symptom of our affluent culture. In fact, more than 60 percent of adults age 25 to 34 are homeowners.[13]

The irony is that our affluence has only served to intensify our financial worries and insecurity. A generation with more than ever, but enjoying it less and less.

Added to this new affluence is the impact of young adult women on the work force—from 34 percent in 1950 to 69 percent in 1983. Careers have become a legitimate life choice. How does this affect relationships, marriage and family issues?

CHURCH INVOLVEMENT

More disturbing than the above statistics is the fact that young adults continue to express their attitudes toward the church most conspicuously by their absence. In an article in the Orange County Register (a southern California newspaper), a reporter gave the sobering conclusion to a nationwide Gallup poll on religion. "Religion's importance in everyday life increases with age—the strongest believers are 55 and older."[14]

It is necessary for us to understand the relevance of these facts if we are to embark on an effective ministry with young adults—a population that mostly avoids and ignores church. In 1958 almost 50 percent of adults under 30 attended church. By 1980, the number dropped to 30 percent. The percentage of persons over age 50 who attended church stayed relatively the same over the span of 22 years.[15]

The Alban Institute, a research group in Washington, D.C., has provided helpful research on young adults and the church. In a survey with young adults that traced one's "church involvement journey," the Alban Institute found that, "A period of intense involvement followed by burnout, and a re-evaluation of involvement in the early thirties is not uncommon for those who find their way into congregational life."[16]

Why the dropout rate? Why the decline in overall involvement? Some of the answers received don't sound that different from those our parents may have used:

"I've had a bad experience with organized religion."

"Christians are hypocrites."

"The church is just a ceremony."

"I was turned off by evangelism."

"When the time is right, I'll go."

While such comments may be true, I doubt that they provide the fundamental reason for the slide in attendance among young adults. Our culture is rapidly changing, and organized religion is paying a price in members. Young adults as a whole are more educated and sophisticated. Fearing the ultimate questioning of church doctrine and convictions of moral practice, the church avoids encouraging young adults to use their intellectual struggle. The result? Young adults who have no time for what they see as non-relevant religious platitudes.

Another reason for declining church attendance is the impact of an increased affluence. Martin Marty observed that "lifestyle is the main factor in determining who goes to church, and the country's 'yuppie' lifestyle isn't a churchgoing lifestyle."[17]

Marty is not suggesting that all young adults are "yuppies." Thanks to the pervasive presence of media, we live in a culture that has been saturated with the values that say we need to consume, achieve and "have it all."

A third reason for the drop in church attendance is increased mobility. Almost 50 percent of young adults move on an average of once per year. It is no wonder that there is a reluctance to sink roots into a church community that may only be available for a year. I often hear young adults refer to the time when they "hope to settle into a church that they enjoy." In the meantime, with little time available and "things" that need to get done, church becomes an occasional experience.

Unfortunately, churches have traditionally not positioned themselves to be helpful to people in transition. Consequently, we've not only missed the boat, we've missed it long after it left the port for open seas. Perhaps we have contributed to the phenomenon of young adult mobility. Can the church learn to touch young adults in the midst of mobility?

A fourth reason for the attendance decline may be the church's attitude regarding evangelism. There are two unhealthy extremes. One is the laissez faire, "We've got what you need. Come and get it." With such an attitude, it is easy to criticize young adults because they don't ever seem to show the commitment to "take us up on the great offer." And those who do come are the visibly needy, and we can find no neutral ground. The other extreme is to join the ranks of the majority of social institutions and become a merchandiser. "Step right up. We've got what you need here. And the first 10 receive a free ..." Can evangelism be reduced to a better brand of entertainment? Is hype necessary to build ministry?

A fifth reason for the drop in attendance is the result of our own self-fulfilling prophecy. Our stereotypes only reinforce themselves and promote distance. Far too many church leaders attribute non-church attendance to laziness, lack of belief, self-centered behavior, or a failure of parents to inculcate a sense of duty.[18] We reap what we sow.

It is time to take an inventory. Based upon what you have just read, are you hopeful for the opportunities of ministry with young adults? Are you excited about what the next 12 months will hold for you and your ministry opportunities?

Many people read what has been written and respond with discouragement. Still others, who do not see statistics and trends as particularly relevant, turn immediately to Section Three of this book hoping to find a "cure-all" program that will magically remedy the decline of interest. They have missed the point.

Rather than discouragement or apathy, I see hope. Never before has there been such a vast resource of untapped leadership ability. Young adults are not only tomorrow's church; young adults are today's church. The potential is unlimited.

KEY POINTS

1. According to Gail Sheehy, young adults constitute a range of persons sharing significant development issues. Here are the descriptions:
   - Ages 18 to 22: Pulling Up Roots
   - Ages 22 to 28: Trying Twenties
   - Ages 28 to 32: Catch 30
   - Ages 32-Plus: Rooting and Extending
2. We now live in a nation where almost *one-half* of all adults are single.
3. Twenty-five percent of Americans between 25 and 35 have college degrees.
4. Careers have become a legitimate life choice.
5. Young adults continue to express their attitudes toward church most conspicuously by their absence and disinterest.

REVIEW QUESTIONS

1. Does it make sense to look at young adults through Gail Sheehy's adult development stages? Is it helpful to you? Why or why not?
2. Did any of the statistics surprise you? Which ones? Why?
3. What percentage of adults attending your church are between the ages of 20 and 35?
4. Five reasons for declining church attendance were discussed. Do you have any to add?

   Which of the five most effect your church?

   What should be the church's response?

5. After reading this chapter, how would you describe your attitude toward young adult ministry in your church?

CHAPTER 2

A Cultural Backdrop

And they went away in the boat to a lonely place by themselves. Now many saw them going, and knew them, and they ran there on foot from all the towns, and got there ahead of them. As he went ashore he saw a great throng, and he had compassion on them, because they were like sheep without a shepherd; and he began to teach them many things (Mark 6:32-34).

Jesus' compassion led him to action. He did something with his compassion. He taught. He fed. His actions, however, were not arbitrary. They were aimed at specific needs. It is clear that Jesus addressed the people where they were. His compassion touched *real* people, with *real* needs, in *specific* situations. Jesus *knew* the people to whom he was ministering. The same must be true for us in young adult ministry. *The effectiveness of our ministry is tied to a clear understanding of the needs of those to whom we are called to minister.*

Earlier in this book, you took a personal "stereotype inventory." Do you remember what you wrote? Do you still agree with your original observations? Are you seeing young adults accurately? In order to be truly effective in our ministry, we must understand the needs of young adults. Stereotypes and misconceptions can cloud our understanding.

It has become common information that the church is usually 10 to 20 years behind the culture in responding to societal trends. Why is that? And are we following the same pattern relative to young adults? Is it possible for us to change this pattern and set the pace toward effective ministry with young adults? To do that, it means becoming serious about our role as "social critics." It means looking with a realistic eye at the trends, movements and belief systems which are shaping the next generation. The Gospel becomes the Good News when it touches real needs. Could our ineffective programming with young adults be tied to our misunderstanding of them and their world? There are three significant aspects that influence young adults and their world. Let's look at them together to gain a better understanding:

•**The cultural backdrop.** Into what kind of culture have our young adults been raised? What are the influences that made them who they are today? This chapter highlights in detail the cultural backdrop of today's young adults.

•**The pressure points.** What are issues of concern for young adults? Where are the areas of negative pressure? Pressure points affecting young adults will be discussed in the following chapter.

•**Coping mechanisms.** How are young adults responding? How do young adults face the world in which they live? What are the consequences of a pressure-cooker world? Coping mechanisms also are discussed in the following chapter.

It cannot be "business as usual" in the church. Our world is changing too rapidly; it affects the people with whom we minister and the way they receive the Gospel message. Can we learn something about ministry by a serious reflection of the culture around us? The answer must be yes. For young adults are a reflection of the society in which they were raised. And a ministry to the whole person cannot assume that an individual can be removed from his or her background and culture. How has that culture influenced young adults?

WE ARE A "POSTPONING" GENERATION

Our world is larger than ever. Airline travel is no longer a novelty, but a necessity. World travels are easily a topic of routine conversation. The choices before us are unlimited in jobs, schools, degree programs, automobiles, home entertainment equipment, television stations, restaurants, clothing styles, magazines, music styles, churches, vacation opportunities, books and marriage partners.

The reality of increased mobility only serves to multiply the options before us. Young adults are able to move jobs, careers, homes and social environments with an uncharacteristic ease. It is a culture where 44 percent of those in their early twenties can expect to move once every year.[1]

This multitude of options has only served to create a young adult generation very cautious about commitments. Gail Sheehy observes:

> The response of many of today's young men and women to the pressure to make decisions about the future is—not to. The most notable characteristic of the post-counterculture generation is that both men and women are postponing the major commitments of life. Faced with decisions usually made in the Trying Twenties—should I marry? Should I have children? Should I commit to this career path or that one?—the preferred decision among a large segment of educated young Americans is no decision at all. Put it off. Keep all the options open.[2]

Sheehy says the motto of our new freewheelers is, "Don't lock me in!" As a result, some of the decisions they are postponing will become "no's" by abstention. The pattern for this society in the last quarter of the century is one of people making few commitments of any kind.[3]

An ad for Michelob beer captures our generation's battle cry, "Who says you can't have it all?" The effect of our generation's battle cry is apparent by its consequences. The first is boredom. In a culture with so many choices, why are we so bored? A social researcher in Newsweek says, "This generation [of young adults] is very bored. That's why you have things like restaurant madness."[4] Choices. Too many choices.

On the one hand, young adults are driven to achieve. On the other hand, young adults face the unpleasant reality that their new-found affluence is not capable of affording or supporting the expected lifestyle. "Few can afford to buy today the houses they grew up in; two children now come at the price of four; and the dual careers demand that the balancing act be done with one hand behind one's back."[5]

Another consequence of our postponing generation is a "wait-and-see" attitude. "Marriage with Susan would be okay, one 27-year-old man told me, "but I don't want to close the doors yet. What if I make a mistake? There may be someone twice as good around the corner." He's right. There may be. (Although there might be someone "twice as good" for Susan, too.) And the product of our mobile, affluent culture is a "hold-out-until-all-of-your-options-are-in" stance toward life.

There are two immediate impacts that a "postponing" attitude has on church life and ministry. The first impact: Mobility is a fact for young adults. In that case, if you are easily bothered by mobility, transiency, turnover and transition, then ministry with young adults is not for you. It will not be long before you will be frustrated and resentful. Our frustration only serves to breed the second effect. We make the mistake of addressing a symptom: "These young adults are so non-committal! You can't get the young adults to do anything!" Is that really the issue? Or are young adults merely reflecting the culture in which they were raised? And if the latter is the case, what is the church's role in creating an alternative environment? An environment where commitments can be made without being seen as a threat to one's identity and security.

The second impact is the lack of rootedness expressed by our young adults. This has been the first generation whose parents have been unable to pass on family and traditional values due to geographic distance. Young adults move away from home early—and stay away. That in itself is not negative, but it does have an impact. Young adults find themselves without a community and looking for a place that can provide meaning. "Most young people search avidly for a cause greater than themselves, in the service of which it will make sense to be an adult."[6] "But," say most, "that cause can wait until I'm settled."

WE ARE IN AN ERA OF SELF-PROTECTION

One of the natural outworkings of young adult development is the need to find something in which to believe. The age in which we live makes that process increasingly more difficult. Only a superficial look at the last 25 to 40 years gives us a picture of increased suspicion and mistrust. And for good reasons. The world itself has been a pattern of self-destruction. All of our structures of hope have slowly crumbled or have been challenged, or have revealed clay feet. In Sheehy's words, the result was that:

> ...with the 1970s the young were washed back in the apathetic aftermath. No more utopias. Some observers say that as a result of their reduced hopes, college students today have a revived sense of optimism. It remains to be seen what or whom they will invent to put their faith in. The current ideology seems a mix of personal survivalism, revivalism and cynicism. Uppermost, once again, is the pragmatic—gaining skills as a means to a paying job.[7]

In a recent conversation with a professor at a large California state university, I asked about the "causes" that motivate the students of today. His response was immediate. "In the '60s and even '70s, we witnessed the obvious presence of a cause—be it anti-establishment, peace, anti-Vietnam or 'get high.' But now the 'cause' is pragmatism. What do I need to do to get the best opportunities for the best jobs?"

Self-preservation, indeed self-preoccupation, is a consequence of our age. Different from the "me generation" of the '70s, where the goal was self-actualization, the '80s have become the generation of self-preservation. Whereas the '70s found young adults risking reputation, friends and career on journeys to find themselves—via yoga, meditation, psychotherapy, T-groups, brief excursions out of the mainstream of society, back to the farms and into the woods—the '80s bring us a new cautious spirit. The selfishness now shows itself in a "state of transcendental acquisition, in which the perfection of their possessions enables them to rise above the messy turmoil of their emotional lives."[8]

As the conditions of the world grow worse, the natural inclination is to become more self-protective. And given our new affluence, it is not surprising.

What effect does such a pull toward self-protection have on young adults? The consequences are obvious. First, there's an increase in the anxiety or fear of the future. "Will I be able to raise a family in a safe world?" "Will I be able to find a spouse who will stay 'till death do us part'?" "Will my spouse and I be able to maintain this hectic career pace just to maintain our lifestyle?" "Is it possible to find a niche in such a dog-eat-dog world?"

Of the single young adults that I have talked with over the last three to five years, easily 75 to 85 percent have expressed a desire for marriage, while in the same breath adding that they didn't want "to get trapped," or end up "the same way my parents did." The result is an "I'll-play-it-safe" attitude.

In sharing this concern with a minister friend, he remarked, "I've never heard any of the young adults in our church expressing those fears or concerns." My response was immediate. "I believe you. We are not listening. Some reasons could be that your church may not allow an environment for such expression. Also, young adults' concerns are expressed in other ways, namely the obvious lifestyle of postponement, and the extreme caution shown in relational commitments."

As we talked, he said he understood what I was saying, but wished to think the young adults in his church were different.

It will become apparent when we talk about the role of the church, that a significant part of young adult ministry is in creating a healthy environment for dialogue, struggle and questioning. Ministry begins with listening.

Another obvious consequence of our self-protection is the cautious approach to relationships. Our need to avoid personal or relational tragedy too often leaves us immobilized, unable to make commitments. We may find a need to be "moralistic" about those who do fail in order to justify our own fear.

A recent article in the Los Angeles Times focused exactly on the reasons for cautious commitments:

> Relationships ... a need to give and a need to not be taken. And yet being human (and ever hopeful) we seek closeness with another person ...
>
> That we continue to isolate ourselves is not an act of cruelty or calculation, but one of fear ... And so we approach male-female relationships with the same expectations that we have of matters ruled by science and law. Then we recoil in anxiety when events aren't unraveling as we know they should ... The specter of these uncertainties turns us inward ...
>
> This is hardly a way to begin a union. And yet we do. To God, government or just one another, we enter the relationship with one foot on the boat, the other firmly on the pier, ready to jump upon first notice that the unionship is sinking. And of course, sink it eventually does. There's no voyage without a full crew ...
>
> Intimacy. In intimacy, we risk learning something heinous—that is, human, something that would bind us closer than could any shared joy. We instead opt for the sale surface and keep our conversations to what's in the news, or what's going on in our friends' convoluted lives—anything that keeps the self separate and therefore certain.
>
> Realtors call it "mingling."[9]

It is not that we need to look very far to find reason to justify our fear. In a world where approximately one in two marriages fail, there is a reason to take a second look. The casual attitude toward long-term relationships has affected us all. Sheehy touches this nerve in a story in her book **Pathfinders**: "Running into an old friend who had dropped out of sight when a lover she adored moved in, I asked how the relationship had turned out.

" 'Oh,' she said with a cavalier flick of the hand, 'just another one-decade stand.' "[10]

And the evidence against risking commitment continues to mount. A recent comic mirrored our approach to relationships. Sitting on a couch, a woman says to her boyfriend, "I know we seem perfect for each other, David, but let's check it with the computer just to make sure." Sheehy adds some more insight:

> As I got to know the young men I interviewed, I noticed something odd. Their posture was laid-back, but beneath the surface there was an edge. These pacesetters talk of a life suffused with the soft glow of nonstructured time and unlimited personal space, of loosely arranged but loving relationships, of the body as temple and the mind as instrument for their personal expressions. But beneath the rhetoric was the rigid success ethic instilled by their parents. These postponers seemed to be leaning against a velvet-sheathed sword. And underneath that edge, there was something else: a refusal to choose, to commit, to give up any pleasure for the pursuit of meaning and direction that might be more lasting.
>
> Although the lowest-well-being young professional men did not usually see themselves as longers, the sad echo throughout their self-descriptions was an impaired capacity to form friendships or to love. Some of them had prolonged ties to their parents, if not by living in the same house with them, then by remaining at least partially financially dependent. So bound were they emotionally that even if they tried, they could not achieve intimacy with anyone else.[11]

Churches only seem to add fuel to the fire. They—or should I say we—encourage young adults to "settle down and get married," without providing either an environment for healthy dialogue regarding relationships or a strong premarital or pre-engagement program where couples know they can get solid feedback on their situations. And there is an overwhelming absence of support structures for marriages and persons committed to long-term relationships.

Church leaders also have been reluctant to encourage healthy models for strong relationships. A healthy model would include honesty about real emotions and conflict resolution. Such honesty is considered by many to be "unspiritual." So for models in church, we see people with "we-never-have-any-problems" smiles.

It is true that it is easy to scapegoat the "church," but after all, we are talking about ways in which the church can become more effective in ministry with young adults. Scapegoating is not our desire—responsibility is our goal.

WE HAVE ENTERED THE BIOTECHNIC ERA

In this era:

•**Self-esteem is measured by performance.** While this may be no new revelation, it is of significant influence in the way the church approaches ministry. We're trained by our culture to be in control, get our act together, accumulate necessary trinkets on the road to "success." In short, we become somebody by what we do, not who we are. Are our churches any different?

The picture is one of a treadmill. In **Pathfinders,** one young adult describes her life plan:

> 'To run as hard as I can to get ahead of the game now, accumulate a terrific amount of expertise, cram three years of experience into a year and a half so that at my peak for attracting the best mate, I can get married and step off the treadmill and coast for a couple of years while I start a family. By then I'll have made myself so valuable that everyone will want me when I'm ready to come back.' She could regain her spot on the treadmill without having lost a beat.[12]

Newsweek adds the "testimony" of a 25-year-old young adult who likes condo ownership because, "It makes me feel smart and gives me more control over my life." (A life that sometimes seems to be moving very fast.) "I don't think earlier generations of young people were as consumed by time as we are," she says. "We seem to be moving every minute. If we lose our appointment books, we're through. Too often, we are so preoccupied with the destination, we forget the journey."[13]

•**We are defined by what we consume.** US News and World Report says, "By the end of the decade, baby-boomers will easily account for over half of all consumer expenditures."[14]

Robert Gribbon is helpful in clarifying this point.

> The baby-boomers were the first generation raised with television as its primary storyteller. TV did function as a socializing agent, transmitting a vision, but its primary purpose was to create a world into which individuals could fit by being consumers.[15]

If the church is not careful, it will simply become another commodity, or commodity dispenser. We do young adult ministry by the "shopping mall model." We provide a variety of alternatives to occupy a person's time, or to relieve a person's boredom. We treat people as consumers. "If you add this activity to your life, you'll be okay."

As our world changes, so does the context for effective ministry programs. Young adult ministry cannot develop under the declaration, "We've always done it this way before." Our ministry must be aimed at real people and at specific needs. Our ministry must be armed with intentions to create environments for wholeness.

KEY POINTS

1. The effectiveness of our ministry is tied to a clear understanding of the needs of those to whom we are called to minister.
2. It cannot be "business as usual" in the church. Our world is changing too rapidly.
3. We are a "postponing" generation.
4. We are in an era of self-protection.
5. We have entered the biotechnic era.
   •Self-esteem is measured by performance.
   •We are defined by what we consume.

REVIEW QUESTIONS

1. Do you agree with this statement? "The effectiveness of our ministry is tied to a clear understanding of the needs of those to whom we are called to minister." Why or why not?
2. How does our "postponing" generation affect young adults?
3. What are some of the ways "self-protection" shows itself in your own life?
4. Did anything in this chapter help you see young adults from a different perspective?
5. In what practical ways does the information in this chapter affect the church's role in ministry with young adults?

CHAPTER 3

Pressure Points and Coping Mechanisms

Ours is a unique time. Faster pace, greater options, increased mobility and more pressure than ever before.

Underneath the good-looking, healthy faces of today's young adults lie hearts made increasingly fragile by the pressures of our time. What are those pressure points? Where will the well-protected armor give way? Does the church have a role in confronting such pressure points? How do young adults face the world in which they live?

In my seminars on relationships I begin with the premise, "The first step of growth is honesty." The same holds true for ministry as well. If we wish to aim at real people, and touch real needs with the Good News, it is necessary to begin with an honest look at the pressure-cooker world we call home. The purpose of this chapter is not introspection or blaming, but understanding. And the truth we began with deserves repeating: *My effectiveness in ministry grows with my understanding of the target—young adults.* Following are some of today's pressures that young adults are facing, along with coping mechanisms and consequences to those pressures:

THE PRESSURE THAT IT IS NOT OKAY TO BE "JUST ORDINARY PEOPLE"

"She's the ultimate '80s woman—fit, trim, lively, independent, career minded," says Leslie Adisman, fashion editor of Seventeen magazine. "She's alone, no husband, no boyfriend, no children clinging to her."[1]

That's the picture Madison Avenue and the media give. Ordinary has become an indictment rather than a description. The media says,

"If you're living life right, you're in ecstasy most of the time."

The pressure is subtle, yet constant. Pressure increases with all of these thoughts: "Am I good enough?" "I'm in control. I can't let anyone know I'm not in control." "I need that job promotion desperately. With it comes respect." "Are you going skiing with us to Tahoe this year? Why not? Everybody's going."

We live in a world where more is never enough. Coping mechanisms and consequences are evident. We cannot be content, so we fantasize about those who do "arrive" by reading about lifestyles of rich and famous people; we sacrifice the values of our "ordinary life" of relationships, family and personal solitude to pursue the ecstasy that will let us "be somebody." And we complain to those around us that "life is not fair."

Listen to Rob Lewis, a 28-year-old attorney with Denver's largest law firm, who was quoted in Newsweek:

> Our professions have become very important to us and we're willing to perhaps sacrifice other things for them—marriages, families, free time, relaxation. Our marriages seem like mergers, our divorces like divestitures. (I have) gone through a number of important relationships which have failed because my commitment to my job was greater than my commitment to the relationship. If it was a tossup between getting the deal done and coming home for supper, the deal got done.[2]

In one of my seminars there was a young woman who was completing the sentence, "Life is _____." She really struggled to find the right word to describe life. She kept repeating, "Life is so ... Life is so ..." Finally, she blurted out, "Life is so *daily*." After we finished laughing, we realized how profound that statement was. For it is that very fact that causes me discomfort. Life *is* so daily. And because I cannot handle "ordinariness," I forsake life to pursue the call to be the "ultimate '80s man or woman."

Effective ministry can happen when we understand this pressure. Unfortunately, we are tempted to carry the pressure into the church. We have become the church of the "evangelical superstars." There is the pressure to look, act and talk "spiritual." We think that somehow God cannot handle it if we are normal.

That's not good. I talk with many young adults who mention this pressure when referring to reasons why they are not involved in church. "With all the pressure to succeed and be together in the world," said one young man, "I don't need that from the church too." I understand his point.

By the same token, there has been a positive backlash to this cultural pressure. A recent cover story in the Los Angeles Times was titled "Growing Number of Yuppies Show Preference for Downward Mobility." The article begins, "They have opted out of high-paying, high-stress careers."[3]

"Having it all" may turn out to be "having too much." We've already discovered that the era (or perhaps, media event) of the "yuppie" may be coming to an end. It does not take long for people to wonder whether the climb to the top was worth the climb.

There's a healthy, new willingness to redefine what we mean by success. And the church needs to be a part of that redefinition process.

THE PRESSURE TO BE SUPER-SEXED

Books, magazines and videos on technique and sexual expression line our newsstands and bookstore shelves. We have become technicians rather than lovers. Even with the emphasis on celibacy as a viable lifestyle and the epidemic occurrence of sexually transmitted diseases, there has been no drastic decrease in sexual activity among single persons. Statistics tell us that somewhere between 50 and 90 percent of single adults (depending on which survey you believe) maintain some form of an active sex life. In fact, 30 percent of divorced persons maintain an active sex life with their former spouse.[4] But statistics are not at issue here; the issue is direction.

How do we cope with a world bombarded by the reality of sex as a commodity? How does this pressure impact young adults? Can the church form an appropriate response? As one pastor expressed it to me in his straightforward way, "What can we do to make sure our young adults aren't jumping into bed with each other?" I had no answer for him then. I still don't. Because I don't believe sex is the issue. Identity is the issue. But we have made sexuality in the church an issue of behavioral chaperoning. To view issues of sexuality merely as behaviors which we must either stop or permit gives us a wrong perspective of ministry too. I find the church usually responding to the issue of sexuality in one of these three ways:

•**Silence.** "If we say nothing and pray, we can hope for the best." Besides, if we speak to the issue, we might show our ignorance! There is the assumption that dialogue encourages experimentation. Indeed, just the opposite is true! Lack of dialogue reinforces repression. And it is a psychological truth that what you repress owns you. There's no outlet from which we may receive perspective, understanding or direction.

•**Legalism.** This is the most popular response. It sets up the church, or pastor, as a moral police officer who gives public declaration about which behaviors are okay and which are wrong. As a single young adult I found myself looking for the pastor who allowed the things I wanted to do!

Legalism says that righteousness is based on what you don't do. We live to be exonerated by the rules. Legalism draws lines. It defines life by righteous limitations. When you cross the line, "You're bad." When you stay on this side of the line, "You're good." The question is not, "What is right?" but, "What can I get away with and still have it be God's will?" Ministers become police officers and Christians become expert lawyers, always seeking the necessary loophole. Legalism dehumanizes.

I attempted a legalism structure on sex for one group of young adults. There were two typical responses: They would do whatever they were told not to do and live with the guilt; or they would do all the right things, but for all the wrong reasons. That's when I began to realize that legalism doesn't start with the heart. It starts with a need to perform.

•**Ignoring it.** This approach takes the view, "It's their lifestyle, why should we bother? What's done in private is private." Our apathy only points to our own fear about our need to wrestle responsibly with our values, choices and relationships.

I believe that all three approaches are ineffective and ultimately oppressive, however, there *is* a fourth option.

•**Pro-life approach to sexuality.** Jesus came not just to "keep us from doing wrong," but to allow us to "live life to the fullest." He came to change the way we look at wholeness and righteousness. Wholeness begins in the heart. Pro-life morality changes the question from "what" to "why." Jesus focuses on the consequences and personal responsibility. The issue is on what happens to us as a result of our choices. "Rules break," Jesus is saying, "but people tear, and I don't want you to tear."

In fact, down deep, Jesus' concern is inherent in all of us. For every one of us is "looking for life." We live better lives when there is the presence of peace, nurture, wisdom and health. Pro-life says that when you foster those virtues, correct or righteous decision-making will be an automatic byproduct.

Pro-life is not easy to teach; and it is definitely not easy to practice. After doing a workshop for ministers on the issue of pro-life morality for young adults, there was a good deal of discomfort. "You have no right and wrong with your system," said one leader. "What if they still choose to go to bed with each other?" asked another. "How do we let them know it's wrong?"

I understand where the questions were coming from. But they missed the point. My concern as a minister or leader is not to keep my young adults "out of bed" or away from sex. With enough guilt I could do it—leading a group of people who do all the right things for all the wrong reasons. "Pharisaism" is what Jesus called it; and it kills like cancer.

My concern is to give young adults a place where they can be honest about the gift of their God-given sexuality. And to teach them and myself how to receive a love from God that is not based on performance, technique or righteous limitations. If God's unconditional love begins to "own me," it affects my decisions. "Jesus evidently didn't want people to neurotically concentrate on 'not sinning' but rather to focus on loving God and people."[5]

My focus is on wholeness, nurture and health. Now pro-life does not just apply to single persons, but to everyone. Because marriage does not guarantee that all my sexual behaviors are pro-life. It calls for personal responsibility.

Young adult ministry at its best is an environment that nurtures personal responsibility. How do we face the pressure of our super-sexed generation? We slowly learn to let God love us. Legalistic environments only reinforce the performance mentality that young adults live with daily in the world they encounter. The church must be different.

THE PRESSURES OF LONELINESS AND ISOLATION

"No man is an island," John Donne prophetically observed. He's right. We fear isolation above all else. And that fear is reinforced on a daily basis as we come in contact with an internal sense of "aloneness," (that nagging that rears its ugly head when we least expect it). For loneliness seizes me most acutely in a crowd. When I'm surrounded by laughing, confident people—all of whom, I'm sure, find life more appealing, enjoyable and purposeful. So I retreat in my silence. Or worse, I overcompensate with my wordiness and laughter.

Not everyone is willing to confess to a fear of loneliness. I've discovered a common response to questions of loneliness: "Lonely? Not very often. I've got too much to do to have time for loneliness." In our pressure-cooker performance culture, loneliness is seen as "failure" and something to be avoided at all costs. What exactly is loneliness? Andrew Greeley says:

> There are two kinds of loneliness that afflict human life. The first is the loneliness that comes from the human condition. It can be mitigated and alleviated but it cannot be eliminated. The other is the loneliness that we choose freely. It can always be conquered if we choose to do so.[6]

If we do not understand the first loneliness Greeley speaks of, we will not have an adequate response to the pressures that face young adults today. For above all else, loneliness is an indication of our incompleteness—of our brokenness. Such loneliness cannot be removed; in fact, must not be removed. For to come to terms with our incompleteness is to understand the confession necessary for ultimate healing. Henri Nouwen goes further to add:

> The Christian way of life does not take away our loneliness; it protects and cherishes it as a precious gift. Sometimes it seems as if we do everything possible to avoid the painful confrontation with our basic human loneliness, and allow ourselves to be trapped by false gods promising immediate satisfaction and quick relief. But perhaps the painful awareness of loneliness is an invitation to transcend our limitations and look beyond the boundaries of our existence. The awareness of loneliness might be a gift we must protect and guard, because our loneliness reveals to us an inner emptiness that can be destructive when understood, but filled with promise for him who can tolerate its sweet pain.[7]

We've made a mistake if we see ministry with young adults as programs which are designed to take away loneliness. Such a philosophy only increases our busyness. We advertise that we exist "to take people's loneliness away." The result? Incessant activity; increased hype; and a fear of silence, thinking and dialogue. We are afraid to be real.

But there's good news. Once I acknowledge my incompleteness or "loneliness" (which certainly doesn't disappear once I marry) then I can take steps to develop community. I can overcome what Greeley calls "existential loneliness" or voluntary isolation (personal withdrawal). Now I can see people not as objects to take my loneliness away, but as *fellow journeyers.*

Community is fundamental to Christian faith and growth. Community is fundamental to young adult ministry. Community is our need to find fellow journeyers. Unfortunately, we have been conditioned to seek people out for the purpose of "loneliness exorcism."

Singles bars are evidence of this reality. On any given Friday or Saturday night, I could take you to any number of singles bars near my home in southern California and we would find wall-to-wall people. Why? What is it that causes so many to gather? I've heard preachers deal with the singles bar scene by preaching simple judgments against them: "Those people only gather in those 'flesh pits' for sex and alcohol!"

While it's true that many persons who go to singles bars have sex and/or drink alcohol, I am convinced that those are not the primary reasons they go. I don't think they are looking for "skin," I believe they are looking for "kin." The fundamental need is community. Singles bars are symbolic of the pervasive crying out for a place to belong. What is the church doing to create community? Fellowship has got to be more than people spilling coffee on each other after church!

Young adult groups are very often Christianized singles bars. And singles bars are not the issue here. The issue is our need to take away people's loneliness by keeping them busy. Ministry begins by acknowledging our loneliness and recognizing that community is a place where we can be real—and where we can belong. How do we respond to this pressure of loneliness? The answer is graphically pictured in a theme song, "You wanna be where everybody knows your name." We need to belong.

THE PRESSURE TO FIND SECURITY

Change is not easy because it threatens our security. Change affects our lifestyle, our emotional life, our self-esteem, and even our physical well-being. We fuel the fire by valuing comfort above all else. And we find ourselves anxious about security.

Because many young adults find themselves in a state of transition, the issue of security gets full attention. There is insecurity over the future. "Will I ever marry?" "Will I be able to marry again?" Such insecurity produces a hesitancy in decision-making. "I'll do

such and such *when* ...," or, "*If only* this would happen, *then* ..."
There is the assumption that, "I've got my whole life ahead of me
Whatever I need to commit to can wait."

Along the same line, there is insecurity over marriage. "Is it worth
the price I need to pay?" "Is it possible to find the right person in
today's crazy world?" With security as a primary goal it is very understandable to see a significant number of single young adults opting
for a commitment to career development over relational development. Such a focus makes sense with our cultural success/achieve-
ment orientation. "Relationships don't seem to be a good bet these
days," was the way one 26-year-old male expressed his opinion to
me. "You get so used to working," said another 29-year-old. "It's
easier than personal relationships. It can be an escape from them."[8]
Young adults are asking, "Is it possible to have a good marriage
and a successful career? And what if we want a two-career family—is
that possible?"

There is also insecurity over money. "I know we make more than
our parents," said one young adult, "but it doesn't seem to change
the fact that there's never enough to go around." It can be a frightening experience to think about what it will cost to send our children
through college. What will our retirement fund look like? Will social
security exist? Is there anyone to help us face these insecurities with
sound practical advice on money management?

With the increase of family violence (of every four households in
America, one experiences some type of family violence) there is
insecurity in the family system itself. We find persons moving from
one unhealthy family system to another. The result? Insecurity.

A ministry with young adults must honestly face the issues of
security and insecurity without pretending the latter will go away
with time. An insecure environment must be replaced with a secure
environment. Elements of trust and openness are vital.

I see two immediate consequences of our preoccupation with
security or insecurity. The first is hurry. We are driven: rushing here
and there; accumulating people, trinkets and experiences that will
serve to build a fortress against the realities of life. What are we
in a hurry for? What do we hope to find?

The second consequence is our preoccupation with our need to
"be actualized," to be somebody. We are hoping to ward off insecurity with an exterior of "togetherness." We have arrived. So take
est, do therapy, jog, do church, and answer Redbook quizzes on
romance. What we're looking for is security. What we fail to see

is that security is not resolved externally. Security must change us from the inside.

That is why trust and openness are vital to young adult ministry. In a pressure-cooker world, we must offer a place for young adults to be real.

KEY POINTS

1. Young adults face the pressure that it is not okay to be "just ordinary people."
2. Young adults face the pressure to be super-sexed. The church usually responds to the issue of sexuality in one of these ways:
   •silence
   •legalism
   •ignoring it
3. A better approach to sexuality is pro-life. Pro-life changes the questions from "what" to "why." The issue is on what happens to us as a result of our choices.
4. Young adults face the pressures of loneliness and isolation.
5. Young adults face the pressure to find security.

REVIEW QUESTIONS

1. Do you think today's world places greater pressure on young adults? Why or why not?
2. Can you relate to any of the following pressures? If so, in what ways?
   •pressure that it is not okay to be "just plain"
   •pressure to be super-sexed
   •pressures of loneliness and isolation
   •pressure to find security
3. What are some of the ways (positive or negative) young adults cope with such pressures?
4. How does legalism fuel the fire of the pressure to be super-sexed?
5. Does the church have a role in confronting any of these pressure points?
6. Someone said, "The church should be there with answers for today's problems." Do you agree or disagree? Why?

CHAPTER 4

Obstacles to Effective Ministry

For which of you, desiring to build a tower, does not first sit down and count the cost, whether he has enough to complete it? Otherwise, when he has laid a foundation, and is not able to finish, all who see it begin to mock him, saying, 'This man began to build, and was not able to finish' (Luke 14:28-30).

As a young pastor was leaving one of my leadership workshops, he bubbled with enthusiasm and said, "I can't wait to get started! After I initiate these principles, we'll have the biggest and best young adult ministry in town!"

I admired his confidence and did not wish in any way to dampen his zeal. We always could use more zeal for dreaming "big" for ministry. But, we would be naive to assume that ministry with young adults could be considered easy or completed by instituting certain principles. If we have learned anything from the first three chapters, it is this: There must be more to ministry with young adults than a big program.

Young adults are real people with real needs. They live in a pressure-cooker world and are crying to be known. Their cry may not be obvious or even audible, but that is the nature of this ministry. We must begin with the idea that we are on a journey to get to know people, to uncover unrealized potential, to provide the freedom to ask, question and talk, and to give permission to find fulfillment in involvement and leadership. As we've said earlier, the potential of young adult ministry is limitless. However, we must do our homework. The time set aside at the end of each chapter for inventory, review and discussion is vital. It allows us to know our ministry is headed in the right direction. Ironically, the time spent in group discussion using the questions at the end of these chapters is itself ministry.

Before we look at the appropriate response to what we've read in this section, let's take some time to count the cost of young adult ministry. What are the obstacles? Are there any unseen barriers? Must we remove any internal stereotypes or myths about young adults or ministry with them?

Some of the following obstacles you may relate to; some may seem irrelevant. Regardless, each is important to confront. They are listed randomly—not in any particular order of importance.

MISUNDERSTANDING THE UNIQUE CHARACTER OF YOUNG ADULTS

Invariably, in my weekend travels, I will encounter a church where young adults will express their concern on this very issue. "There's no place for us here," they will begin. Further questioning reveals what they mean. Their church usually has an existing college group (sometimes college and career) consisting of young adults ages 18 to 25. But these young adults discovered that around age 23 or 24, they were too old for that group and were ready to move on. Unfortunately, the average age for most church "single groups" is 38 to 42 or older. The young adults ages 24 to 35 are lost in the middle.

I am not saying that there cannot be a "singles group" for persons age 24 to 35. There *can* be, but that is not the issue. The issue is that a group for younger singles will be much different in emphasis than a group for older singles.

The only other options for young single adults are to get married and hope to find a ministry to young marrieds—which is also hard to come by—or to become scarce or drop out.

The importance of coming to terms with this obstacle is preventative. It will keep us from attempting to duplicate a college group for young adults, or from assuming they can be easily channeled into a church singles group. In fact, very few young adults will even respond to the designation of "singleness." Even though it is a fact that many young adults are single; their preference is for adult, young adult, career adult or even career singles. The issue becomes more complicated given the continuing relationship between newly married young adults and their single friends. Are the "newlyweds" allowed to come to a "career singles" group?

By understanding the unique character of the young adult population, you know that one program will not cover their entire needs. Young adult ministry should encompass several programs aimed at the specific needs of this diverse age group.

INADEQUATE MEASUREMENTS FOR SUCCESS

It is not as if young adult ministries have not been attempted. In fact, many churches have launched what they hope will be the right idea for luring their young adults back to church. There is a high degree of expectation and hope. Unfortunately, many, if not most, of the start-up groups fail or become small remnants of the faithful who commit themselves to the never-ending task of maintenance.

Good intentions aside, what happens next? Do the remnants of the faithful struggle to continue programming for a few young adults? Do they give up altogether and say, "It's not worth this effort. Nobody cares anyway." Or do they evaluate to see why the ministry isn't reaching more people and what they could do better?

Even with the opportunity to do an adequate evaluation, I have discovered that most pastors cannot remove themselves from the fact that this was a failure and therefore a personal reflection on them and their church. Robert Gribbon is helpful in his observation:

> Among pastors there is a frequent syndrome of frustration, guilt, and sometimes anger because they feel that they ought to do something with young adults but find themselves unable to do anything successfully. In some cases this leads to the conclusion that it is not possible or necessary to work with young adults and the attitude that nothing needs to be done because 'they'll come back when they're ready.'[1]

Our measurements for success have within them a self-destructive element. Our criteria have been relatively simple:
- large numbers or at least a "respectable attendance"
- identifiable group
- busy calendar of activities
- good reputation among the congregation as a whole

The frustrations inherent in such criteria are self-evident:
- motivation becomes aimed at keeping numbers
- our focus can easily move to entertainment
- avoid anything which may affect our "reputation"
- business only serves to create "burnout"

In my own ministry, the greater the pressure of the above criteria, the greater my anxiety over why all the young adults in our congregation were not attending my young adult group. When numbers would fluctuate, it became necessary to defend my ministry by finding some reason for the drop in success. Meetings with other ministers became seedbeds for comparison and jealously, wondering why they had a more successful young adult group than I had. All the while, I was missing the point of ministry.

Don't get me wrong. I am not saying that numbers, calendars and programs are to be avoided. In fact, I have run young adult ministries where all three were present. But numbers, calendars and programs cannot become the reasons for our existence. If we learn anything from our overview of young adults, it is this: *Impersonal programming will fail.* I was busy, but I was not necessarily touching lives. Again Gribbon is helpful:

> The informal and occasional ministries with young adults were undervalued, and the clergy often felt like failures, because the criteria for 'success' were the establishment of a young adult program and frequent attendance of young adults at Sunday services. Attendance and activity are the usual success criteria for congregational ministries, but we maintain (and will later explain more fully) that these are not appropriate or achievable goals for young adult ministry. Where attendance and activity are the goals, most ministries with young adults will be frustrated; but on the other hand, it is difficult for congregations to invest large amounts of time, money, and energy in ministries which do not 'pay off' in terms of increased activity and attendance.[2]

VIEWING YOUNG ADULTS AS PRODUCTIVE RATHER THAN DEVELOPMENTAL

One of the expressed frustrations with young adults is, "They are not givers. They are only here for what they can get." The frustration is understandable. The church is definitely dependent upon resources donated or given to them. It is no wonder that church members are seen as potential donors, volunteers or workers. It also is no wonder that this viewpoint or frustration becomes an obstacle to young adult ministry.

In the first place, when you treat people as "takers," you never have an environment to make opportunity for giving. Why? Because you never "expect" it of them. And we continue to resent young adults, even though we treat them the way we do not wish them to act.

In the second place, we begin to value people for what they can give. And our criteria for "gifts" are external at best. We begin to measure program success by what it "produces." What it "gives back" to the church. In other words, there's got to be a payoff.

Such an attitude will make a truly successful young adult ministry virtually impossible. Why? Because people are not commodities, they are developmental beings. And as we have said before, the twenties are a time of testing the waters of life. Gribbon puts it this way:

> Young adulthood is like a time of blossoming—it is not fruitbearing, it is not 'productive'—it seems more concerned with the ephemeral and with display. But without the blossom, there is no fruit. If we do not encourage the full development of the individual in the young adult years, there will be no productive years.[3]

The call of the church is to create that environment of nurture for a "budding plant."

AN INADEQUATE VIEW OF SCRIPTURE

The minister remarked to me that he was grateful for the fact that all his young adults had a proper understanding of the Christian faith and lifestyle. I wasn't quite sure what that meant—nor was I sure I wanted to pursue it—but nevertheless, I asked him to continue. "Last week," he said, "I led a discussion on the serious moral questions of our culture: abortion, pornography, premarital sex and homosexuality. And everyone in the class was in agreement about the biblical perspective."

I couldn't resist, "How many were in the class?"

"Twelve," he replied, "and they are faithful."

No wonder, I thought, when they're spoon-fed. Retreating to childhood authority figures is definitely easier than growing up. But I was still uncomfortable with his comments. They disturbed me, and I wanted to know why. I have since uncovered the reasons for my discomfort.

Having everyone in agreement on social and moral issues is not necessarily admirable, especially if there is no environment for questioning or disagreement. Moral choices are of consequence if they are "owned" moral choices. Neither my parents' choices, nor my church's choices are enough to get me through life. The issue, of course, has nothing to do with abortion or premarital sex—let alone this minister's assumption that such issues are "the serious moral questions." The issue is creating a place where the Christian Gospel can become personal and real.

The church falls short in its ability to provide such a place where it practices an inadequate view of scripture. The outcome is an inadequate view of reality.

I find it ironic that in a time in which many Christians are demanding insistence upon the "inerrancy of the Bible," they practice ministry as if God is totally untrustworthy. Let me explain. If the Bible is true and God is real, it has obvious consequences on our ministry. For example, one consequence is that reality can be trusted. Why is this an important fundamental issue in young adult development? Trust is primary. When trust breaks down; development breaks down.[4]

How is trust cultivated? By transferring authority from parent to church? By enforcing adherence to an inerrant Word? By having all young adults agree on a common moral code? The answer is no to all questions.

Trust begins when one is allowed to test and see that God is trustworthy. Allowing young adults the opportunity to test their faith leaves many ministers with a sense of paranoia. "We'll lose them," is the fear. Perhaps. But is God real and trustworthy—or is he not?

If God is trustworthy:

•we are free to minister without any need to dominate or control.

•we are free to minister without paranoia over how our reputation will be affected by who is, and who is not there.

•we are free to prioritize. To say "no" to some activities to focus on what is "best."

•we are free to persevere, realizing that we may only be planting seeds and never see a "harvest."

We become less protective. Less fearful of our "program reputation." Less anxious about how success is measured solely by numbers. A better measure for success is making sure our programs offer resources to help people face life's limitations; words of forgiveness, grace, reconciliation and renewal; and a vision for the future.[5]

Such a realization only serves to give me hope. What a foundational realization for my ministry: God is trustworthy. Andrew Greeley's observations regarding the trustworthiness of God are a necessary beginning to a healthy ministry foundation:

If Reality is benign or gracious, then it is ultimately safe to take and be taken because no matter what happens, a gracious Reality will protect one. If, on the other hand, Reality is malign, capricious, arbitrary, then love is a risky business and surrender bound to end in disaster ... I would argue that he who is a Christian, that is to say, one who is fully committed with his total personality to the revelation of God as contained in his words through Jesus Christ, does not hesitate; he is on the side of Father Teilhard's interpretation. While the thought of conquest and surrender may strike terror in his heart, the terror is not strong enough to stop him. I am not saying that only the Christian is capable of friendship; but I will say that a convinced, committed Christian has a far better motivation, a far deeper rationale for friendship than anyone else. The Christian knows that the Really Real is gracious.[6]

The second consequence is that we are free from the need to bring closure to struggle and doubt. Questioning need not be an enemy to successful programming. Discouraging struggle is no longer my goal. It is almost as if I must protect God's reputation—for I am sure he cannot handle the young adults who find the need to question their faith and the foundational structure of the identity.

A MYOPIC VIEW OF COMMITMENT

"How do we retain the young adults that come to our church?" "It seems like our back door is larger than the front door." "They'll *only* come for a few weeks, and then they'll be gone." "Is there any way to keep young adults committed?"

I can relate to the concern and the frustration. The reality is simply that 50 percent of young adult groups turn over every six months. National surveys tell us that 80 percent of young adults say that religion is important in their lives but only 25 percent attend church regularly.[7] And given the cultural backdrop of our postponing generation, church simply becomes another option among many. In fact, it is not at all uncommon to find anywhere from 25 to 50 percent of those young adults who attend church to be affiliated with two or three different congregations simultaneously. Gribbon adds:

> More importantly, young adults are in a highly independent, transitional period in their lives. They are unlikely to make long-term commitments to any organization or institution. They are trying to make sense of life for themselves and their faith is likely to be highly

individualistic and expressed in a personal searching and questioning.[8]

If I take all this personally, it can take a serious toll on my ministry, not to mention my emotional wellness. My typical response is to show disdain for the "blatant disregard for commitment" among young adults.

Left to fester, my myopia only infects the rest of my church life. Two assumptions must be called into question:

•that commitment can only be defined by the long-term;

•that significant ministry can only be done where there is frequent involvement.

Granted, long-term commitment and frequent involvement are essential for the development of Christian maturity and a healthy community. But here we are talking about young adult ministry, and two things are essential: We must affirm where young adults are, and we must take advantage of every opportunity we have to touch them where they are.

I used to be so concerned about those young adults who were infrequent in their involvement that I did not take adequate advantage of the opportunities I did have in building steppingstones to greater commitment. For example, if a person couldn't commit to me for one year, I should have asked for a one-month commitment.

DEFINING MINISTRY SOLELY BY OUR NEED TO BUILD A PROGRAM

Aside from the pastor's visitations, almost all ministry in congregations is thought of in terms of program. Thus, when attention is drawn to the needs of a particular group, such as young adults, the common response is 'we ought to have a program for them.'

However, it is characteristic of young adults to be critical of institutions, impatient with traditions, highly mobile, and engaged in an independent and individual period of searching and transition. Their most important needs are not met by affiliative groups and their faith is seldom expressed through religious membership and institutional loyalty.[9]

Robert Gribbon is right. There is more to ministry than a blurb in the bulletin that says, "Young adults meet here on Thursdays at 7 p.m." This fact is repeated throughout the book because it remains, in all probability, our number-one temptation. Settling only for program saps the very lifeblood out of ministry.

"But," you might protest, "this is supposed to be a book about successful programs for young adults." In one sense that is true. But a successful program is impossible if it is *only* a program. If a program is not first and foremost a ministry, then it is idolatry, developed either for reputation, congregational pressure, or to prove that "our church can do what First Church down the street could never do."

We've all either known of or been a part of young adult groups that have been launched with a flash and some hype, only to plummet to earth before they ever reach orbit. Why? Because they lack the wrong programs? I doubt it. Bad programming can affect a group, but it can never kill a ministry. It is because they never started on the right road.

Where does that right road begin? With an honest look at the obstacles that threaten to cause us to settle for less than the best.

KEY POINTS

1. An obstacle to effective ministry is a misunderstanding of the unique character of the young adult population.
2. An obstacle to effective ministry is an inadequate measure for success.
3. We see young adults as "productive" rather than "developmental."
4. We have an inadequate view of scripture.
5. We live with a myopic view of commitment.
6. We define ministry solely by our need to build a program.
7. With an honest look at the obstacles that threaten to cause us to settle for less than the best, we find the right road to effective young adult ministry.

REVIEW QUESTIONS

1. Why is it necessary to identify obstacles to effective ministry?
2. Which of the six obstacles mentioned do you see as the most serious threat to your own ministry? Why?
3. Are there more effective ways to determine success? Are numbers an essential in determining success? Why or why not?
4. What are some creative and practical ways a church can create

an environment where young adults are allowed to express struggles, questions and concerns?

5. Can you think of any ways in which the transitional nature of young adults can be used to an advantage in ministry?

6. What are the practical ways that we keep a balance between "ministry" and "program"?

CHAPTER 5

The Keys to Success and Effectiveness

The process of ministry is akin to sending a city Boy Scout troop on a mission to capture a dairy cow. There is just one problem: The city boys never actually have seen a dairy cow. Will they even recognize the object of the mission when it stares them in the face?

The same is true for those looking for an effective young adult ministry. What does a successful church with a successful ministry look like? Will we know it when we see it?

As we move toward our section on strategy and programming, let's pause for a moment to reflect on a series of images of success. Call them marks of success, if you wish ... or visible distinctions.

We'll begin by posing a question: If your congregation is effectively incorporating young adults, what would be its visible distinctions? In other words, what would be considered an effective response to what we've learned in the previous chapters?

We are drawing up a blueprint, not of program ideas—yet. But of the heart and spirit of an effective church. When Jesus saw the needs—he did something. He took specific steps.

So as we build our young adult ministry, it will be characterized by specific steps or certain unique flavors. If the ministry touches the young adults of this generation, the necessary foundational ingredients will be clearly visible. Following are some characteristics of an effective, successful congregation:

A CONGREGATION THAT GIVES AWAY RESPONSIBILITY

The scenario is all too familiar. "When the young adults care enough to commit themselves to our church, we can minister to them. The problem is getting them to care—getting them to feel ownership with the church. How can we get them to take more responsibility? Will they ever be committed?"

There is no need to argue some of the realities of our cultural overview in previous chapters. Young adults *can* be selfish, indulgent, irresponsible and noncommittal. So what else is new? Is there anyone in our culture who is not tempted by any and all of those lifestyle choices? The question becomes one of focus. Unfortunately, most of us live with the assumption that the best way to encourage responsibility is to make people feel guilty for their non-commitment and hope that our appealing to their "low threshold" of guilt will motivate responsibility. Sometimes we believe such an assumption because we are convinced that non-committed people in our church are a direct reflection of our reputation as a leader. It becomes an unending cycle—guilt produces more guilt.

In talking with young adults around the United States, I've had a pleasant shock. Lack of responsibility (seen as apathy or selfishness) is not always due to non-commitment. When I asked about young adults' lack of responsibilities in their local churches, the responses varied: "No one asked me." "What would I do?" "There are others who could do a better job." "I've only been here two months." "No one knows who I am." "People will think I am too young."

Congregations that successfully incorporate young adults into the church body have this in common: *The churches do not ask for responsibility; they give it away.* There is a significant difference. One assumes that people are not committed; the other assumes they are, but the commitment needs channeling and an opportunity for expression.

Giving away responsibility begins at the basic level of allowing varying degrees of participation. How often does it happen that we criticize those who hold back their involvement? How often do we stifle the enthusiasm of those who can't wait to be involved in anything and everything the church does? Perhaps young adults hold back their involvement and have their enthusiasm stifled because they haven't been asked.

This is a philosophy that sees young adults as givers, not just takers. Unfortunately, many begin to approach ministry without questioning the stereotype they carry regarding young adults. Giving away responsibility begins by getting to know our young adults. (There are some very helpful tools for doing this in the last section of this book.) Such an effort communicates very clearly to young adults that, "You are a significant part of this church—and that is important to us."

Giving away responsibility also means letting your young adults dream about the ministry and direction of the church. Sponsor a "Dream Session" as outlined on pages 140-141. When you let people dream, you begin to give the ministry away. That is the secret of success. By your actions you affirm that the people are responsible.

Giving away responsibility means *using* your young adults' input and ideas. Do you have a worship planning committee? Are there any young adults on that committee? (Do you allow *any* input to your worship planning?) What about your adult education department? Are there any young adults giving input? Does the pastor allow feedback to his or her sermons? Effective ministry means listening to young adults' feedback, ideas and input.

A CONGREGATION THAT FOCUSES ON A "FAITH THAT MATTERS"

There is a strong correlation between success with young adults and a ministry that is based on the necessity of faith development. The focus is on nurturing people.

In the first chapter, we touched on the development cycle of a young adult. Ages 18 to 32 are marked by questions and experimentation. It is the time for establishing a tentative "life structure." A time for developing a value system through which the world will make sense. A time for undertaking the risks involved in building relationships and making commitments.

In the same way it is a time of searching faith.[1] Corresponding with our identity development—the need to question and differentiate one's self from the authority structures of one's childhood—is our faith development need for meaning. It is what James Fowler refers to as the "synthetic-conventional faith" in his book **Stages of Faith**. In his scheme, such a stage of faith begins in late adolescence, where the forming of identity and the shaping of a personal faith are crucial. As in Sheehy's Pulling Up Roots, this is a time for new stories, a new people and a new community of faith. Young adulthood brings the stage Fowler calls "individuative-reflective faith." It's purpose is the "reflective construction of ideology, and the formation of a vocational dream."[2]

Identity development and faith development go hand-in-hand. And the church needs to understand this reality. Religious faith simply cannot be a hand-me-down. "Tell me the old, old story" doesn't cut it with young adults, unless you have in your church only a handful of young adults who were raised in that church and have been content to do what Sheehy describes as "identity foreclosure." As a protective device, you assume the identity of your parents (or some other authority structure in your life—such as church) and make no attempts to ask whether such an identity is relevant to you. Granted, such a young adult group would be easy to handle, very cooperative and cause little anxiety. But would it be effective ministry? No.

Effective ministry with young adults is marked by an invitation to ask questions. Such an approach to ministry is neither easy nor convenient, but it touches real lives.

Faith-development ministry sees young adults not as "payoffs" in numbers, donations and volunteers, but as "flowering fruit trees"—developmental and not static. Robert Gribbon adds:

> Christian theology is distorted if theory is used as a ladder which people must climb. As desirable as growth is, no one is saved by growing up. All of us, infants, young and old are acceptable and saved solely by the grace of God. We can therefore accept and affirm individuals at every stage of development. We can nurture growth and respond appropriately, but growth, like life itself, is always a gift from God.[3]

Effective ministry means creating environments where I can "practice my faith." What does that look like practically?

For one thing, instead of giving young adults lectures on missions from old missionaries—who may be impossible for anyone to relate to—give them a job. In one church, the young adults adopted an orphanage in Mexico and built a dorm and chapel for 100 orphans. It was "their project." And they learned more about a faith that matters by shoveling cement and sand than they would have from any 12-week series in Sunday school.

For an effective young adult ministry, it is also necessary to be willing to "scratch where they itch." Sponsor workshops on faith issues that matter; for example, "Making Effective Moral Choices," "Sex and Dating," "Success and God: Do They Mix?"

Unfortunately, churches have a tendency to present such topics by giving answers to their young adults. That's not what they need. They need a place to ask questions, and challenge the "answers" they have tried to live with for five to 10 years.

A CONGREGATION THAT
CREATES OPPORTUNITIES FOR BELONGING

Erik Erikson said that the central theme for young adult development is "intimacy." If our Trying Twenties find us fighting with the authority figures of our past, and attempting to carry out a value system that matters, it is also the time when we come face to face with our potential isolation. This is why many young adults foreclose on their identity. They don't attempt to own any world view or, as Levison calls it, "dream."[4]

Why? If you begin to search for meaning to life, what if no one is there for you in your searching? What if you are all alone? Staying safe, say many, is better than potential isolation. By the same token, many superficial relationships are preferred to one or two committed ones. Again, it is protection against potential isolation.

Young adults need people. They need places to belong. And the most effective ministries are those which provide such belonging opportunities. "That sounds too easy," you may say. "The trouble is that most young adults will not seek out a church as a place to belong." You are right. But that doesn't take away the point here. Effective churches are those who have made it clear to the young adults involved that they are accepted and valued.

Small groups are the most essential link in this chain of effectiveness. Small groups can be growth groups—groups that meet eight to 16 weeks for the purpose of talking over an issue relevant to personal, relational or spiritual growth. Or, small groups can be minichurch groups—home studies committed to several weeks of sharing, studying, goal-setting and reaching out. Steps for beginning a small-group program are included in the last section of this book.

A CONGREGATION THAT
IS LINKED TO THE COMMUNITY

Most of us still operate in a church model similar to the 1950s. It says that the church is the community center. All activities are held at the church facility, and people from the community come to that facility. Evangelism becomes simply a matter of opening the church doors and advertising the fact that, "We are available; come and get it." That model is no longer viable. As Carol Weiser correctly observes, "Baby-boomers are not going to come to church simply because the institution exists."[5] To effectively touch people, we must be willing to go "to where they are."

Two suggestions come to mind. The first is the realization that effective programs do not necessarily need to be linked to church facilities. Local restaurants, community facilities and homes all can serve as non-threatening environments to initiate young adult programming. The second is the need to be involved in community affairs and events. In what ways are we "among the people"? In what ways could we interact with young adults in their environment?

A CONGREGATION THAT SHOWS SENSITIVITY TO NEWCOMERS

Acceptance is a significant issue for everyone. But it is particularly significant for young adults. Realizing that the majority of young adults are single and that the primary task of the twenties is sorting through identity and intimacy issues, belonging is important. Belonging begins with the introduction of newcomers.

There is a lot "on the line" when someone visits a church or a young adult group for the first time (especially for the first time in many months or years). There are stereotypes, expectations and the need for affirmation. Young adults bring with them the reality of a pressure-cooker world, where acceptance is measured by performance and achievement. To be truly welcomed, with no need to perform in return, is a rare and pleasant experience.

It is too easy to send double messages. On the one hand, we say, "You are accepted here." On the other hand, we show unnecessary concern over where newcomers have come from, and what they have been involved in, and what level of belief and commitment we might expect from them.

Does your church (or young adult group) have a "theology of welcoming"? It begins with semantics. First-time individuals are not visitors, but newcomers. There is a difference.

It is also important that newcomers do not feel left out because they don't understand the "inside story." Many groups or congregations have found it helpful to assign a member or regular attender to each newcomer. As a newcomer enters, he or she is introduced to a "newcomer host" by the greeter. The host is responsible for introducing the newcomer to a variety of people, answering questions, and introducing that newcomer to the group later in the evening (or morning). A full description of the "newcomer host" program is in the last section.

We also need to be aware that a sure sign of acceptance is a clear communication that we will not be offended if a person does not choose to be a regular part of our group or church. Disappointed, yes; offended, no. Effective congregations are not soliciting members, but building a family.

A CONGREGATION THAT GIVES YOUNG ADULTS OWNERSHIP

It is essential that young adults have their own turf if a young adult ministry is to be effective. However, not all young adults desire to be in a young adult group. Many are content to be actively involved in other areas of church life. And many avoid any area of involvement.

Whatever the case, ownership is essential. When you give ownership and give validation, whether it's with a weekly young adult study group, a concert, a seminar or an annual young adult sponsored Sunday service. The message is clear: When you give ownership to any of those ministry functions, you validate their importance. Imagine what a young adult hears when he or she is told that, "The church is really supportive of a young adult sponsored event, but we don't have any money for you. You'll need to clear all your decisions through the pastoral staff. By the way, the only room left for you is the church basement." Is there any incongruity there? Of course, there is. It is equally incongruous when the leadership of the church announces the beginning of a young adult ministry, and then goes on to program for the young adults as if they are merely the "recipients" and not the "owners." And we wonder why we are not effective in touching young adults where they are.

The primary building block in the second section is the affirmation that unless the young adults *own* and are a part of *building* a young adult ministry, the ministry is destined to serious anemia or even failure.

A CONGREGATION THAT IS AFFIRMING OF DIVERSITY

Unity of purpose and direction does not mean the absence of difference. Effective ministries learn ways to incorporate such differences. This is important for young adult ministry if the church desires to reach beyond the handful of young adults who have remained connected with the congregation.

The congregation communicates loudly and clearly that one does not have to give up "distinctives" to begin the Christian journey. Are there ways in which we imply to people that in order to be accepted they must change the way they look? where they spend their time? how they talk? Are the people involved in congregational leadership clones of the pastoral staff? Do we have a theology of affirming diversity?

Effectiveness. Success. Neither one is a possession. They are both journeys. Journeys that require ongoing choices. Evaluation and re-evaluation. For, after all, we're building a family—not simply an association, group or club. And the journey toward effective ministry begins with an accurate view of our target. What are we aiming for? We should seek to become congregations that ...

- give away responsibility
- focus on a "faith that matters"
- create opportunities for belonging
- are linked to the community
- show sensitivity to newcomers
- turn programming ownership over to the young adults
- affirm diversity

Robert Gribbon sums up the need for our effectiveness. He asks why young adults need the church. "Their search could be better characterized as a diffuse seeking for friends, for a community of shared value, for support with life tasks, and a personalized but structured relationship with ultimate reality."[6]

The good news is that the effective church can be all those things. Let us begin that journey toward effectiveness—today.

KEY POINTS

1. An effective congregation is one that gives away responsibility.
2. An effective congregation is one that focuses on a "faith that matters."
3. An effective congregation is one that creates opportunities for

belonging.
4. An effective congregation is one that is linked to the community.
5. An effective congregation is one that shows sensitivity to newcomers.
6. An effective congregation is one that turns programming ownership over to the young adults.
7. An effective congregation is one that is affirming of diversity.

REVIEW QUESTIONS

1. Is there a difference between asking for responsibility and giving it away?
2. Are there any creative ways your church or young adult group could give away responsibility?
3. What is a "faith that matters"? How do you apply this principle practically?
4. "Belonging" sounds good on paper. Can it ever become a reality? Why or why not?
5. Does your church have a "theology of welcoming"? If so, describe it.
6. What are the ways one can tell if the young adults own their ministry?
7. In what ways can any of the keys to effective ministry mentioned in this chapter, help you in your ministry with young adults?

Effective Ministry With Young Adults

CHAPTER 6

The Heart Behind the Ministry

Effective ministry is intentional ministry. It does not happen spontaneously or accidentally. It happens with right choices, a strong foundation and focused planning. This, of course, does not mean that we deny the "spontaneous" role of the Holy Spirit. On the contrary, a fresh touch of the Spirit has meaning when it is received as a gift—and not a demand.

This section begins the process of responding to the needs we saw in the first section. Where do we go from here? How do we respond to the needs we see in our generation? Where can the church begin to create an effective model for ministry with young adults?

It is important that we do not begin this section overwhelmed by the overview we just completed. There are a variety of possible feelings when we clearly see the task before us. We may feel overwhelmed, shocked, sad, dismayed, even hopeless, confused or inadequate.

All of these feelings are understandable. But it is important to stop—and remind ourselves that the reason for our honest assessment in the first section is not to take hope away, but to encourage an understanding of young adults and to build a lasting hope.

No one said young adult ministry would be easy, so there is no need to paint a rosy picture of our culture. Nor is there any reason to pretend that an effective young adult ministry will not require wise choices, hard work and a strong foundation. But now that we recognize the cost, let's move ahead to discover the steps that are necessary to minister to young adults.

There's something prophetic about the story from Morris West's book **The Shoes of the Fisherman**. It draws our attention to the fundamental issue of ministry. Where is our heart? The following excerpt illustrates a pope named Kiril who understood "the heart behind the ministry":

> 'What did His Holiness have to say about that?'
> 'He wants the child made a ward of the Church. He wants the girl provided with employment and a dowry. Once again, you see, there is a question of precedent. But I admire his attitude even though I am not sure I can agree with all of it. He has a soft heart. The danger is that it may be too soft for the good of the Church.'[1]

Kiril came to the ministry with no ax to grind, nothing to prove, no one to impress. He was called. He was not driven, coerced or compelled out of guilt. He was doing what he believed God wanted him to do.

When I took a position as a minister with single adults, I began to survey the Bible in order to discover scripture passages which confirmed single adult ministry and young adult ministry. I found none and that frustrated me. Now, I'm glad I was unsuccessful in my search. I was looking for a Bible verse that would give credibility to my pre-existing program. The Bible doesn't outline programs. The Bible shows us God's heart for people. In my enthusiasm to accomplish something for God, I almost overlooked the fundamental questions, "Is my heart in what I am doing? Am I called to this ministry?"

There *is* a difference between programs and ministry:

- Programs focus on techniques—ministry focuses on people
- Programs look for numbers—ministry sees changed lives
- Programs need quick answers—ministry understands grace in uncertainty
- Programs see the course—ministry sees the hearts

It's an issue of balance. It's an issue of priority. Kiril (the pope in West's quote) understood balance and priority. He understood ministry. It was not a steppingstone to some other "real ministry."

I'm uncomfortable with people who see their ministry with young adults as a rung on the ladder of church-ministry progression—until they can get a "real job."

I've discovered that I will be successful with young adults when

I understand that this is the "real job." This is where God called me to be. Granted, I am not doing this forever, but that bridge can be crossed when God moves me on. But now I must find meaning in the knowledge that I am called to minister to young adults.

How do you know if you're called? Well, if you are called, you are compelled to do it and your heart finds joy in your call. But you say, "I'm an assistant pastor, and the senior pastor said that I am in charge of young adults. Is that a call?" Or, "I'm a lay person, but I have a strong desire to see what our church can do with young adults." Or, "I'm a senior pastor and I know that our church needs to address the needs of young adults, but it's never been an interest of mine. Where do I start?"

All these are legitimate questions. A call is not necessarily an emotional experience. It is simply the confirmation of God—through a still small voice, confirmation of others, confirmation of scripture or a place where my sense of joy meets the world's needs.

Ministry begins with the heart. Unless we understand that principle, ministry is reduced to the implementation of programs. And it's important that we continue to emphasize this principle as we walk through this book. Our temptation will continually be to skip to the final section, where program ideas are discussed. Granted, programs are necessary; however, programs are only as effective as the heart that creates the vision. Although we seek to be effective and innovative, we wonder why we are so often frustrated and exhausted. We've lost our perspective on the question "Why?" Why ministry? Why ministry with young adults?

It is a tragedy that so many churches program for young adults but don't know *why*. Having a young adult program because it's "the thing to do" is not an adequate reason. Sometimes our reasons are known; sometimes they are not. "Why?" may never have been asked. *Ministry must begin with an adequate foundation. The foundation is laid when one begins to answer the question "Why?"*

In order to understand the necessity of building an adequate foundation for ministry, we must go directly to the ministry of Jesus himself. Here we see balance and focus—a model for the "true heart" behind the ministry. In Mark's Gospel, Jesus reveals his heart to us:

> The apostles returned to Jesus, and told him all that they had done and taught. And he said to them, 'Come away by yourselves to a lonely place, and rest a while.' For many were coming and going, and they had no leisure even to eat.

And they went away in the boat to a lonely place by themselves. Now many saw them going, and knew them, and they ran there on foot from all the towns, and got there ahead of them. As he landed he saw a great throng, and he had compassion on them, because they were like sheep without a shepherd; and he began to teach them many things.

And when it grew late, his disciples came to him and said, 'This is a lonely place, and the hour is now late; send them away, to go into the country and villages around about and buy themselves something to eat.'

But he answered them, 'You give them something to eat' (Mark 6:30-37a).

It is important for us to see and apply three principles from this story to our ministry with young adults:

WE MUST SEE JESUS' HEART FOR PEOPLE

Mark 6 says that Jesus looked and saw people. He didn't see opportunities, problems or program ideas—at least initially. First, he saw people.

Today Jesus is the same. He sees people. He sees Valerie, a 31-year-old, always-single career woman. A woman with energy, zest and leadership ability. And a woman scared by the reality of alcoholic parents. Valerie finds personal relationships difficult. Trust is not easy; staying busy and successful is easier.

Jesus sees David, a 26-year-old newlywed. A seminary graduate, eager to do ministry. Talented, energetic and personable, David still wonders if it will be possible to experience the life and ministry to which he feels called. He wants to be more than mediocre and second-best.

Jesus sees Debbie, a 22-year-old, part-time college student. A young woman with a sincere heart and a strong desire to be a faithful Christian. But Debbie sometimes feels overwhelmed by the pressures for perfection, and her fear that she may not become all that she has set for herself to become.

Jesus sees Louise, a 29-year-old single parent. She has three children and an absentee husband. Her life is torn by memories of childhood abuse and emotional trauma. Louise perseveres, looking for a place to find healing, and a place to give the talent she knows is buried somewhere underneath her fragile exterior.

Jesus sees Tony, a 28-year-old unmarried man. Women frighten him. What's worse, he fears that he might have homosexual feelings. He feels guilty most of the time, and longs for a place to find a "family" who cares.

Jesus sees people. And he calls us to see people. The heart of the Gospel is the heart of our Lord seeking to restore people. It is the heart of our Lord seeking to heal, to mend, to redeem, to make whole, to set people free to realize a potential beyond their wildest dreams.

Where do we see this heart of Jesus? from a distance? through the scriptures only? No. To understand the heart of Jesus, and therefore the heart of ministry, we must see him from the perspective of our being sheep without a shepherd on the hillside of Galilee.

"Now you're in prison again."

"In a way, but I hope to break out of it."

"We're all in prison, one way or another."[2]

The conversation from **The Shoes of the Fisherman** illustrates that the message of the Gospel is clear: "While we were yet sinners Christ died for us" (Romans 5:8). When we personalize that verse, the heart behind the ministry begins to make sense. Ministry makes sense because I know what it means to be a sheep without a shepherd and to have Jesus have compassion on me. Ministry makes sense because I know what it means to have Jesus heal me when I'm sick, mend me when I'm wounded, comfort me when I'm discouraged and nudge me when I'm complacent.

The first section of the book referred to statistics and trends. It pointed to a variety of issues that characterize the young adult culture. It opened windows into our understanding of the particular needs of young adults. We misunderstand, however, if we come away from those chapters with a commitment to minister to "them." We should not think of ministry as "us" and "them."

We are called to minister because we too are in need of ministry. It is no longer "us" and "them." It is "us." We begin to understand ministry when we begin to see the heart of Jesus for us.

In Luke 4, we see Jesus beginning to flesh out his statement of purpose,

> The Spirit of the Lord is upon me, because he has anointed me to preach good news to the poor. He has sent me to proclaim release to the captives and recovering of sight to the blind, to set at liberty those who are oppressed, to proclaim the acceptable year of the Lord (Luke 4:18-19).

Jesus answered the question "Why?" It created the foundation for his ministry.

WE MUST RECEIVE JESUS' COMPASSION TO BECOME A HEALING PLACE FOR OTHERS

The numbers of sheep on the hillsides have not diminished. Where will they come to know the compassion of Jesus? When will they come to realize hope? How will they come to understand the good news that the Gospel is relevant to their lives?

Jesus communicates his love through those whom he has loved. Those of us who have experienced his love, become "conductors" of his love. Jesus now sees the sheep on the hillside through our eyes. We are "ambassadors" of his compassion.

The effectiveness of a ministry can be measured by the degree to which we continue to receive healing in our own lives. In other words, we are able to minister to others once we have been ministered to. Henri Nouwen clarifies this issue in his book **The Wounded Healer: Ministry in Contemporary Society:**

> How does our Liberator come? I found an old legend in the Talmud which may suggest to us the beginning of an answer:
> Rabbi Yoshua ben Levi came upon Elijah the prophet while he was standing at the entrance of Rabbi Simeron ben Yohai's cave. He asked Elijah, 'When will the Messiah come?'
> Elijah replied, 'Go and ask him yourself.'
> 'Where is he?'
> 'Sitting at the gates of the city.'
> 'How shall I know him?'
> 'He is sitting among the poor covered with wounds. The others unbind all their wounds at the same time and then bind them up again. But he unbinds one at a time and binds it up again, saying to himself, "Perhaps I shall be needed: if so I must always be ready so as not to delay for a moment" (from the tractate Sanhedrin).
> He is called to be the wounded healer, the one who must look after his own wounds but at the same time be prepared to heal the wounds of others ... Thus like Jesus, he who proclaims liberation is called not only to care for his own wounds and the wounds of others, but also to make his wounds into a major source of his healing power.[3]

At a recent seminar, one young pastor seemed perplexed by the "wounded healer" message. "You see," he told me, "my young adult group is a healthy group. I don't think they are in need of much healing."

His comment exposed an unfortunate myth about healing: It is only for bleeding hearts, social downcasts, relational losers and the emotionally imbalanced.

He went on, "In fact, I spend a lot of energy attracting healthy people. We don't want to be a group that attracts losers. If I start talking about healing, the healthy people will leave."

I understand his concerns. Anyone who does young adult ministry wrestles with the tension of the need to attract "healthy" people. But healing is for healthy people too. If I assume that I am exempt from my need to receive love from Jesus, I cannot be a conduit of that same love to others. And I have found that in my own ministry, underneath the "I've-got-my-act-together" mask, is loneliness, fear of inadequacy, anxiety about future decisions, the need to be loved and the need to be needed. The fact is that we are all incomplete. We cannot make it alone. Ministry happens when we learn how to receive.

Ministry is not reserved for those of us who "have our act together." In this culture, you must not appear weak, especially if you are the leader. As we indicated in the first section, the young adult of today is under tremendous pressure to be strong and in control. The concept of becoming wounded leaders goes against our grain. The struggle is nothing new. We see the apostle Paul facing the same issue:

> Blessed be the God and Father of our Lord Jesus Christ, the Father of mercies and God of all comfort, who comforts us in all our affliction, so that we may be able to comfort those who are in any affliction, with the comfort with which we ourselves are comforted by God. For as we share abundantly in Christ's sufferings, so through Christ we share abundantly in comfort too. If we are afflicted, it is for your comfort and salvation; and if we are comforted, it is for your comfort, which you experience when you patiently endure the same sufferings that we suffer. Our hope for you is unshaken; for we know that as you share in our sufferings, you will also share in our comfort (2 Corinthians 1:3-7).

I remember Jean. She talked to me after one of my conferences. She was concerned that she didn't have an adequate ministry for young adults because she didn't have as many programs as the church where I was a pastor. My response was, "Tell me a little about last week. What was it like?"

She told me about a lunch meeting with a 28-year-old woman facing the loss of her children through a custody battle, late-night phone calls with a graduate student who was discouraged and hurting, "pick-me-up cards" to two young women she knew who were going through difficult times after the end of serious dating relationships, and she continued with other stories.

Jean may not have had a refined group with several programs, yet she had a ministry. And Jean needed to be free to hear that affirmation. Any "program" that Jean now begins to develop will become more effective because its foundation is in Jean's *heart* behind the ministry. Jean was a healing place for others, because she knew the healing touch of Jesus.

PROGRAMMING CAN BE EFFECTIVE
WHEN DEVELOPED OUT OF A DEVOTIONAL LIFE

Jesus was effective because he spent time withdrawing to be with his Father. "And in the morning, a great while before day, he rose and went out to a lonely place, and there he prayed" (Mark 1:35).

Skill, excellence, and quality programming are necessary and worthwhile goals. But just as cars need fuel, people in ministry need "alone time" with the Father. Skill, excellence and quality programming do not make a ministry. Yes, we need them; but even more, we need men and women whose lives are faithful to the Father. Jesus' power was directly proportional to the time he spent with God. A devotional life is a renewed life. A life that can stay fresh in a stale world.

If I am too busy and do not have time to be "ministered to," then my ministry becomes an *occupation* or *job* rather than a *calling*. A job is something you do to the satisfaction of an employer. A calling is an obligation beyond pleasing someone. A job can grow stale; a calling can be renewed. Ben Patterson says:

> With the exception of simple fatigue, all loss of motivation is a form of forgetfulness. It is losing touch with the 'why' of ministry, being cut off from the Vine whose branches we are; and then keeping busy enough, or noisy enough, or narcotized enough to not have to face up to the fundamental disjointedness of our lives.[4]

Jesus needed time with the Father in order to combat dryness, frustration, imbalance, temptation and lack of focus. If Jesus made such a priority of it, how much more do we need to withdraw? Where do you go to withdraw? What steps do you take to stay fresh?

Renewal does not happen spontaneously. It requires choices. We can stay fresh because we make decisions. The following are practical steps for you to stay fresh and renewed in your ministry:

•**Schedule evaluation.** Your calendar reflects your theology of renewal. Our schedule can betray a difference between what we believe and what we practice. Take out your calendar. Look over this month, last month and next month. Have you scheduled any alone time? think time? study time? family time? leader-development, discipleship or mentoring time? Are any of those categories blocked off on your calendar? See the following example of schedule evaluation. "If only I had one more day" or, "If only I had one more hour in each day" are the responses I usually get. In fact, there is really never enough time. If I want to add any of those commitments to my life, I must make time. It's a choice.

SCHEDULE EVALUATION

MONTHLY

S	M	T	W	T	F	S

Look over the past two months in your calendar. Fill in the approximate hours (per day or per week if you prefer) given to the following areas:
Alone Time _____
Think Time _____
Family Time_____
Study Time _____
Job (non-study) Time ____
Friend Time _____
Play Time _____
Ministry Time (if you are a lay person and church work is not a part of your job)____

Are there any areas which require change? additions? deletions? Who will hold you accountable to any changes you wish to make? (continued)

	WEEKLY						Fill in a "normal" week. What percentages of each day are given to:
S	M	T	W	T	F	S	Work _____
							Play_____
							Family _____
							Study _____
							Self _____

After I presented the idea of evaluating schedules, one young minister asked, "But what about my ministry? If I begin focusing on these commitments, I won't have any time to run my programs."

"You're right," was my response. "But who told you it was your responsibility to run your programs? That's the job of the people. Your job is to make people effective programmers."

For ministry to be effective, the programming must be owned by the people. If I practice that, I will begin to let go of my need to run everything, be at every event, chair every committee and host every get-together. This important principle will be covered in detail in the final section.

How often should we do a schedule evaluation? I recommend that we begin each week (either Sunday evening or Monday morning) with a look at how we've prioritized our time. If you are married, it's important that your spouse be a part of this process.

•**Renewal retreat.** I find that in my life, it is necessary to withdraw often for a complete retreat. So I spend three days per month in a monastery in southern California. It is isolated and quiet. It allows me to refuel, re-evaluate, refocus, recommit and rejoice. But what if you don't have that much time? Then take as much time as you can, even if it is only a half hour per week. You will never *have* the time to develop a lifestyle of withdrawing; you must *make* the time.

A retreat can be any place that is away from the interruptions of your normal life. Where do you go to gain perspective on your life? to dream about the future? to spend uninterrupted time with God? Choose a place where you will not be interrupted for 24 hours. Then use the following sample retreat agenda for your alone time with God:

A PERSONAL 24-HOUR RETREAT

6:00 p.m.	30-Minute walk (or 30 minutes of silence in nature)
6:30 p.m.	Read Six Psalms
7:00 p.m.	Light Snack
7:20 p.m.	Personal Reading and Journaling
11:00 p.m.	Sleep
6:00 a.m.	30-Minute Walk (jog or aerobics)
6:30 a.m.	Shower
7:00 a.m.	Read Six Psalms
7:30 a.m.	Breakfast
8:00 a.m.	Guided Prayer

•adoration/thanksgiving
•confession
•intercession
•petition
•adoration
Read Hymns (three or four)

9:00 a.m.	Stretch
9:15 a.m.	Personal Reading and Journaling
11:30 a.m.	Lunch
12:30 p.m.	15-Minute Walk
12:45 p.m.	Brief Nap or Rest
1:30 p.m.	Read Six Psalms
2:00 p.m.	Setting Goals
3:00 p.m.	Stretch
3:15 p.m.	Personal Reading and Journaling
5:00 p.m.	20-Minute Walk
5:30 p.m.	Journaling and Reflection (of last 24 hours)

•**Accountability.** Staying fresh in a stale world is difficult because most of us are isolated. We have many friends and acquaintances, but it's rare to find one who is committed to the task of keeping us fresh.

Goals of an accountability relationship are:

•letting another or others evaluate my priorities

•not needing to prove my worth by performing

•being seen for what I can become and challenged to move that way

•being free to be me

Accountability is usually not a well-received word. We conjure up images of parental authority, loss of freedom and independence, compromise of identity. Those are normal reactions, but very unfortunate.

Accountability is God's way of reminding us that not one of us is an island. It is easy for me to fool myself, rationalize bad choices and behaviors, and justify sloppiness or laziness. It is not so easy to do with a friend who is committed to the process of mutual growth. I have friends who do that for me. They say in effect, "We love you too much to let you settle for mediocrity." Accountability is not fun or easy. But it's worth the price.

You cannot begin an accountability relationship with just anyone. Think of existing relationships in your life where there are trust, reciprocity and respect. Make a commitment with one or more of these people to form an accountability relationship (or group). Agree on the goals of an accountability relationship.

When you meet periodically, use these discussion questions to see if each of you is on target and moving toward self-improvement. Review the relationship periodically to see if expectations are being met.

•Am I needing to hide less about who I am?

•Am I becoming more confident in my identity?

•Am I setting goals for areas of personal growth?

•Am I excited about my accountability relationship—looking forward to the times we get together and the support I draw from it?

If you have not scheduled a regular time to be involved in an accountability relationship, do so now. The relationship will help you evaluate your goals, keep you on target and challenge you toward improvement.

•**Networking.** If it's true that we cannot make it alone, we need others not only for accountability, but for support as well. It makes a big difference to me when I know that there are others who can relate to what I am doing. Ministry becomes all the more difficult when I feel all alone.

I'm a believer in networks—a formal (or informal) association of persons who are brought together by common interests, vocations and callings. Networking may mean a lunch once every other month with three or four other young adult pastors or leaders in your city. Or it may mean a telephone call every now and again, just to pick one another's brain, and to say, "I'm praying for you. How's it going?"

How does a network begin? You can start one. Why wait for someone else to get motivated? Just think of a few people who are in similar vocations or friends who have common interests; call them and arrange to meet at a favorite restaurant for lunch. Do this once a month or more. It's easy to do and also keeps you refreshed and renewed for ministry.

Effective ministry is intentional ministry which begins in the heart. It happens with right choices, a strong foundation and focused planning. It flows from the heart of God through the heart of a devotional life.

KEY POINTS

1. Effective ministry is intentional ministry. It does not happen spontaneously or accidently.
2. The fundamental questions to ministry are:
   • Is my heart in what I'm doing?
   • Am I called to this ministry?
3. I'm uncomfortable with people who see their ministry with young adults as a rung on the ladder of church-ministry progression— until they can get a "real job."
4. Ministry must begin with an adequate foundation. The foundation is laid when one begins to answer the question "Why?"
5. To understand the heart behind the ministry, we must see Jesus' heart for people.
6. As a recipient of the compassion and "heart of Jesus," we become a healing place for others.
7. The effectiveness of a ministry can be measured by the degree to which we continue to receive healing in our own lives.
8. Programming can be effective when developed out of a devotional life.

REVIEW QUESTIONS

1. Where has God's grace been real to you?
2. Does Mark 6:32 apply to you? In what ways?
3. Where do you begin to apply this understanding of a "heart behind the ministry"?
4. Where do you go to continually *revive* your heart?
5. Review the second chapter. Where has God been working in your life in the areas mentioned?

CHAPTER 7

Ingredients of a Solid Foundation

As we said earlier, ministry with young adults is not simply a matter of copying a successful program and hoping for the best. Successful programming (answering the question "Why?") comes out of a devotional life—a sincere heart. That is where ministry begins. But it cannot stop there. It is not enough to be sincere. In the following verses, Jesus speaks of the importance of establishing a firm foundation:

> Every one then who hears these words of mine and does them will be like a wise man who built his house upon the rock; and the rain fell, and the floods came, and the winds blew and beat upon that house, but it did not fall, because it had been founded on the rock. And every one who hears these words of mine and does not do them will be like a foolish man who built his house upon the sand; and the rain fell, and the floods came, and the winds blew and beat against the house, and it fell; and great was the fall of it (Matthew 7:24-27).

Jesus' parable speaks of a strong faith foundation. That teaching is applicable to young adult ministry. Without the right foundation, there is no guarantee as to the strength or future of the building.

What constitutes a solid foundation? It is our theology of ministry. It is our reason for being. It is the grid by which all of our programs are evaluated. It determines the direction our group is headed. The fact is that all of us operate from some foundation. Many of us, however, have never stopped to look at what that foundation includes. Unfortunately, we have not stated our theology of ministry.

When you build a foundation—your theology of ministry—you are declaring your non-negotiables. "This is where we stand."

Although I cannot lay your foundation for you, I can get you started with some important non-negotiables for young adult ministry. These principles will insure that your foundation is a strong one.

Following is an illustration of the six ingredients you'll need to build a firm foundation for young adult ministry. The ingredients are discussed in detail throughout the rest of the chapter.

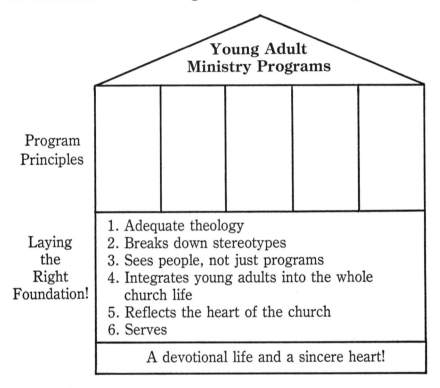

**Young Adult
Ministry Programs**

Program
Principles

Laying
the
Right
Foundation!

1. Adequate theology
2. Breaks down stereotypes
3. Sees people, not just programs
4. Integrates young adults into the whole
   church life
5. Reflects the heart of the church
6. Serves

A devotional life and a sincere heart!

A FOUNDATION WITH AN ADEQUATE THEOLOGY

You can tell a church's theology, not by the creedal statement they have in the foyer by the door, but by how it is practiced in their programs. Many ministry problems are not program problems, but theological problems. For example, one gentleman approached me to get my opinion on why his church's young adult program was not working. When I inquired about the program, I was informed that only a handful were attending and the morale was low. They met on Friday night in the church and called it "The never-married Christian group." No wonder they were failing! Their church creedal statement affirmed equality through creation, but their program reflected a segregation by marital status. What we say about young adults in our church must be compatible with our theology.

Do you want to have an effective ministry with young adults? Take a look at the theology of your church. There are several issues to examine:

•**Personhood.** What does the Bible say about personhood? Are some persons better than others? Is there a hierarchy of spirituality? Do we accept people where they are despite how they got there? Are young adults complete persons? Is singleness an okay life choice? Is marriage really a prerequisite for completeness? How do we communicate our theology of personhood?

•**Family.** Have we adequately defined "family"? Most of our church curriculum addresses the "nuclear family"—father working, mother home with children—and yet statistics tell us that less than six percent of American family structures are nuclear.[1] What does that say to the church? How does the Bible define family? What about a young couple (age 24 to 28) who are postponing children until their thirties? Are they still a complete family? What about the young couple who are unable to have children (a group of 12 to 15 percent of all married couples)? Is a 33-year-old single parent with her two children a family? Is a single 26-year-old a family unit? How do we communicate our theology of family? What does it mean that the church is "family"? Do our young adults sense that reality?

•**Evangelism.** Once we've decided to have a ministry with single adults, we open the church doors and say, "Okay, you can come to our church now." Is that evangelism? How did Jesus evangelize? What does it mean for us to go where the people are? The tragic statistics in the first section of this book already affirmed that most young adults are not coming to the church. The church must find ways to go to them.

•**Commitment.** I agree with Terry Fullum when he said in an interview with Leadership journal, that we assume "noncommitment" on the part of our church people. This is especially true with young adults. We talk to them as if they are uncommitted. Guess what happens? They become uncommitted! Listen to our language: "Oh, he's still unattached and noncommittal." "You know single people—they will never commit themselves." "You just can't count on young people these days!" We end up getting the church work done by the people with the lowest threshold of guilt. Is that what the Bible means when it speaks of commitment? Look at Ephesians 4:11-15 and 1 Corinthians 12 as Paul talks about the role of each part of the body. How can you communicate this to your church? to your young adults? Read Terry Fullum's illustration:

> We have a number of clergy and lay leadership conferences here every year, drawing people from all over the world. And we house them in the homes of the parish. For many years, I used to go to the congregation and say, 'A conference is coming up, and we need 200 beds; please sign up.' We always got what we needed, but it was a hassle.
>
> Then one day, I realized all that wasn't necessary. I went before the congregation one Sunday and said, 'You have heard me ask for beds for the last time. From now on, we will assume that if you have an extra bed in your house, of course you would let someone use it. Because everything you have belongs to the Lord and you've consecrated your home to his service, naturally you would make it available to his servants. So we have made up a bed bank for the parish, and we'll assume yours are available. If for some reason you cannot host a guest, you let us know—otherwise, we will assume commitment rather than noncommitment.'[2]

How does this illustration apply to our churches? with our young adults? Where do we begin?

A FOUNDATION THAT BREAKS DOWN STEREOTYPES

The message of Galatians is blunt: Stereotypes create barriers to the work of the cross. Programs give people things to do, but ministry begins to break down barriers.

> For in Christ Jesus you are all sons of God, through faith. For as many of you as were baptized into Christ have put on Christ. There is neither Jew nor Greek, there is neither slave nor free, there is neither male nor female; for you are all one in Christ Jesus. And if you are Christ's, then you are Abraham's offspring, heirs according to promise (Galatians 3:26-29).

I like the poem by Robert Frost that begins with these words, "What is that thing that does not like a wall, but breaks a hole big enough for two to walk through abreast." The poet was speaking about a wall in his back yard separating his neighbor's orchard from his. But it is also a graphic statement about the reality of Jesus. He is about the business of breaking down walls.

A young adult program will only be as effective as the environment in which it exists.

A FOUNDATION THAT SEES PEOPLE, NOT JUST PROGRAMS; THAT BUILDS COMMUNITY, NOT JUST AN ORGANIZATION

Ministry is more than programs which occupy people's time. It is a family and community environment which is nurturing and developmental.

We find ourselves tempted to compare our programs with those around us. If the church down the street begins using a guitar, we need to use two! Our "ministry" quickly degenerates to a "dog-'n-pony show" with the emphasis on creating the "biggest," the "best" and the "busiest."

To focus on people is not easy. We always will be tempted with new programming. As long as you're in church work, there always will be someone telling you that, "There is something you're not doing—and you need to be doing it now!"

Jesus' ministry was effective because he knew how to say no. He knew how to prioritize. He didn't see everyone. He didn't do everything everyone asked him to do. He stayed close to his Father, and out of that relationship found the resources to focus on his calling. The result? Jesus loved people.

A FOUNDATION THAT INTEGRATES YOUNG ADULTS INTO THE WHOLE CHURCH

Why is it that many young adult programs seem like only a satellite or programmatic necessity to the church? Very often churches are threatened by vitality and energy. It is the threat of something new.

Integration is not easy. It does not happen spontaneously. It requires work and effort. We can begin by creating an environment and structure that emphasize integration. We can begin by re-educating our church from the pulpit. We need to see young adults as *givers*, not just as *takers*. When seen as takers, is it any wonder that integration is difficult?

Do a current assessment of your church. How many young adults are involved as Sunday school teachers? Do any serve as deacons and elders? Is any member of your pastoral staff under 35? Is there a program to develop ministry interns? Are young adults invited to serve on church committees? What about your new member program?

I recommend that you create an integrative environment for new members of the church. Have your new members' class in a small group of eight or 12 persons for a six- to 10-week period. Make sure the groups are integrated (single and married, old and young). The message comes clear: People who are not like me don't bite, and they are just as important to the body of Christ as I am. Maybe, just maybe, I can learn from them!

A FOUNDATION THAT REFLECTS THE HEART OF THE CHURCH

If a ministry with young adults is not the desire of the church, and is not supported by the senior pastor (or leadership team), the likelihood of creating an effective ministry is very small. In each area of church ministry, there needs to be consensus in direction.

On the other hand, the absence of pastoral support should not be used as an excuse. In such a situation, determine that the process of change can begin with you! Make it a priority to sit down with your pastor and share your heart and vision for ministry with young adults.

It is important to have staff support. As a ministry with young adults builds, some programming ideas will be controversial; for example, ministry on off-campus facilities such as restaurants, and ministry with divorced persons, etc. The more support from church staff, the more effective the young adult ministry.

A FOUNDATION THAT IS "SERVING"

Nothing will kill a program faster than to let it exist for itself only! I've been a guest at many programs where they seem to gather for the sole purpose of bemoaning their current marital status. That is why I am not in favor of identifying the group solely by the marital status. Self-serving groups isolate and insulate themselves by becoming problem-focused. To focus on "my singleness" is not going to effectively motivate me to move on with my life and grow as a Christian.

We grow only as we serve. The irony, of course, is that many young adults, who are "too busy" or who are in a crisis, don't feel as if they have anything to give. But therein lies the mystery of the Gospel:

Even in times we believe we have nothing to give, we grow by giving away ourselves.

We need to give ourselves and our people a sense of mission. In my ministry with young adults at the Crystal Cathedral, we adopted an orphanage in Mexico. There we built a dormitory and a chapel, and provided food and clothing. Making monthly trips to the orphanage, we soon discovered that the people benefiting most were not the orphans, but us!

Make sure that your ministry is built with an *equipping* focus. We cannot overemphasize the importance of every member of the body doing his or her part. I've found that this emphasis is healing as well as affirming. Do you want to see healing take place? Give a needy person a job in the church.

The more we see our focus as outward, the more we will see our ministry defined by the needs of the community.

KEY POINTS

1. When you build a foundation—your philosophy of ministry—you are declaring your non-negotiables. "This is where we stand."
2. A solid foundation has an adequate theology.
3. A solid foundation breaks down stereotypes.
4. A solid foundation sees people, not just programs; sees community, not just an organization.
5. A solid foundation integrates young adults into the whole life of the church.
6. A solid foundation reflects the heart of the church.
7. A solid foundation is "serving." The more we see our focus as outward, the more we will see our ministry defined by the needs of the community.

REVIEW QUESTIONS

1. Why is it important to begin with an adequate foundations?
2. Which of the six foundation principles make up your church's present foundation for ministry? Or is your foundation non-articulated?
3. What are some ways in which inadequate theology affects pro-

gramming? How does Terry Fullum's illustration relate to your church and young adult ministry?

4. What are the prevalent stereotypes in your church regarding young adults? older adults?
5. How can we re-educate ourselves and create an environment that emphasizes people, not status?
6. List creative ways that you can integrate young adults into your church.

CHAPTER 8

The Ministry Planning Arrow

With a strong foundation, effective programming can become a reality. Without it, the results are destined to be frustrating, super ficial, short-lived or built only on hype.

At a recent young adult ministry workshop, one young pastor wondered whether so much concern for foundations was necessary. "I love the Lord and feel called to do ministry. So why can't I just find a 'working program' and get started?" he asked me during a break. Fifty percent of his job description was young adults, in a church where 30 percent of adults attending were between the ages of 20 to 35. What an opportunity he had. No wonder he wanted to "hurry" the process along. By the time the workshop ended, he agreed to not shortcut the developmental process. A foundation must precede a program.

Six months after the workshop he called me. "I'm excited. Our programs are working. But I realize I'm not just doing programs for programs' sake. I know why I'm here. That sense of purpose has only increased my love and commitment to the young adults I'm working with. It renews my hope!"

I could use phone calls like that in regular dosages. It was good to hear his affirmation.

Our need now is to make the foundation process as practical as possible. Let's walk through a six-step process of building a foundation, or of re-evaluating an existing foundation. To help us, we will use a ministry planning arrow. To make most effective use of this planning experiment, I recommend one or both of the following:

•**Read the chapter as an overview.** Once complete, set aside one to three hours to walk through the process personally.

•**Calendar a full day or weekend to walk through the planning process with your leadership team.** The most effective size for a leadership team is six to 12 people. If you don't have a leadership team, gather several interested people together and form a brainstorming group. Use the sample retreat schedule outlined on pages 14-15.

The most important thing to remember is: *Allow others to be involved in the planning process. Don't plan solo and expect to sell "your" ideas to "the group."*

Are you ready to begin the process of building a foundation? Use the following arrow for notes and brainstorming. (Instructions are included in the six steps.) Draw the arrow on notebook paper and make copies for each member of your leadership team.

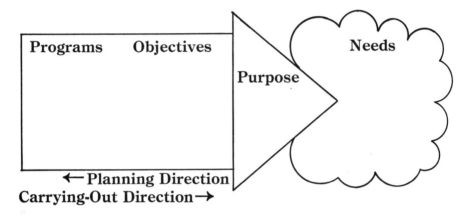

STEP ONE: PRAY

Prayer keeps our ministry focused on God, not on ourselves. This important step was discussed in detail in the previous chapter. Effective ministry is based on a devotional life—a sincere heart.

We need to be careful not to perpetuate the methodology that works out all the details and then feels compelled to bring God in to "bless our work." It is easy to take prayer for granted—as an afterthought. That's why it is important that we continue to remind one another of its necessity.

Prayer is not simply a means of securing God's validation. It is a way in which we learn to listen to God. For God wants far more for us than we could ever dream, ask or think (Ephesians 3:20).

Make it a habit to have a prayer time when you don't say anything, don't ask anything and don't tell God anything. Just listen. Place a blank note pad in front of you. Start writing anything that comes to mind: ideas, thoughts, dreams, desires.

I've found it helpful to use a separate piece of paper specifically for writing down the things that distract me. For example, "I need to pick up the dry cleaning." "Did I remember to water the lawn?" That way, I can clear my mind of my daily worries without thinking I'll forget to do them.

Prayer puts me in the right place before God. It allows me to do ministry with a sincere heart.

STEP TWO: AFFIRM YOUR FOUNDATIONAL PRINCIPLES

No one gets on a rapid-transit bus without first checking to see where it's going. The same should be true for young adult ministry. In which direction are you headed? What biblical principles are you building your ministry upon? What's important as the distinguishing characteristics of your programming emphasis? What are the foundational principles of the church of which you are a part?

In the previous chapter we discussed six non-negotiables as foundation stones for ministry. Review that chapter as you begin to articulate those principles which are essential for your direction. What are your non-negotiables? Will you try to break down stereotypes? Will you look at people, not just programs? Is "service" your focus? Write your non-negotiables in the space below the arrow.

STEP THREE: IDENTIFY NEEDS

Jesus was effective because he knew what people needed. He saw that the people were "like sheep without a shepherd." Jesus had a target; he knew what he was aiming at. There is no ministry without a target.

It's time to brainstorm. What are you aiming at? Picture the people to whom you minister. Whom do you see? Picture their faces. Their circumstances. Their needs. What do you see that makes you sad?

What do you see that makes you angry? Are there any issues over which you get concerned enough to "pound the table"? When Jesus saw needs, they evoked intense emotions. He cried. He felt compassion. He threw people out of the temple. He was sad. Jesus knew what was at stake.

Let him open your heart to see where people are incomplete, where they hurt, where they face life alone and afraid. On the arrow, list those need areas that come to mind.

Before we complete our brainstorming time, it is important to take some time to distinguish between "felt" and "unfelt" needs. Many people advocate that ministries be built on meeting the "felt needs of the community." That is, those needs which are not only visible, but apparent to the person who is in need. Felt needs are essential. But if that's all there is, it can be an unhealthy approach to ministry.

Jesus saw felt needs, but he always looked beyond them to the deeper unfelt needs. For often, felt needs are merely symptoms. And in our hurry to do ministry, we touch only symptoms and never reach the cause. That's why those foundational principles (our non-negotiables) are so essential. They keep us from being "symptomatic" and from being focused on "felt needs" only. For example, earlier we discussed a foundation based on six principles or non-negotiables (the need for integration, reaching out beyond our narcissism, etc.). Those issues are important areas of need, but they may not be felt.

Look at the needs you have listed. Are any of them symptoms of greater areas of need? Let me give you some examples:

Felt Needs	Unfelt Needs
Lack of Purpose	Discipleship Relationships
Moral Uncertainty	Spiritual Direction
Anger and Pain From End of a Relationship	Healing Process in the Context of a Small Group
Money Problems	Financial Planning and Budgeting
Loneliness	Community or Small Group Involvement

STEP FOUR: PURPOSE

The needs to which God has called you to address will determine the specific focus of your ministry and thus your programming. Not all programming is created equal. We cannot overlay a generic board on any and every church. Your ministry will be determined by the needs you have uncovered. This is where the process gets exciting. Why? Because a purpose statement keeps you focused in the right direction.

That's why it is important that a purpose statement be articulated, written down and made public. An alarming number of ministers respond with a blank stare when asked the following question, "What is the purpose for your program?" Answers range from "We've always done it this way!" to "The pastor asked me to do it."

Your purpose statement is a general statement reflecting the direction you want your programming to take. Most of us have been in ministries where we have wondered why certain programs exist, but have maintained them, thinking (or hoping) there was a good reason. The purpose statement provides a way to scrutinize our programs.

Now it's time to form a statement. Ask everyone in your leadership team or brainstorming group to write three or four sample purpose statements. They should be only one to three sentences in length. Begin the sample statements with, "In response to the needs we see, our purpose is ..." Then compare statements. Refine what you've uncovered. Rework it together and come to a consensus. Write the final, agreed-upon purpose statement in the arrow.

A purpose statement is important because it sets the tone for your ministry. It was my policy to begin every meeting by reciting the purpose statement. "Hello. Welcome to First Church. We get together here every Wednesday night for the purpose of ..."

Every week newcomers, as well as old timers, heard the purpose statement. It started to sink in. "So that's why we're here!"

It also is necessary to have the purpose statement available in printed form such as a brochure, flyer or business card. It helps us effectively communicate why we're here.

Following are three examples of purpose statements. Use them to help you create your own.

•As the young adult community, we want to engender and call our people to a deeper sense of belonging—accepting and affirming each other as a Catholic family.

•The purpose of Cornerstone ministry is to encourage married and single young adults to a progressively deeper commitment to God, the body of Christ, and the work of Christ in the world through worship, instruction and community.

•Sonrise is a ministry committed to glorifying God. It encourages Christlikeness by building a creative community which meets individual needs, and by accepting his Lordship over relationships, careers and every aspect of life.

STEP FIVE: OBJECTIVES

Now we begin the process of fleshing out our purpose. Objectives are broad, non-measurable categories or areas of focus. They indicate the involvement necessary to fulfill your purpose statement. The following example is the purpose statement from a young adult ministry in Thousand Oaks, California.

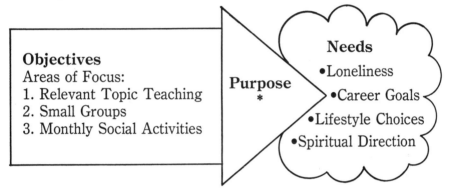

*"We were all called to be whole and healthy people in an unwhole and unhealthy world. And no one of us can make it alone. We get together once a week to look at issues and tools that will help us make wise decisions and become whole persons."

Let me contrast the previous illustration with another church's purpose and objectives:

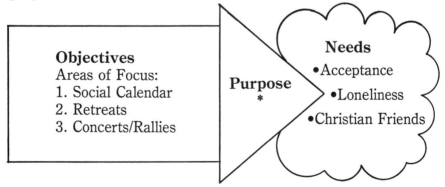

*"We exist to create an accepting and caring environment where

young adults can find positive fellowship."

By setting objectives, we are free to focus. Objectives of a young adult ministry allow you to target activities to fulfill your purpose. If the purpose is "an accepting and caring environment where young adults can find positive fellowship," there are activities you don't have to plan (such as teaching seminars). Objectives free you to target needs.

STEP SIX: PROGRAMS

Based on your arrow, what specific programs do you need? Will some programming ideas be more appropriate than others? For example, if your purpose is positive fellowship, you can plan activities such as progressive dinners, game nights, "Friday Night at the Movies" (rent a video and pop popcorn), etc. You also can plan for specific groups such as singles and young marrieds. Keep reading! The final section includes guidelines and ideas for programming.

KEY POINTS

1. With a strong foundation, effective programming can become a reality.
2. Allow others to be involved in the planning process. Don't plan solo and expect to sell "your" ideas to "the group."
3. The first step to build a firm foundation is to pray.
4. The second step is to affirm your foundational principles.
5. The third step is to identify the needs of the young adults.
6. The fourth step is to create a purpose statement.
7. The fifth step is to list objectives.
8. The sixth step is to create programs to fit your objectives and purpose.

REVIEW QUESTIONS

1. How do you respond to the "process" of planning? Have you set aside time to walk through the planning arrow with your group? (For the remainder of the questions, use the blank planning arrow found on page 91.)
2. What are the non-negotiables for your ministry?

3. Have you identified target need areas? Have you distinguished between felt and unfelt needs?
4. What is your purpose statement?
5. What are the three most important objectives for your ministry?

CHAPTER 9

A Biblical Foundation for Leadership

You've worked through a philosophy of ministry. You've developed a direction and purpose statement. Now it's time for a sizzling young adult program, right? Not quite yet. A common thread of all the stories I've heard of failed young adult programs has been the lack of direction and leadership.

Leadership. That one word evokes a myriad of emotions. Mention the word leadership and the responses vary:

"Training leaders is too much work."

"We need strong leaders. I'm not sure what they look like, but we need them!"

"You just can't count on those young adults."

"My people are too busy."

"I get them trained, and they get married and leave."

Where do we begin in unraveling this puzzle called leadership development? Young adult leadership development is very important. The ministry belongs to the young adults themselves.

I once saw a bumper sticker that said: "Where are the people? I must find them for I am their leader!" Sound familiar?

My constant task—as director or minister—is to find ways to turn the ministry over to the people. I do that most effectively if I see my role as a "leader developer." I'm here to build, grow and train leaders.

The fundamental problem with leadership is a problem of definition. To help us gain a better view of leadership, let's look at the following verses:

And his gifts were that some should be apostles, some prophets, some evangelists, some pastors and teachers, to equip the saints for the work of ministry, for building up the body of Christ, until we all attain to the unity of the faith and of the knowledge of the Son of God, to mature manhood, to the measure of the stature of the fulness of Christ; so that we may no longer be children, tossed to and fro and carried about with every wind of doctrine, by the cunning of men, by their craftiness in deceitful wiles. Rather, speaking the truth in love, we are to grow up in every way into him who is the head, into Christ, from whom the whole body, joined and knit together by every joint with which it is supplied, when each part is working properly, makes bodily growth and upbuilds itself in love (Ephesians 4:11-16).

There are four important biblical principles that will create the foundation for the development work we will begin to do in the next chapter. All of the biblical principles have practical applications, and when applied can bring an individual and group to life.

A LEADER KNOWS HIS OR HER IDENTITY IN CHRIST

It's clear from the Bible that at one level all Christians are leaders. That doesn't mean that everyone is a leader and no one is a follower. It means that no one is exempt from doing the ministry. Ministry is not a job reserved for a special few called "leaders."

Therefore, if any one is in Christ, he is a new creation; the old has passed away, behold, the new has come. All this is from God, who through Christ reconciled us to himself and gave us the ministry of reconciliation; that is, in Christ God was reconciling the world to himself, not counting their trespasses against them, and entrusting to us the message of reconciliation. So we are ambassadors for Christ, God making his appeal through us. We beseech you on behalf of Christ, be reconciled to God. For our sake he made him to be sin who knew no sin, so that in him we might become the righteousness of God (2 Corinthians 5:15-21).

What does that mean? It means that as a young adult coordinator or director, you are not the only "hired gun" in town. And that the leadership team is not the only group responsible for making this ministry work.

We get stuck when we assume that "leaders do the ministry, the rest of us get ministered unto." According to the Bible, that's not true. We *all* do the ministry. Does that mean we all have the same levels and areas of responsibility? No, of course not. But that comes later. We must begin with this affirmation: *As a Christian, the choice to be a minister is not an option.*

People need to hear that affirmation. Just because I'm the pastor, or the vice president or the chairperson, doesn't make me special. I have more responsibility, but I am not any more important to the group than the others.

We get ourselves in trouble when we start to believe that the group can't make it without us. If 2 Corinthians 5 is true, then others can do quite well without me. (Remember Jesus telling his disciples that they would even do "greater things"?) And maybe I should stop my attempts at building a kingdom, and get about the task of equipping *ministers.*

Begin telling your group who they are in Christ. "You're ministers! It's not a question of whether you want to be. The question is where and how well are you doing?"

Every year, I presented a four-week series to our young adult group on the subject of our role as ministers. Why? Because we need to update the way we think about leadership. According to Ephesians 4 and 2 Corinthians 5, everyone who is a believer is involved.

Below is an overview of the four-week series on leadership.

OUR ROLE AS MINISTERS

SESSION ONE: OUR IDENTITY IN CHRIST

(2 Corinthians 5:17-21)

Every Christian is a minister. There is no vote. There is not an elite group of "those who minister," and the rest of us are "ministered unto." This is "our church," not "my church," or the "pastor's church." As ministers, God has done the following in each of us.

•He has given us his Word (2 Timothy 3:16-17; Ephesians 3:1-5, 7-11).

•He has equipped us with his power (Ephesians 1:18-20; 3:14-20).

•He has given us his character (Romans 8:29; Ephesians 4:13).

•He has equipped us with spiritual gifts (Ephesians 4:7-13; 1 Corinthians 12—14).

Questions:

1. Would it make a difference if we say every believer is a minister?

How would that affect your church or group?

2. How do we communicate this truth?

3. What does this truth do to your understanding about your identity in Christ?

SESSION TWO: OUR SIGNIFICANCE TO THE BODY

(1 Corinthians 12:12-26)

We need the body and it needs us. There is no such thing as a hierarchy of "superior giftedness." Simply because someone is "the pastor," doesn't mean he or she is more necessary for the body. In fact, the Bible is clear that the weakest most vulnerable parts are most necessary.

Our goal with one another is *building-up*. I need to see that the Christian faith is no longer something I (or you) can do in isolation. We have a role as builders in each others' lives.

Questions:

1. Why do we see some persons as essential for the body, and others as dispensable?

2. How does 1 Corinthians 12 change the way we should view each other?

3. In what ways does the principle apply to leadership?

SESSION THREE: OUR SPIRITUAL GIFTEDNESS

(1 Corinthians 12—13; Ephesians 4; 1 Peter 4:10)

•**Faith.** You must believe you are gifted. God doesn't ask us to do what he hasn't equipped us to do (John 15:16; 1 Corinthians 12:7).

•**Prayer.** God doesn't want us to pray only that we'll satisfy a curiosity. He asks of us a commitment (Colossians 4:2-4).

•**Awareness.** Be aware of the gifts available.

•**Responsibility.** In what type of service are you presently involved?

•**Common sense.** Consider your desires; consider the needs of others; consider your experience; confirm others.

The purpose of my gift is not to wear an identification badge, but to propel me into service. Read 1 Peter 4:10. How do we find our niche?

Questions:

1. What does 1 Peter 4:10 mean practically to you?

2. Are you aware of your niche? Explain.

3. Are any of the five steps listed helpful? In what ways?

SESSION FOUR: OUR JOB AS SALT AND LIGHT

(Matthew 5:13-16)

God says that we are *models* (1 Thessalonians 1:7) and ambassadors (2 Corinthians 5:17). What does that mean? It means we don't just float through life in a vacuum. We are bearers of God's message of peace. We have the message that turns the world upside down (Acts 17). We do not live only for ourselves.

What does it mean to be salt?

•Salt brings out taste. Brings out the best in people.

•Salt is a preservative. A preservative against moral decay.

•Salt adds zest and excitement. Are you fun to be with?

Questions:

1. Does it make a difference that you are God's ambassador? If so, in what ways?

2. How does our call to be salt affect our leadership position?

3. In what specific ways can you be more like salt?

It is typical for people to come to me and say, "Terry, there's a problem in our group; what are *you* going to do about it?"

My response, "I don't know. Let's brainstorm together. What are *we* going to do about it?"

Granted, I may end up being the individual to deal specifically with the problem, but I don't want to let that person off the hook by letting him or her think this is "my ministry" and I'm the only one who can deal with it. I communicate the message that *we* are involved in this ministry *together*.

A LEADER IS COMMITTED TO THE GOAL OF THE BODY OF CHRIST

A leader knows where the body is going. Why does your group exist? To create a successful program? To provide fellowship for young adults? To create an environment for healthy relationships? To an extent all are true. But they can only happen when we understand that the foundational reason we exist is "to equip the saints for the work of ministry, for building up the body of Christ, until we all attain to the unity of the faith and of the knowledge of the

Son of God, to mature manhood, to the measure of the stature of the fulness of Christ" (Ephesians 4:12-13).

Becoming Christlike and mature is not an individual endeavor, although most of us live as if it were. "It's me and Jesus, and he wants me Christlike." That's only partially true. In fact, "Christlikeness" is always mentioned in a plural context in the Bible. In other words, *I* become Christlike only as *we* become Christlike. It is no longer sufficient for me to focus on my own personal and spiritual development as if I were an island, and ignore other people's need to develop spiritually. The young adult group can no longer be just a smorgasbord for "my needs." My needs are met only as our needs are met. I become Christlike, only as we become Christlike. My focus changes from "me-centered" to "us-centered."

This focus also makes a difference in the way we recruit involvement. While it is true that people are needed to set up chairs, make coffee, plan parties and organize retreats; they do not exist only for those tasks. These tasks all get old if they are an end to themselves. Why do we set up chairs? Because ultimately it helps in the process of creating a ministry where "Jesus changes lives." Jesus is in the process of developing what C.S. Lewis calls "little Christs"—people "infected" with the life of Jesus himself.[1]

That is what ministry is all about. Creating a place where people can be accepted—right where they are—and transformed by Jesus.

Everything that is done to create that place is important. Just because I make the coffee, it doesn't mean that I am any less important to the group than the one who leads worship. I need to see my role as important in building "Christlikeness."

Many of my leaders labored under the assumption that their role was less significant because it was not a part of the spiritual life of the group. One young woman said to me, "I enjoy planning the parties, but I know the real ministry takes place in your Bible study." That's not true. If every believer is a minister and a leader, then it even further breaks down the distinction between the sacred and the secular. The party and the Bible study must be planned with the same purpose in mind: to create a place where Jesus can become real. That does not require religious words, Bible verses or stained glass. It requires real people who are themselves changed by Jesus.

Whether you plan or participate in a Bible study or a party is not the issue. The issue is the intention or goal of your involvement.

A LEADER UNDERSTANDS
HIS OR HER NICHE IN THE WORK OF THE BODY

A leader is more than just a title or position. Titles do not confer leadership. Neither does a majority of votes. Areas of giftedness determine what niche of leadership I undertake.

That's why I'm not an advocate of elections for leadership positions. In the following chapter you will read that "selective leadership" is preferable. Why? Because the focus is on plugging people into places where they fit, not simply filling positions because the organizational chart says there is a vacancy.

There is a reason the apostle Paul began his speech on spiritual gifts with this sentence, "Now concerning spiritual gifts, brethren, I do not want you to be uninformed" (1 Corinthians 12:1). The fact is, things have not changed. Most Christians are very uninformed regarding spiritual gifts. For effective ministry to take place, we need to confront that void.

When was the last time you taught your young adult group about spiritual gifts? It is a complex and scary subject to tackle, especially if you don't feel theologically qualified. But you need not make it so complex, that only aggravates the problem.

We need to teach spiritual gifts as building blocks for finding your niche. To do that, we must begin with the following assumptions.

•**The Bible does not create a complete list of all spiritual gifts.** It is giving us a framework to understand the importance of gifts and what that means to ministry.

•**A spiritual gift is not merely an identification badge.** "Hi. I'm Terry and I have the gift of administration." As a badge, a gift is meaningless. A gift is only a gift when it is used. Gifts are discovered, not just in teaching sessions, but by putting people to work.

•**A spiritual gift cannot come from a begrudging spirit.** Just because a person is a talented teacher doesn't automatically mean he or she is gifted in that area for ministry. So often we look for obvious talents, and miss areas of giftedness. *My spiritual gift is that place where my sense of joy touches a real human need.*

•**A spiritual gift is not a title but a way of touching needs.** So it is not a noun, but a verb. Not host, but hospitality. Not giver, but giving. Not teacher, but teaching.

For some very practical help in the area of spiritual gifts, I recommend Rick Yohn's book, **Discover Your Spiritual Gift and Use It.**[2]

One of the key ways to implant this third principle of finding the right niche, is to allow people the opportunity to dream. Where will their joy touch a sense of need?

A LEADER KNOWS ULTIMATELY WHO OWNS THE BODY

It is normal to take responsibility for things for which we have no responsibility. We see it happen as soon as someone assumes a leadership role. With that role I also assume that I am responsible for the well-being and success of the group. It is reflected in my language. It becomes "my group," "my committee," "my ministry," "my party." But at a deeper level we may be planting seeds of unreal expectations.

According to Ephesians 4:15, it is not my group, or my committee; they belong to Christ who is the head. There is a big difference. What does that difference mean? It means ultimately that I am free. I am free from my need to:

•worry about who attends and who doesn't attend

•feel anxiety over the fact that my committee isn't accomplishing as much as "your committee"

•worry about my reputation based on "what others think" of my ministry

•harbor resentment because the people aren't appreciating all my hard work for them

When I take responsibility for the outcome, I focus on all the wrong issues. Does that mean we give up our desire for excellence? No. But it means that excellence is a by-product, not a goal. Faithfulness is the goal. If I understand that, then it changes the way I do ministry. If God is indeed my owner, I am free from my need to:

•perform

•impress

•entertain

•manipulate

Instead, I am free to:

•risk failures

•compliment another

•give the ministry away

•share the rewards
Leadership begins with the right foundation.

KEY POINTS

1. Young adult ministries which start with a flurry, slowly fail because of lack of leadership.
2. A leader knows his or her identity in Christ.
3. As a Christian, the choice to be a minister is not an option.
4. A leader is committed to the goal of the body of Christ.
5. A leader understands his or her niche in the work of the body.
6. A leader knows ultimately who owns the body.

REVIEW QUESTIONS

1. When you hear the word "leader" what synonyms come to mind?
2. Is it true that *all* Christians are ministers? What difference does that make practically? What are the ways you can teach that truth to your young adults?
3. Why are people involved in leadership roles in your young adult group?

Obligation	Reputation	Requirement
Elected	Guilt	Service
Enjoyment	Compassion	Pity
Empathy	Fun	Other _____

4. Are the four biblical principles on spiritual gifts helpful in sorting through this complex issue? Why or why not?
5. Where can you begin to emphasize "sense of joy touches a real human need" in your life and ministry?
6. Do you agree with this statement? "If I believe this group belongs to Christ, I am ultimately free." Why or why not? How do we apply that principle?

CHAPTER 10

Leadership Development: The Unfinished Task

I am often asked, "What is your main responsibility in your ministry with young adults?" My initial answer is one word: *equipping*. It is my job to find leaders, train leaders, develop leaders, encourage leaders, and to set leaders free to do greater things than I could accomplish. That's the job description of a young adult pastor or ministry leader.

Now that we have an adequate biblical understanding of leadership, we can begin to equip those around us for leadership. Where do we begin such a task? What are the practical steps? Let me suggest 10 practical principles:

BUILD YOUR MINISTRY WITH SELECTIVE LEADERSHIP

Mass recruitment does not work. This sentence is all too familiar, "We need a leader, would anyone like to volunteer?" The result is that we end up with leaders who we wish were not there, or they are there for the wrong reasons. And because these individuals have taken the trouble to volunteer, it becomes additionally difficult to remove them from leadership, change their role or offer direction. Far too often we feel obliged to use persons against our better judgment. When we lead out of desperation, we end up with a desperate ministry. Volunteerism is not an effective way to build leadership.

Are we saying that we never use volunteers? No. We are saying that volunteering is not "the" reason to entrust a person with leadership.

Let's use Jesus' model. He personally *selected* his disciples. We get frustrated because we look around and say, "But there are no leaders around here to select from! That's our problem!" Remember, Jesus didn't select "finished-product leaders." They were raw material only! His purpose was to select in order to develop and equip. That's where we should begin.

Here are some important steps to take when selecting leaders:

•**Pray**. Jesus spent a full night in prayer before he selected the disciples. It's important that we begin there, because we need "divine eyes" for this task. With our human perspective we may be looking for persons with the wrong motive. We need the Spirit to open our eyes to undiscovered potential.

•**Observe.** Watch those persons who display leadership ability or exhibit leadership potential. Keep track of your observations. Keep a "Leadership Potential List" at your desk and jot down names of people who are leadership development material. Never assume that once you select leaders you're finished with the process. Always be ready with new leaders.

The "Leadership Potential List" has been very helpful to me. It has allowed me to focus my thinking and energy in the direction of encouragement and leadership development. Following is a sample list:

LEADERSHIP POTENTIAL LIST

Name	Areas of Interest/ Giftedness	Notes (include current or past involvements, personal observations)

•**Ask.** Let people know your interest in them. For example, "Hi Sue. I think you've got some real gifts and abilities and that you are strongly committed. Would you be interested in talking about how those abilities would be used in a leadership role in this group?"

If the person says "no," find out why. It may be a very valid reason. Perhaps he or she simply misunderstands the expectations of leadership, or perhaps the person is sensitive to a negative experience in the past. If he or she says yes, move on to the next step.

SPEND MORE TIME WITH A FEW— THE LEADERSHIP CORE GROUP

Jesus spent most of his time with a few people. As is often the case, leaders in church ministry are involved in everything from leading the singing to sweeping the carpets. And those of us in young adult ministry find ourselves racing from planning parties to buying doughnuts. Result? All the time is absorbed and there is nothing left for personal renewal or leadership development.

By nature we find it difficult to transfer leadership because we are afraid to let people fail. "After all, it might reflect back on my reputation!" "I just know they can't do it as well as I can." So we rescue our leaders. And if someone drops the ball, we pick it up. Such rescuing only encourages people to continue to drop the ball.

Let me give an illustration from my time at the Crystal Cathedral. One of our large successful programs was held on Tuesday nights. The program began at 7:15. Different people were responsible for room set-up and coffee. One evening, 10 minutes before the program was to begin, there was no sign of any set-up or coffee. Panic set in and I did what any good leader does! I set up the chairs and made the coffee. Right move? Wrong. My chair-and-coffee committee got word and began to think, "This is great! If we don't show up, Terry will always cover for us." The next time it occurred, I decided to practice what I preach. *I allowed my leaders to fail.*

When the people started arriving and 7:15 rolled around with no chairs and coffee, it was simple. We said to everyone entering, "Tonight you must find your own chair, and if you want coffee, you'll have to wait." Bad for our reputation? Perhaps. Good for leadership development? Definitely. That same evening two guys came up to me to express concern over no chairs and coffee. The outcome? They set up chairs and made coffee for the next two years. If I'd continued rescuing there would've been no new involvement.

This process begins when you set aside specific time for the primary purpose of encouraging and building up leaders. Look at your current calendar. Are there any blocks of time devoted specifically for leadership development? You need to set aside time to develop "discipleship" relationships with a few of your leaders. The purpose is to focus on their spiritual growth. To give input and direction. To attempt to model a lifestyle of leadership. Leaders who do not receive will soon become dry, and one cannot draw water from a dry well.

Above all else, your leadership core must be a nurturing group. Assigning tasks and accountability to tasks are secondary.

The most important hour on my calendar was for our leadership team prayer and Bible study. We met on Tuesdays from 6-7:15 p.m., prior to our evening gathering. The group was mandatory, for the purpose of study and prayer only. If anyone had any business or announcements, it waited until 7:00. We had 30 minutes to focus on personal and group spiritual growth. We carried 3x5 cards with one another's personal prayer requests and praise reports. I brought extra cards in case people forget theirs. We alternated study leadership weekly and walked through studies such as Galatians 5: "The Fruit of the Spirit," 1 Timothy: "The Role of a Leader," and Mark: "Jesus' Leadership Style."

Evaluate your calendar by doing the following exercise. Think about all of the activities you do in a "normal" week then look at the calendar below.

First, place an "x" in the times you have designated for yourself or your family. Next, block off time according to the category of activity. Use the following letters:

G-Time with entire young adult group
SG-Time with portion of group or small group
L-Time with leadership team or leadership development group
I-Time with individual leaders
O-Office or paperwork time

	S	M	T	W	T	F	S
6 a.m.-9 a.m.							
9 a.m.-noon							
noon-5 p.m.							
5 p.m.-9 p.m.							
9 p.m.-11 p.m.							

What percentages of time are you spending with each category? Are they healthy allotments? Most people who fill out this chart find that very little time is spent encouraging and building up leaders. What are some readjustments that you can make in your schedule? It is important to make time for your leaders so they can be encouraged to share the responsibility of ministry.

MAINTAIN AN ONGOING LEADERSHIP DEVELOPMENT GROUP

This group is in addition to the leadership core group. I recommend an ongoing group for the purpose of developing potential leaders, because your first task in leadership is to begin to find someone to replace you. Start developing now. The group can meet twice a month for one hour. The purpose of the group is to understand leadership. What is it? How do we develop leadership? Does it require specific skills? What motivates us as leaders? How can we be servant-leaders? The group is for those persons whom you have been listing on your "Leadership Potential List." Allow each group to run for six to eight sessions. Continue to bring new people into the group. Remember, the focus is on the "leaders not yet developed." Pages 100-102 include an outline on what to cover each week with your leadership development group.

There are other helpful development tools. I recommend quarterly retreats (two for full weekends, two for Saturdays only) for current leaders as well as potential leaders. The purpose of a retreat is to withdraw in order to focus. It allows relationships to be strengthened, commitments to be revitalized, and groundwork to be laid for a healthy camaraderie. For a sample retreat schedule, see pages 14-15. In addition, it is important to give the leaders an opportunity to be affirmed and to affirm one another, recognizing that each is important to the body of Christ. Such retreats also give us time to focus individually and as a group on the following questions:

- Am I clear on what a leader is and does?
- Where am I being nurtured?
- Do I meet the qualifications?
- What are my responsibilities?
- Who am I responsible to?
- Do I understand the structure of our group and the church?

By now you may be throwing your hands in the air and saying, "How do you have time for all those groups and retreats?" Good question. The answer is, "I don't." I must make time. Realizing that to make time for something means to prioritize. So instead of attending *all* the group parties and functions, I am selective. Instead of counseling anyone, I limit the number. Why? So I have time for my leaders; so that they can be the ones who do the ministry.

You also may need to train persons, who in turn train leaders. The right people can be given the responsibility of the leadership development group or the retreat ministry. The key: Always look for a way to duplicate yourself!

And remember, effective leadership development is not just for the purpose of filling vacancies for a young adult program. It should be seen as an opportunity to create leaders that can affect a variety of areas in the church. Don't be confined to programmatic barriers.

DEFINE SPECIFIC LEADERSHIP QUALIFICATIONS

What is expected of your leaders? Are there requirements which must be met? Are these qualifications known? What kind of people are you looking for?

"Aim at nothing and you're sure to hit it" applies to leaders as well as programs. Often our qualifications are unspoken. We have a difficult time finding leaders because we haven't clearly defined leadership qualities.

Take some time now to make a short list of what qualifications you desire. These questions may help you as you list:
- Is it necessary that the potential leader be a Christian? How long?
- Is it necessary that the leader be a church member?
- Should he or she have former leadership involvement?
- Should the leader have been in the group for a certain period of time?
- Should he or she be single or married?

These leadership qualities can be combined into a job description which will be discussed later.

In using Jesus' model, three qualifications become apparent. The potential leader must have:
- a learner's heart, a willingness to be taught, a flexible spirit;
- a growing spirit, an individual who is not content to stay put but wants to be more of what God wants him or her to be; and
- a giving spirit, a freedom to move outside of the personal boundaries of self, to see the needs of others and a hurting world.

FOCUS ON SPIRITUAL GIFTS

We believe the biblical principle that each Christian is blessed by God with spiritual gifts. Those gifts are for the purpose of equipping the body of Christ. Therefore, it is important to direct persons into areas where their gifts can be used. This is often difficult because many Christians aren't aware of their spiritual giftedness.

It is important to begin to educate your people about gifts. In so doing, you become aware of where people are gifted and where they could be used in the ministry. In our leadership development program, we administer the "Modified Houts Questionnaire."[1] This test allows people the opportunity to become aware of possible areas where God has gifted them.

FOCUS ON POSITIVE LEADERS

Negative leaders cannot lead, they can only organize mass commiseration rallies! In selecting leaders, focus on those who by their attitude seek to be a part of the solution, not the problem. Often, we allow those who are most vocal with a negative opinion to be the leaders. That's unfortunate. Sometimes it is difficult to ignore the squeaky wheel, but that can be done only as we make concerted efforts in developing.

DEVELOP MALE LEADERSHIP

Sound chauvinistic? It's not meant to be. The guideline is not to exclude women in leadership. In fact, with young adult ministry, finding qualified women is usually the least of our worries. It doesn't take long, however, before one hears the fated question, "Where are all the good men?"

There is a sociological phenomenon relative to young adults: Men are attracted to social groups where male leadership is visible. Unfortunately, strong male leadership does not spontaneously appear. It must be developed. If you want good men, you must go after them. Spend time with them. Make it a priority.

ASK FOR A SPECIFIC TIME COMMITMENT

Often we ask someone to be a leader for an undetermined amount of time. Usually that means until the leader is burned out, until someone else comes along, or until Jesus comes again. We can avoid that trap by setting clear expectations with regard to a time frame. I recommend six months. It is a time commitment people can "put their hands on," and they are more likely to fulfill their obligations when the commitment is clearly defined.

PROVIDE SPECIFIC JOB DESCRIPTIONS AND A STRUCTURE

Again, we must avoid the trap of undefined expectations. People need to know what's expected of them. It is helpful to put expectations on paper. In that way, everyone involved can be clear as to the lines of authority, and what is and is not required of them. The following are specific examples of job descriptions.

RETREAT AND CONFERENCE COORDINATOR

Spiritual Gifts Helpful: administration and serving.

Purpose: to plan and organize a total of _____ retreats and conferences (winter and spring retreats, camping trips, etc.). This person is appointed by the coordinator of young adults for a term of six months.

Responsibilities:

1. He or she is a committed Christian, and attempts to practice that faith in his or her daily life.

2. He or she is an active member or currently in the process of becoming a member of a local congregation.

3. He or she will be present for Sunday morning worship services and his or her respective Sunday school class.

4. He or she is an active member of the leadership core group and will attend all scheduled meetings.

5. He or she plans and distributes a six-month "Retreat, Conference and Event" calendar.

6. He or she oversees a committee of four to six persons who assist with the following: flyers, publicity, program, facility, agenda.

7. One month prior to the event, the following is to be detailed and ready for distribution to the group: the event name, date and theme; location with maps; cost (adult? child? minimum deposit? maximum cost? full-pay deadline?); tentative agenda; registration details.

The following two outlines are from University Presbyterian Church in Seattle, Washington. The leadership team for their young adult group "Cornerstone" is organized in this manner. Depending on your group's size and needs, you may not wish to implement all of these areas:

RESPONSIBILITY AND AUTHORITY OF YOUNG ADULT LEADERSHIP

1. Plan Sunday Morning Young Adult Class

- topic
- speakers
- music
- announcements/bulletin board
- call to worship
- greeters
- logistics/facility set-up

2. Monthly Newsletter
   - church-sponsored activities
   - staff phone numbers and ministries
   - scripture included with logo
   - professional quality

3. Spiritual Events
   - retreats
     a. planned by a separate committee with at least one staff member included
     b. speaker must have pastoral approval
     c. semi-annual minimum, open to entire group
   - seminars
     a. spiritual instruction and discussion
     b. monthly
   - monthly informal worship time

4. Social Events
   - target (one to two per month)
   - encourage non-staff organization
   - subject to pastoral approval

5. Mission Outreach and Service
   - encourage support of group, church, local and world ministries
     a. prayer
     b. finances
   - encourage participation

6. Community/Individual Growth
   - small groups
     a. topic selection
     b. organization
     c. selection of facilitators
   - discipleship
     a. facilitate
     b. sustain
   - "body-building"

7. Long-Range Planning and Direction
   - needs assessment
   - evaluation
   - quarter-to-quarter continuity
   - preparation and selection of future leadership

YOUNG ADULT LEADERSHIP ORGANIZATION

1. Composition
   - six to eight members (equal male-female ratio)
   - proven leaders in our church
2. Areas of Personal Ministry
   - staff facilitator
   - small groups
   - spiritual development
     a. discipleship
     b. events
     c. community-building
   - social development
   - outreach
   - communication
     a. newsletter
     b. bulletin board
   - session committee representative
3. Term
   - two terms annually
     a. January through June
     b. July through December
   - six-month minimum commitment
   - two consecutive terms maximum
4. Selection
   - current leadership selects incoming leadership
   - four current leaders carried over from preceding term
   - staff facilitator
     a. selected by current leadership
     b. approved by pastor
     c. selected from current leadership
5. Meetings
   - weekly
   - content
     a. prayer

  b. planning
  c. sharing and Bible study
6. Facilitator's Responsibilities
  •meet regularly with pastor
  •plan and facilitate weekly leadership meetings

After you have provided job descriptions such as these, the next step is to establish a structure to implement them. There are two ways to approach structure. The first is to begin with an arbitrary organizational structure such as this:

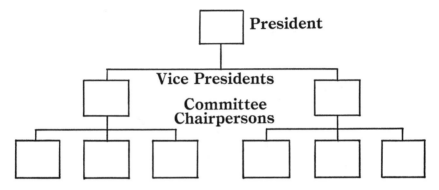

Because I have practiced ministry with this model, I am aware of some inherent weaknesses. An arbitrary structure is established irrespective of need areas. Because the structure was already intact, that dictated our areas for ministry. Anything new had to "fit" into the existing structure. Many of our leaders did not feel connected in any strong way with the needs—or reasons why they were there in the first place.

I recommend a structure that may be fluid from year to year. The number of responsibility slots available are determined by the number of need areas you have chosen to focus on at this point. In that way, you're not assigning someone to a position just because there has been someone in that position before.

To form a structure to fit your needs, ask these questions:
•In our planning where are the areas of need we want to address?
•How many people do we need to carry out those responsibilities?
•Do we have persons in our church or group called to those areas of ministry?

Identify the areas of need. Clarify your expectations for that role of responsibility. Go to work.

PUBLICLY AFFIRM LEADERS

Leaders are not members of a secret committee. Your group will function with greater effectiveness if people know where and to whom to go for a given need. Sometimes we want to avoid bringing any attention to our leaders for fear that a clique will emerge. Cliques are not built on public affirmation; cliques arise from inadequate teaching. If you're doing your job during your time with your leaders, then your leaders will know that leadership makes them servants, not lords.

There are two helpful tools for public affirmation. The first is clear communication. Whenever anyone assumes any leadership role in your group, be clear and upfront with the group as to the person's responsibilities. If you have a monthly calendar, it's a good idea to publish the names (and possibly the phone numbers) of each member of your leadership team and his or her role.

The second tool is a litany of commitment (see the following example).

Every six months we planned a special meeting that focused on leadership. At each of these meetings, I gave a lecture on biblical leadership, and had our leaders come forward for prayer and public commitment. The litany also incorporates the body. Leadership is not just an "us-and-them" proposition.

LITANY FOR NEW LEADERS

Far from being a "functional role," the capacity you are about to assume is truly a "calling of ministry."

_____ is a community where one can experience the acceptance of Christ, healing, caring and growth, and have the environment for making positive lifestyle choices. Do you desire to model those purposes in your own lives?
(We do)

The growth of the community can only be as effectual as the growth of the leaders. Do you commit yourselves to pursue your own growth, desiring to be faithful in your personal walk with Jesus Christ, desiring to understand the relevance of the Bible for your own lifestyle; and seeking to direct your own goals to attaining Christ's likeness?
(We do)

As it can be said that the growth of the leader is essential, so too, honesty makes a leader great. Do you desire to follow Christ's example in dealing honestly with your own emotions, and Christ's admonition to deal honestly with your own weaknesses and failures, knowing that the admission of weaknesses only serves to point us to our strength?

(We do)

It has been said that Jesus Christ is faithful to complete the work he has begun in us. Do you desire to allow him free reign in your lives, stretching, shaping and molding you, as you serve in this capacity?

(We do)

Do you, the members of _____, desire to show your support as a community by pledging to allow these—your leaders— the environment to do the job to the best of their ability, to support, encourage, and pray for them and to join with them in this next six months of growth?

(We do)

It is important to understand that these 10 steps of leadership development do not eliminate problems with leaders or potential leaders. We set unreal expectations for "structures." Our hope is that they will eliminate problems and inconveniences. The 10 steps given are to provide a structure not to eliminate problems, but to deal with them. We are too easily given to knee-jerk reaction to problem solving. Solving problems with no context.

A relational context is essential for solving problems. Problems are effectively addressed and solved when relationships are intact. That context provides the right environment.

The process of leadership development never ends. I had always hoped it would. That is why I got discouraged whenever I would "lose" a leader, or be disappointed by someone because I had not realized that developing leaders would be ongoing. It began to set me free to see leadership development as my primary task. The joy of releasing people to their God-given potential, of seeing people function as servants.

Easy? No.

Worth the effort? Definitely.

KEY POINTS

1. Build your ministry with selective leadership.

2. Spend more time with a leadership core group.
3. Maintain an ongoing leadership development group.
4. Define specific leadership qualifications.
5. Focus on spiritual gifts.
6. Focus on positive leaders.
7. Develop male leadership.
8. Ask for a specific time commitment.
9. Provide specific job descriptions and a structure.
10. Publicly affirm leaders.
11. A relational context is essential for solving problems.

REVIEW QUESTIONS

1. Do you agree or disagree about the principle of selective leadership? Why?
2. Review the calendar on page 110. Does your schedule need reprioritizing? In what areas?
3. Does your church or young adult group have anything like a leadership development group? Could a leadership development group be beneficial to your ministry? In what ways?
4. What qualifications do you think are necessary for leadership in your church's young adult ministry?
5. Do you use job descriptions? What do you think of the examples provided in the chapter?
6. Sketch out an organizational structure that would be most suited to your ministry needs. Do you need to make any changes in your current structure?

CHAPTER 11

Help! I'm From a Small Church

"This is easy for you," one director of young adult ministry challenged me after a workshop. "You've always been at large churches. You've had money, resources, space and people. What about those of us in small churches? We've got about 30 young adults in our entire congregation. Where do we begin a young adult ministry? Is it even possible in a small church? Our entire membership is less then 200!"

I know his concern is valid. I served for three years in a church of less than 100 members. Small churches do not have the resources of a big church, and there's no need for us to pretend that they do. Nevertheless, it is wrong to assume that small churches are exempt from certain ministries. Exempt from certain areas of programming—due to personnel, space, resources—perhaps. Exempt from ministry—never.

Any ministry attempt that begins with the assumption that "small churches can only provide second-class ministries" is destined to be anemic or to fail. Smaller in size does not imply less in quality or impact, however, such stereotypes are difficult to overcome. We live in a world of the super church—big congregations, mega-bucks and entertaining programs. What's a small church to do?

Before we look at ideas for effective ministry with young adults in a small church setting, it is first necessary to examine our faulty assumptions. Right ministry can come from right thinking. Faulty assumptions will only short-circuit the process along the way. Let's take an inventory of faulty assumptions:

WE ASSUME THAT A SUCCESSFUL YOUNG ADULT PROGRAM MUST BE BIG

You may feel intimidated when someone asks, "How many young adults are in your program?" And you answer, "We don't have a program." We have a problem if we automatically assume that ministry and program are synonymous. Using numbers as a measurement for success is a wrong motivation for ministry. Some argue that this thought is an excuse for staying small. It can be, but that doesn't deny its truth. It is worth repeating: *To focus on "building a big group" is a wrong motivation for ministry.*

Not all churches are prepared to have a young adult group, or a full-scale active young adult program. And if that is so, small churches need to take hope. Just because a small church cannot conduct a large group or program doesn't mean that it cannot have an effective *ministry* with the young adults. Effective ministry begins with the "spirit" of a congregation modeled by its leadership. And that can happen in a church of any size. It happens when we choose to take seriously the personal and faith development of young adults. And we reflect that decision in the way we preach, the way we talk about singleness, the way we give away responsibility, the way in which we develop leadership, and the way in which we show concern.

WE ASSUME THAT WE ARE IN COMPETITION WITH LARGE CHURCHES

Nothing can be more discouraging than to continually compare notes with a larger church and feel as if you're coming up short every time. Big programs can be very intimidating. It always discourages me when church leadership gatherings degenerate to a comparison of size and "who's doing what better than who." We leave such meetings with feelings of inadequacy and failure.

We don't need to play such games. Ministry is not a competitive sport. Competition leads to one-upmanship which infects our ministry with a cancerous feeling of resentment and jealously. With competition, our focus is wrong. People simply become pawns on our road to success. If everyone in the body of Christ has his or her own niche of effectiveness, then we need to choose to avoid competition however difficult that may be.

WE ASSUME THAT SMALLNESS IS A LIABILITY

A human tendency is to focus on what we "don't have." And carried to its logical conclusion, it sounds like the Alfred E. Neuman quote, "Most of us don't even know what we want, but we're sure we haven't got it."

A common assumption for our personal identity is to assume that we never have enough to be okay. Such an assumption makes it difficult to be grateful for anything. We can always find a reason to be unhappy, dissatisfied or unfulfilled.

I'm never in favor of maintaining the status quo just to maintain, but I am convinced that effective ministry begins with a spirit of thankfulness, and not a spirit of wishful thinking. I hear too many leaders begin their conversations with, "If only ..." Even if they are right, what good will it do? I like Bruce Larson's observation, "Life is tough, so now what are you going to do about it?"

The same holds true for small churches. This is who we are, so now what are we going to do about it? That first step begins with a note of thanksgiving about where we are and not anxiety over the liabilities we "need to overcome." In fact, it would benefit us to see the advantages that come with smallness. For example, small churches have a feeling of "family" and closeness. Most people know each other on a first-name basis. Can you think of any advantages that apply in your situation?

WE ASSUME THAT WE MUST MEET EVERY NEED OF EVERY PERSON

I used to believe that if someone was not comfortable in my ministry, I was failing. I don't believe that anymore. Effective ministry does not depend on meeting everyone's needs at any time. I was intimidated when anyone left our church or program. "Why are you leaving? Aren't we meeting your needs? We'll ... we'll do more." "What do you mean, First Church has bigger and better programs than we do?" And there I was, back in the competitive cycle with the larger churches.

For the sake of clarification, continual dissatisfaction can be a sure sign of the need for program and ministry evaluation. What I'm referring to here is that we need not feel inadequate because our ministry program is not appropriate for everyone. In fact, certain programs will *not* be appropriate or applicable to everyone. Smaller churches have the opportunity of creative, specifically focused, long-term developmental ministries in favor of generic smorgasbord programs.

Churches that are above 250 members begin to focus on satellite models of ministry (high school—one satellite, young adults—another satellite, older adults—another satellite, etc.). The bigger the church, the less the satellites know about each other and there is usually a rough transition between them.

In a smaller church, there is a better opportunity to be a part of long-term developmental ministry. Everyone can be involved or be a leader.

Each type of ministry approach has its place. We must not automatically assume that we've "missed the mark" because our ministry is geared toward "developing." Likewise, we should not feel discouraged because our ministry is geared toward satellites or specific groups.

Right ministry begins with right thinking. Right thinking begins with an honest inventory of our faulty assumptions. How do we give up our misconceptions? Deliberately. It means choosing not to give such myths powers by living as if they were true. Do we practice any of the above faulty assumptions in the way we talk? the way we think?

After an inventory of our misconceptions, it's time to look at creative steps for effective ministry with young adults in small churches. In a small church, there is usually only one full-time pastor, and the majority of church leadership comes from lay people or part-time help.

The following steps may be helpful for small churches to minister to young adults:

USE YOUR SIZE TO GET INDIVIDUALLY ACQUAINTED WITH YOUR YOUNG ADULTS

The first step to an effective program is to identify needs. As a small church you can take advantage of your opportunity to talk specifically with young adults that are a part of your congregation.

Why are they a part of your church? What is important to them? What are their particular areas of need? How do they think the church sees them? What role do they want to play in the overall ministry of the church?

Because there is no paid staff, the small church has an advantage. Any specific young adult programming must be initiated by lay leadership. The small church has no choice. It will either be a ministry "by the people" or no ministry at all. With young adults, that can be an advantage. Ownership among the young adults is essential.

To encourage ownership, begin planting seeds, uncovering the visions and dreams that are inside the hearts and minds of the young adults who are currently a part of your congregation. Anyone can begin this process as long as he or she has a sincere heart behind the ministry. If you know of a person who would like to volunteer to begin the process of developing a young adult ministry, let the pastor know and ask for his or her full support.

GET INVOLVED WITH THE LIVES OF A FEW

Small churches should not begin a young adult ministry by imitating a large group "entertainment" orientation. Because of their size, small churches can focus on young adult ministry. They can start slowly. Start small. And start on a solid foundation.

Small churches can focus on growth groups. These are intense groups that create an environment for dialogue on relevant growth issues such as "Single Parents," "Divorce Recovery," "Career Development," "Men's Intimacy," "Women's Intimacy," etc. Growth groups are confined to time limits such as six to eight weeks. In these groups we can get serious about growth. Growth groups are described further in the third section.

Small churches also can sponsor small groups which focus on ongoing Bible study and fellowship. Small groups allow us to be particularly concerned with the reality that the young adult ministry is primarily a developmental ministry. Planting seeds and creating an environment for nurture is more important than focusing on results. Too often, results can only be measured by numbers and involvement.

In a small group, specific attention can be given to follow-up. It is not as easy for someone to "fall through the cracks." We have the opportunity for individual care.

FOCUS ON "MISSION"

One disadvantage to a small church is the temptation to isolation.

One young adult expressed it to me this way, "I was uncomfortable in that church, because it seemed like the people my age were already in their own clique, and they didn't seem to want anyone new."

No growth appeals to some people. It's safe. There's no need to change. Move people from that potential place of stagnation not by just "inviting others to come," but by teaching your young adults to reach out. I recommend that programs have an element of "missions" in them. The need to reach out beyond our little world. A mission focus may mean painting and repairing the houses of the elderly in the church, working on the "soup line" at skid row, taking single parent children out for a day of fun, providing the parents with a day off, or even making and delivering holiday food baskets for needy people in the community. The list is endless. It begins with a little creative "Dream Session" (see pages 140-141).

ALLOW YOUNG ADULTS TO LEAD AT VARIOUS LEVELS OF THE CHURCH

The small church has the opportunity to take seriously its role of leadership development with young adults. Do they have an opportunity to express their views, dreams and concerns? Are they given encouragement and support to implement ideas? Are they invited to participate on committees, to plan events, to plan worship services, to give feedback to the sermon? Responsibility happens when you give it away.

Sponsor a leadership development group. Let it be a place where people are encouraged to own the church and its ministry and no longer wait for the ministry to happen to them.

Small churches. To some it means a burden; to others a blessing. There is no denying the reality that small churches cannot do all that big churches can do. But to assume that such a size restriction automatically affects the quality of a ministry is wrong. The quality of the ministry depends upon the foundation that is laid.

If you are from a small church, don't let the big churches intimidate you. Stay focused on the goal of ministry before you and keep at it.

Start slowly.

Start small.

Start on a solid foundation.

KEY POINTS

1. Smaller in size does not imply less in quality or impact.
2. A faulty assumption is that a successful young adult ministry program must be big. To focus on "building a big group" is a wrong motivation for ministry.
3. A faulty assumption is that we are in competition with larger churches.
4. A faulty assumption is that smallness is a liability.
5. A faulty assumption is that we must meet every need of every person.
6. Use your size to get individually acquainted with your young adults.
7. Get involved with the lives of a few.
8. Become focused on mission.
9. All young adults are to be leaders at various levels of the church.
10. If you are from a small church, don't let the big churches intimidate you.

REVIEW QUESTIONS

1. What are some of the pros and cons of a young adult ministry in a small church?
2. Do we perpetuate any negative stereotypes about small church ministries? If so, what are they?
3. Review the assumptions in this chapter. Do you agree or disagree with them? Why?
4. Which of the assumptions fit your particular situation? Explain.
5. How can a small church situation be used to an advantage with a young adult ministry?

Programming
for
Young
Adults

CHAPTER 12

Principles for Programming

I saw a humorous "B.C." comic strip that was all too true. The character B.C. remarked to a friend who caused nothing but trouble, "Don't just do something, stand there!" I wish that were the case for ministry. "Don't just do something, talk about it!"

The truth is, however, that ministry is only ministry if it impacts what we do. Sooner or later we've got to try something. In the first two sections, we *talked* about young adult ministry. These sections illustrated the need to take that first step of young adult ministry with the right foot onto a proper foundation. The first section asked the question "Why?" The second section asked the question "What?" This section asks the question "How?" In other words, now what are we going to *do* about young adult ministry? How can we program for young adults in our church?

The temptation in young adult ministry is to begin with program. Because of that temptation, "program" has deliberately been saved for this last section.

The planning arrow is almost complete. We've looked at the foundation of non-negotiables. We've specified a purpose and listed appropriate objectives and needs. We've taken an in-depth look at leadership. Now it is time to look at programming.

As we said before, the foundation is the most important part of building a young adult ministry. Just as important is the frame or program principles. Each program is unique in its exterior, but underneath we find a common foundation and frame. This is an illustration of a young adult ministry program (house) complete with a listing of important program principles (frame).

	Young Adult Ministry Programs				
Program Principles	Each program should respond to a specific need	A program must represent a funnel into the church body	The people must own the program	Don't build a program under the pressure of the numbers game	Don't be afraid to end a program to start another
Laying the Right Foundation!	1. Adequate theology 2. Breaks down stereotypes 3. Sees people, not programs 4. Integrates young adults into the whole church life 5. Reflects the heart of the church 6. Serves				
	A devotional life and a sincere heart!				

Before we describe each program principle in detail, it is important to note the following:

1. Don't try to imitate anyone else. Programming cannot be copied. Each program should be aimed at specific needs and influenced by the unique distinctives of your group. There is only one you. And your ministry will be done a disservice if you attempt to build it by imitating another "successful" ministry. Yes, we can help one another. And yes, we can borrow from one another. Why reinvent the wheel? But imitating takes our focus away from ministry and people, and places it on external measures for success.

The key for effective programming is learning; we must always be reviewing and revising. Never assume your programming is exempt from change.

2. Don't try to do everything at once. There will be a strong temptation to start fast and big. And there always will be people who will "help" you by telling you all the things you "could or should be doing." Ministry is not doing everything. Ministry requires priority. We must focus our energies on the few things and be faithful in carrying out those tasks. *Start slowly. Start small. Start on a solid foundation.*

3. Don't be afraid to fail. In our competitive world, even churches want to be biggest and best. And when we see another succeed, we become fearful of trying because, "What would happen if we failed?" You can relax. Failure is a part of ministry. We all fail. But the only true failure is when we attempt nothing, and when we don't learn from our mistakes.

4. Don't fall back into a youth ministry model. Too often our ministry can be reduced to keeping people occupied or busy. Don't forget: This is a ministry to adults—not adolescents.

With those reminders in mind, let's turn our attention to the development of a strong, positive program. To begin, let's do an assessment of your program as it exists (see the following chart). As a leadership team, fill in the first three columns of the overview. Then walk together through the principles in this chapter. At the end of the chapter, look again at this program overview and make any necessary changes and revisions.

PROGRAM PLANNING OVERVIEW

Program Current Structure	Program Purpose	Leadership Required	Area for Change
What events are you currently sponsoring?	What area of need is the event addressing?	How many leaders are needed? What are their roles?	Does this item require revision?

PROGRAM PRINCIPLE ONE: Each Program Should Respond to a Specific Need

We can get into trouble if we are not specific about the purpose of each program, and if we assume that each program will "minister to everyone."

Because our churches are made up of a variety of people, programming must reflect that variety. To help in planning it is important to find out who your young adults are. The following chart is invaluable. The circle represents your young adult group. (This same principle applies to your entire church body as well.) Read the descriptions of each quadrant and the core:

•**Potentials:** Those people around your group. The people who are potential attendees or members: neighbors, classmates, workmates. These are the "special meeting members."

•**Newcomers:** Those people who try your group. They attend one or two Sundays, once a month. They're willing to say, "I'll give this place a try, and see what it has *for me*."

•**Koinonia (community):** Those people who make up the bulk of your group. They are the people who say, "This is *my* church, or *my* group. I belong here." You see them most every week—usually in the same chair or pew!

•**Teaching (disciples):** Those people who take one more step than just attendance. They are involved at a level other than weekly meetings. They attend the Bible studies, make up the small groups, are involved in some form of service, etc. This is the group of people who are serious about growth.

•**Core:** Those leaders who run the ministry. They are the ones who make the "pie" go around. Notice that the core touches all four quadrants. That's because it is necessary for the leadership to be a part of and therefore influence every area of the group or church body.

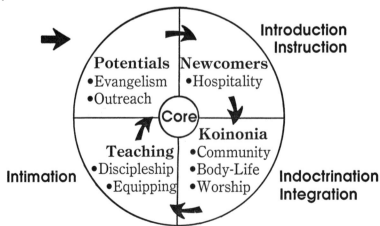

PROGRAM EXAMPLES

Level One: Potentials
Weekend Socials • Concerts
Sports Activities • Beginning-Again Workshops

Level Two: Newcomers
"Talk-It-Over" Groups • New Member Hosts
Weekend Socials • Beginning-Again Workshops

Level Three: Koinonia
Weekend Socials • Weekend Retreats • Sunday Mornings
Board Meetings • Praise'n Sings • Prayer-and-Healing Services
"Talk-It-Over" Groups • Mexico Outreach

Level Four: Teaching
Bible Study • Growth Groups/Small Groups • Seminars
Leadership Training Programs • Leadership Retreats

Level Five: Core
Leadership Small Group • Individual Discipleship
Leadership Development Group

It is important to remember: *Not every program will touch every person in that pie. Effective programming is directed (or focused) programming. It is programming done with a purpose.*

Let me illustrate how I learned this principle—the hard way! We had an existing young adult program called "Talk-It-Over" (see Chapter 15 for more details.) The program was set up as small, non-threatening discussion groups with trained leaders ("enablers"), designed to attract new people to the group and church.

We held the TIOs on Tuesday nights and it was very successful. It wasn't long, however, before I had people coming to me with a complaint about the TIOs. "It's not spiritual enough. If it doesn't become more spiritual, we'll find another church!" So I did what every good minister does—I panicked! After which I tried to respond to their criticism. I began making TIOs more "spiritual." We focused on biblical questions and issues. The result? People quit coming.

Some were bold enough and came to me with their complaints, "TIOs are too spiritual. They're just Bible-beaters." So again I tried to respond. It didn't take long for me to realize Program Principle One: Each program should respond to a *specific* need.

To expect the TIO program to meet every need was naive and unrealistic. So we began directive programming or aiming programs at specific needs. Our TIO program was meant to meet the needs of the top half of the pie—the potential members and newcomers. So that's where we left TIO. It was now free from the expectation that it had to fulfill all needs at once; it was therefore free to be an effective program. After we began directive programming, our Tuesday nights had three programs, each designed to minister to a "piece of the pie." Potential members and newcomers had the TIO program. Koinonia (community) had growth groups. They discussed growth-related issues such as "Relationship Development," "Dealing With Loneliness," etc. The seekers had Bible study.

"That's great if you're a large group," you may say. "What if you only have 20 people and can't run three programs on a given evening?" That's a valid question, but the principle still holds true. Stay focused in your programming. Your alternative is to struggle with a gathering that attempts to be "all things to all people." And although that's a worthy struggle, it doesn't work in one meeting. Once you've discovered the group to whom you are primarily ministering, you can be "set free" to be the best that you can be in that area of ministry. As time goes on your focus may change, but now you have the tools to change with the focus.

You may find that your general meeting is catering to the first slice of the pie. As time goes on, you may have to begin a special Bible study or discussion group for those who are seekers. The study can meet on an alternate night. And here's where you practice leadership development. Having three programs doesn't mean that you run each of them. Begin to look for people who can be front-runners and leaders of any new programming.

Another helpful tool was given to me by Mike Regele, former minister with Salt Company, a young adult ministry of 350 people. He used the following chart to distinguish the variety of persons to whom he ministered. The columns denoting "Come," "Come and Listen," "Come and Grow," indicate various levels of commitment. Mike found it helpful to discover approximately where most of the persons in his group fit, and from that he began to strategize appropriate programming.

	Small Group (six to 15 people)	Medium Group (15 to 40 people)	Large Group (40 plus)
Come			
Come and Listen			
Come and Grow			

To help you discover where most of your group fits, fill in the blanks with: many, some, few or none. This tool will help you focus your programs in the right areas.

PROGRAM PRINCIPLE TWO: Represent a Funnel Into, Rather Than Away From, the Church Body

Let me begin this principle with a story. I was asked to consult at a church interested in developing a strong program for young adults. Their Sunday attendance was about 2,000 and they were surprised that their Friday night Bible study for young adults was only drawing 50 to 60 people. "Are there any programs which would help boost attendance?" they asked. They needed to understand Program Principle Two. In gathering information about the church, I discovered that 85 percent of their Sunday morning attendance was regular attendees (45 percent single adults—most under 35). In addition, 50 percent of their members were in small groups (over 50 percent of the group members were single adults).

The picture became clear and I gave them this assessment: "It's no wonder young adults are not coming to a Friday night special Bible study. Most of your young adults are already involved in significant growth programs, through Sunday worship and home Bible studies."

Their young adult program was an attempt at entertaining the young adults from the church body—persons who were already fully involved. The purpose of programming should not be aimed at entertaining people who are already involved in the life of the church body, but creating a funnel that encourages involvement.

When I first became involved with the Positive Christian Singles program at the Crystal Cathedral, I was worried because every young adult in our church was not coming to "my" program. I had to learn my purpose. It was not to become a self-sufficient entity. It was to become a *funnel.* That's important to learn in programming.

How does one begin to determine the extent or need for developing a young adult program? Look at the following diagram:

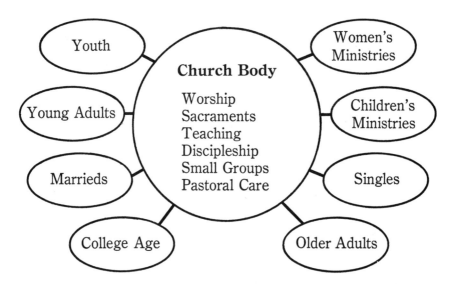

The large circle represents the ministry of your church body. It is not confined to a church building. It is made up of programs which allow the church to celebrate, teach, pray, fellowship and observe the sacraments. Most of the programs are heterogeneous in nature cutting across marital status and age.

Now, what about those circles or satellites outside the larger circle? For example, those programs that are set up specifically to touch needs of a homogeneous unit such as youth, single adults, young adults, women, etc. The issue here is not simply "to have or not to have" specialized programming. The issue is one of direction and purpose.

The potential and temptation of any satellite ministry is that each satellite becomes a congregation unto itself. Because of that temptation, it is important to understand Program Principle Two. Any program such as young adult ministry set up as a homogeneous support structure should serve as a funnel into the body, not as a funnel away from the body. To further illustrate, let's go back to the church I referred to earlier.

The original intention was to draw young adults who were already involved to homogeneous Bible study. They discovered that in their case, it was unnecessary. What evolved was a young adult program that reached out into the community and served as a funnel into the body. Because of the change in purpose, the study was changed from Friday to Thursday (because non-church young adults were already involved on Friday), and from Bible study to topical lectures. Did young adults from the church body attend? Of course, but now because it was ministry to an area that was untouched by other programs.

This program principle is important because it requires each church to program in response to their specific situation, and not simply copy another church's model. Should your church have a program specifically for young adults? Here are some questions which will help you know the right direction.

•Does your theology of ministry see an integrated focus in the ministry of the church body?

•What are the specific needs for a homogeneous support structure? (lecture? study? groups? fellowship?)

•Is there an adequate lay-leadership base?

•Are the social needs of your young adults being addressed in other ways?

•Is there any potential for an ecumenical group formed with two or three other area churches?

PROGRAM PRINCIPLE THREE:
The People Must Own the Program

There is a theory, of course, that says the minister is the "hired gun" in the church, and therefore responsible for everything! Unfortunately, many ministers believe it! And many well-meaning churches have begun programs for young adults only to find them fail. Why? One reason is that if the responsibility for a program rests on one person it will eventually die. *The people must own the program.* Many leaders may say, "But there aren't enough responsible people to help me with the ministry!" I have two responses:

•"Then you don't need to do all the programming you're doing. It's not a sin to cut back!"

•"Then your need is not to build programs, but to build leaders. Spend the next three to four months building a leadership team."

How can we initiate this process of group ownership? We can begin with a Dream Session. You've finished your arrow. It's time to be creative. It's time to dream. Your Dream Session can take place with your leadership team or with an even larger group. It takes about 30 to 40 minutes. Begin by breaking the large group into smaller groups of three to four. Ask this question, "If nothing were impossible, what would you like to see happen with young adults in this church?" Let them start listing their dreams. Remember, this is a Dream Session. It's not the time to discuss the feasibility or even the rationality of the dreams shared.

After 10 minutes, bring everyone to the larger group and begin sharing dreams together. Record the dreams on a blackboard or overhead. There are two very important rules:

•**Each dream must be measurable.** "I want the young adults in this church to be appreciated" is a good dream, but it isn't measurable. "I would like to see young adults involved at all levels of church leadership" is a measurable goal. Remember—these are dreams, don't stop to discuss or say, "That could never happen!"

When Larry Poland conducted Dream Sessions at Campus Crusade for Christ, he had the whole group respond to each shared dream with, "Why not?"

•**Each dream must be accompanied by a name.** Whoever shares the dream must be willing to have his or her name attached to it. This doesn't mean that the person will be required to carry it out alone, but it shows a desire to do something about the dream and not just use this session as an opportunity to complain.

SAMPLE DREAM SESSION

Dream	Name
1. Workshop on career development	Susan James
2. A 10-week series for marriage preparation	Peter Smith
3. A group for couples thinking marriage	Sally Johnson
4. A new-marrieds support group	Matthew Hinson
5. An intercessory prayer group	Bill Walters

After you've had a Dream Session, have the list typed and distributed to all interested persons. Sometime within the next week or two, contact each person and see if he or she is interested in getting the dream started. If not, fine. Two great aspects about the Dream Session are that the people have a time to voice their ideas, *and* you get to see if there is enough incentive on other people's parts to carry out these dreams. You don't have to do all of the programming yourself.

If the person is interested in getting the dream started, see what kinds of resources he or she needs that you can provide. Hook up the "dream" person with other people so he or she doesn't have to "go it alone."

Dream Sessions were without a doubt some of the most exciting times of the ministry at the Crystal Cathedral. We held a Dream Session every six months during our leadership retreat. What a feeling to see 75 people creatively building their own ministry and affirming together, "Why not?!" Did all dreams get accomplished? Of course not. But does that matter? Two things are important here: The people are allowed to dream; and the people are given ownership.

We found that between 30 to 40 percent of our dreams found some completion. That was exciting to me! What was more exciting was the fact that I had nothing to do with any of those coming true. Except to facilitate. The old axiom is true: Introduce them to Jesus. Introduce them to one another. And then get out of the way!

PROGRAM PRINCIPLE FOUR:
Avoid the Pressure of the Numbers Game

It's often the case that one is given the responsibility to start a ministry with young adults, and then is "called to task" for not showing enough growth in attendance. The myth is that numbers are the sole measurement for success. Numbers are important, but they should not be the sole measurement for success. Large groups attract people; but large groups are not built by focusing on numbers. *Successful ministries evolve not from building big programs or big numbers, but from building big people.*

It's easy to be intimidated in the area of numbers. It seems that's the way you measure the effectiveness of your message. The fact is that most young adult programs experience a turnover rate of 33 to 60 percent ever six months. It's normal for people to move away, drop out, or be tempted by more exciting programs.

I learned that my ministry was enhanced as soon as I gave up trying to control the numbers. Because I found that if I was disappointed by the attendance, I would not give my whole heart to the teaching. That was unfair to those who came! So I needed a change of focus.

"God, give me a heart for those who are here."

Although turnover is normal in the group as a whole, your leadership team should experience little or no turnover to be effective. If there is a steady decline in numbers of your group which lasts for at least three months, it may be necessary for you and your leadership team to do some assessment, and see if any alterations in programming are necessary.

PRINCIPLE FIVE: Don't Be Afraid to End a Program to Start Another

Change is difficult in church programming. I'm sure you've heard these words, "We've never done it that way before!" Somehow, we tend to attach an "untouchable" tag to certain programs. *No program is sacred.*

We must be careful, however, not to use change so frequently that we escape any attempt to make a slow-growing program work. Continually assess your programs with your leadership team. If you give a program time and energy and it still doesn't grow, then you can move on to something new.

For your ministry to be healthy, there must be change. How long has it been since you've attempted anything new? How long since an old program has been revised? Remember that organizational structure is not the essence of the ministry. It is what liturgy is to worship. It creates a framework. Focus only on liturgy, and worship is dead.

Yes, you'll meet opposition with change. That's the joy of your job! But if you've done your homework with the planning arrow, and your leadership team supports you, change can be an essential and good move.

KEY POINTS

1. Each program should respond to a specific need. Effective programming is focused programming.
2. A program must represent a funnel into, rather than away from, the church body.
3. The young adults must own the program.
4. Don't build a program under the pressure of the numbers game.
5. Successful ministries evolve not from building big programs or

big numbers, but from building big people.

6. Don't be afraid to end a program to start another. No program is sacred.

REVIEW QUESTIONS

1. Go back to the "Program Planning Overview." Fill in all four columns. Are you satisfied with what you see? Are any changes necessary?
2. Why do you think it's important to have a young adult ministry that reaches out to the community as well as the church body?
3. What is meant by, "The responsibility for a program that rests on one person will eventually die"?
4. What does it take to start building big people rather than big numbers or big programs?
5. Why is change necessary for a healthy ministry?

CHAPTER 13

Where Do We Go From Here?

Whenever I attempt a cross-country journey by car, I find that it is invaluable to use an American Automobile Association map which provides detailed directions and a commentary on certain areas. The same is true with ministry programming. There is no need to build a program by the Braille method. Learning from those who have gone before me is crucial.

So, whether you've been in young adult ministry for 10 years or 10 days, the questions are the same: "What's the next step for a more effective ministry?" "What are the essential steps for putting into practice what we just learned?" To borrow a line from the score of **The Sound of Music,** "Let's start at the very beginning. It's a very good place to start."

We'll begin with the first step—a step that is just as helpful for rejuvenating a long-term young adult ministry as it is for starting a new one. The following review of the steps are not listed in strict chronological order, but can be used as guidelines to assist you at whatever your stage of development.

STEP ONE: FIND OUT WHO YOUR YOUNG ADULTS ARE—TAKE A SURVEY

An effective ministry is an informed ministry. What percentage of your congregation is young adults? What percentage of your community is young adults? What percentage of the young adults in your community are non-churched? What are the reasons that young adults attend your church? What are the reasons their friends do not attend?

What are the stereotypes that currently exist in your congregation relative to young adults? What are the stereotypes that the young adults carry relative to "the church?"

Many churches don't know the answers to the above questions. Many churches haven't asked.

Ill-informed ministries can create tragic results. There's the story of the minister who felt God wanted him to build a complete preschool facility. It was, in fact, a courageous dream. The church raised the money necessary—over one million dollars. Within five years, the preschool was bankrupt and empty. Why? The area where the preschool was built was zoned for expensive housing, unavailable to new families with young children. The result was no business for the preschool. The unfortunate reality is that this information could have been available to the minister if he had only taken the time to ask.

The story illustrates a tragedy beyond what most of us will ever experience, but it does make the point: *Effective ministry and programming begin with effective homework.*

Gather an overview of the age segments in the adult population attending your church. Use the chart below. You can get the information you need from attendance cards (or attendance note pads) common to most churches. Gather the information for four to six weeks before you project your statistics.

Age Group	Never Married	Married	Divorced	Remarried	Widowed	Single Parent	Women	Men
18-22								
23-28								
29-32								
33-35								
36-49								
50-64								
65+								

For gathering specific information, I recommend an all-church survey. They should be small enough to enclose in the church bulletin. Give your parishioners time before or during the service to complete the survey (anonymously) and place it in the offering plate. Several sample surveys are included on the following pages. Use or adapt the one most suitable for your particular church. There is a survey for general information, a survey on church stereotypes, a survey for young adults, and a survey for activities planning. The surveys begin to let us focus on whom we are ministering to and where they are coming from.

SURVEY ONE: Church Survey

Our church is people ... people with specific needs. In order to minister to your needs more effectively, please take a moment to complete the following survey. Names are not required, just general information.

1. ARE YOU: Married _____ Remarried _____ Always Single _____
   Widowed _____ Divorced _____ Other _____
2. AGE LEVEL: 12-18 _____ 19-25 _____ 26-35 _____ 36-45 _____
   46-55 _____ 56-64 _____ 65 + _____
3. NUMBER OF CHILDREN _____. HOW MANY LIVE WITH
   YOU?_____
4. PREVIOUS CHURCH BACKGROUND: (Check one)
   [ ] Baptist [ ] Methodist [ ] Assembly of God [ ] Catholic
   [ ] Presbyterian [ ] Other _____ [ ] None
5. I AM A MEMBER OF _____CHURCH: Yes _____ No _____
   I am in the process of joining Yes _____ No _____
6. I JOINED _____ CHURCH IN WHAT YEAR? _____
   [ ] I am not a member but **I attend regularly**.
7. I ATTEND _____ CHURCH AN AVERAGE OF
   _____ TIMES PER MONTH:
   (Check one) [ ] 1 [ ] 2 [ ] 3 [ ] 4 [ ] 5 [ ] 6 [ ] 7
   [ ] 8 [ ] 9 [ ] 10 +
8. I ATTEND: (Check one or more)
   Sunday Services: [ ] a.m. [ ] p.m. [ ] a.m. & p.m.
   [ ] Home Fellowship [ ] Mid-Week Activity
9. I LIVE IN: (Check one)
   [ ] city [ ] north city [ ] south city [ ] east city [ ] west city
   [ ] other area _____
10. MY INCOME BRACKET PER YEAR IS: (Check one)
    [ ] $1,500-10,000 [ ] $10-20,000 [ ] $20-35,000 [ ] $35-50,000
    [ ] $50,000 +
11. I PRESENTLY TITHE _____% PER MONTH: (Check one)
    [ ] 10% [ ] 12% [ ] 15% [ ] 20% [ ] other _____

I presently do not tithe but I give _____% per month.
12. RATE THE FOLLOWING AREAS OF _____ CHURCH:
    1) Needs Improvement 2) Good 3) Very Good
    Facilities ____ Worship Services ____
    Special Activities (for example: _____, _____) ____
    Total Ministries:
    A) Children ____   B) Youth ____ C) Young Adults ____
    D) Singles ____   E) Music ____ F) Adults ____
    G) Counseling ____ H) Evangelism ____
Please use the back of this card for additional comments.

SURVEY TWO: How Do You Feel About Young Adults?

1. What do you say? Which of these terms seem derogatory of the single young adults in this congregation?
    [ ] eligible bachelor [ ] uncommitted   [ ] old maid
    [ ] non-settled   [ ] single   [ ] divorcee
    [ ] unclaimed blessing [ ] swinging single [ ] other_____
    Do you prefer to use the terms: [ ] family night suppers & retreats
                                              or
                                     [ ] church suppers & retreats
2. How do you feel? When I am all alone, I:
    [ ] feel very lonely [ ] enjoy some soli- [ ] realize I don't
    [ ] other reaction   tude, find it   know how to
        (specify):_____   strengthens me   handle solitude
    When I am with a recently divorced person, I:
    [ ] am afraid to men- [ ] find a chance to [ ] would rather be
        tion the change   help by listening   with someone
        in his or her life   else
    [ ] want to help but
        don't know how
    I think the best ways to meet other people are:
    [ ] church activities [ ] hobby or leisure- [ ] taking educational
                               time groups   courses
    [ ] through other   [ ] at bars and discos [ ] other_____
        friends
3. What do you think? Do you think church leaders should usually be chosen from among:
    [ ] married people   [ ] divorced people [ ] widows or
                                                   widowers

[ ] people who have [ ] all of these
   never been
   married

Does it matter if church leaders are men or women?
[ ] men   [ ] women   [ ] doesn't matter

Which of these statements do you think are true and which are false?

T F All single persons want to be married.

T F Married people are never lonely.

T F All married people are happier than all single people.

T F Single persons have no financial worries.

T F Single persons always get the best breaks on their income tax.

T F Children raised by one parent tend to be less well-adjusted.

T F Many singles relate better to a wider spectrum of persons than do some married people.

T F Single persons pay almost as much for a hotel room as do couples.

T F Single women are often rejected for credit that a married person can get.

T F Single persons are expected to volunteer for more extra-time functions because they have no family waiting for them.

T F Single persons are expected to visit others, but are seldom visited except by other single persons.

I agree/disagree with these statements:

A D I think the women's liberation movement and women's and men's reactions to new roles will call for a new kind of ministry with single persons.

A D Singleness is being accepted more widely now as an appropriate way to live.

4. What would you do? When you go to a church activity, do you go more quickly:
[ ] by yourself   [ ] with someone
                          else

If you were planning a dinner party at your house, would you tend to invite:
[ ] all single persons [ ] all couples   [ ] couples and
                                        singles

When Thanksgiving comes, would you probably include:

[ ] your own family [ ] someone who   [ ] your close friends?
                       might not other-
                       wise have any
                       plans
Would you prefer to attend a church school class made up of:
[ ] all men   [ ] all women   [ ] all couples
[ ] couples & singles [ ] a group your   [ ] a group of mixed
                       own age   ages
[ ] a class chosen
    by individuals
    because of subject
    of the study?
I am: [ ] married [ ] single
    [ ] young adult (ages 18 to 35)
    [ ] middle-aged adult (36 to 64)
    [ ] older adult (65 and older)
    [ ] divorced
    [ ] widowed

SURVEY THREE: Tell Us About You

Our church is making a special effort to check our effectiveness in ministering with young adults. If you are between the ages of 18 to 35, will you take a few moments to complete this questionnaire and place it in the offering plate?

Name _____ Address _____
          (optional)
Telephone_____[ ] Male [ ] Female
                              (optional)
My occupation is primarily: (check one and specify)
[ ] a skilled trade _____ [ ] the service field _____
[ ] business_____ [ ] homemaking
[ ] profession _____ [ ] management_____
[ ] student (specify field and [ ] other _____
    present level)_____ _____
I (check):
[ ] have never been married   [ ] am a single parent
[ ] am married   [ ] am divorced
[ ] am separated
I live (check as many as apply):

[ ] alone   [ ] with my parent(s)
[ ] with one friend   [ ] with two or more friends
[ ] with my spouse and
    child/children age(s) __, __, __
My age is between:
[ ] 18-22   [ ] 23-28
[ ] 29-32   [ ] 33-35
For transportation, I:
[ ] use public transportation   [ ] drive my own car
[ ] am dependent upon a friend
What kinds of activities would you like the church to provide?
[ ] study and discussion   [ ] social gatherings for
    around issues and concerns   fellowship
    identified by a group of
    young adults. List three
    concerns you would be
    interested in considering: _____

[ ] Bible study and discussion   [ ] recreation
[ ] trips and tours   [ ] interest groups (art, crafts,
                                           music, drama)
[ ] retreats for young adults   [ ] programs and activities
                                           with other congregations
[ ] activities that include   [ ] other _____
    children of single parents   _____

Would you prefer activities that:
[ ] separate single and married   [ ] combine single and married
[ ] doesn't matter

I am a:
[ ] member of this church   [ ] greeter/usher
[ ] church school teacher   [ ] member of the young adult
                                           group
[ ] member of an adult Sunday   [ ] church officer
    school class   [ ] choir member
[ ] staff   _____(specify
                                           other activities)

I attend this church because:
[ ] my parents are members   [ ] it has an effective young
                                           adult group
[ ] it is relevant to my life   [ ] it is geographically close to
                                           home

[ ] the people are a family to   [ ] other _____
    me   _____

My special interests, skills and hobbies are: _____

_____

_____

SURVEY FOUR: Activities Planning Survey

To help us plan future activities, please circle any of the following events you would attend. Also, we are looking for people to be a chairperson for each event and be responsible for organizing it and therefore be able to attend it free. If that interests you and you have the ability to plan and organize one of these events, please let us know at the bottom of this form.

Sports
1. volleyball
2. softball
3. racquetball
4. tennis
5. biking
6. basketball
7. football
8. baseball
9. hockey
10. roller skating
11. water skiing
12. fishing
13. snow skiing
14. golf tourney
15. bowling league
16. hiking
17. _____

Theater and the Arts
18. dinner playhouse
19. first-run movies
20. plays
21. musicals
22. art museums
23. church choir
24. art classes
25. photography club

26. other _____

Travel
27. train to: _____
28. bus to: _____
29. carpool to: _____
30. observatories
31. amusement parks
32. other _____

Seminar Topics
33. tax planning
34. nutritional health
35. know what we believe
36. personal finance
37. relational skills
38. assertiveness training
39. sexuality
40. divorce-recovery workshop
41. parent effectiveness
42. small group leader
43. intimacy
44. self-esteem
45. stress management
46. personal appearance
47. job search skills
48. other: _____
_____

Seminar Speaker Ideas (list on back side):
Name: _____ Day Phone: _____ Evening Phone: _____
Address: _____
_____ I would like to serve on a committee for activity #_____
_____ I have contacts which would be helpful in organizing activity
#_____.
Please fill this out, then turn in to the membership table.

Some of you may say, "But your surveys cannot give an accurate picture of the young adults who are not coming to church." Good point. Such information can only come from direct contact. Why not set up a program where direct contact is possible? How about a congregational young adult contact program? The following idea is from the Alban Institute.

SURVEY FIVE: Identifying Young Adults in Your Congregation

The lay ministry study course emphasizes the importance of contact between older and younger adults. This contact and ministry can take place anywhere. At home, at work, on campus or in church. But frequently the contact within congregations has been broken. The following process was designed to help a group of older adults begin to personally identify young adults in their congregation.

Materials:
Each participant should have a pencil and at least five 4x6 cards.

The Purposes:
1. To expand your personal contacts with young adults. You are creating a list of young adults whom you personally know something about.

2. To learn. By finding out more about some specific individuals you also will learn more about the diversity of young adult life-situations in general.

3. To help your congregation build a list of young adults. People who are known and who may be involved in some future ministry with young adults.

4. To minister. As you talk to individuals out of your concern for young adults, you are doing more than gathering information. Your call expresses the concern and interest of the congregation.

Individual Instructions:

1. On a 4x6 card, write down the name of a young adult whom you know in your congregation. Leave room for an address and phone number. (Fill in the address and phone now if you know them.)

What other general information do you know about this person? Is he or she living with parents or independently? employed? attending college? involved in some church activity? married? Note this information on the card.

2. Using one card for each individual, write down the names of some other young adults in your congregation whom you may not know as well.

3. During the next two weeks, we will try to find out a bit more about some of the young adults that we have identified. Right now, in the training session we will be concerned with two planning tasks.

Action Process:

•How do we go about gathering more information about these individuals, and why?

•If we are having a hard time identifying young adults in our congregation, how do we expand our basic list of possible contacts?

In Your Small Group:

•Share the names you wrote on the cards. Remove any duplication of names.

•Plan to make some information calls during the next two weeks.

•You may plan to expand your list. Or, you may wish to role play a telephone call.

There are a number of ways to find further names of young adults in your congregation. One of course is to ask the young adults whom you know already. Another way is to check your congregational directory or card file—often it has been found that the children listed with congregational families in the records have grown up and become young adults. Another way to gather the names of young adults is to ask people who have recently worked with a senior high group, or who have worked in other ways with young adults. Some young adults may be church school teachers or members of the choir.

Below is a list of some activities to help you gather the names of young adults affiliated with your congregation. On the right hand side is a space to write in the names of whoever in your group volunteers to undertake that activity. Not all will be appropriate for your congregation, and you may think of others.

Now, in your group, plan what you will do to enlarge your list of young adults.

Activities to Identify Young Adults	Individuals Responsible
1. Talk to ministers	_____
2. Ask church school coordinator and teacher	_____
3. Check congregational directory or file	_____
4. Look at record of marriages for recent years	_____
5. Ask youth group leaders	_____
6. Put announcement in bulletin for young adults and parents of students	_____
7. Check record of confirmations, adult baptisms, new memberships for appropriate past years	_____
8. Make an announcement in church	_____
9. Who in the group will be responsible for coordinating these activities?	_____
Phone Number	_____

Making Information Calls:

When you call someone or speak to him or her in person, identify yourself, and say that you are a member of a group in your congregation that is concerned about your congregation's ministry with young adults. Simply explain that you are in the process of trying to gather some information about young adults who have been related to the congregation, and ask if they might help you.

The following memo was prepared by a ministry group in one congregation which was in the process of identifying young adults affiliated in some way with the congregation. The ministry group was working from a list of names which was out-of-date, and they were making some calls to learn where these young adults were now. Some of their suggestions may be helpful to you.

All Saints Telephone Call Guide:

As an initial project, the Young Adult Action/Study Group is planning to gather some basic data on young adults in the 18- to 21-year-old age bracket.

The basic information that we need at this point is the current address, telephone number and status. That is, are they away at school, attending college locally or working full-time?

In addition, the phone calls to gather this data will communicate the basic fact that there is a concerned group at All Saints. We also expect that there will be some feedback or pastoral information to which we will listen and make notes.

Each member of the young adult Action/Study Group will need to make around 19 calls. As a first step, we are asking each member of the group to make 10 calls, and then contact the group coordinator.

The Purpose of Your Call Is:

•**To gather data** such as current address, phone number, status.

•**To communicate** the fact that there is a group in the church interested in young adults.

•**To minister** by non-judgmental listening and interest. To use feedback and pastoral information for future ministry.

Suggested Sample Dialogues:

1. "Hello, I'm ... from All Saints Church. We're trying to gather some information about our young adults. May I speak to (name) please?"

2. (If person is living away) "Well, we would like to know about those who are living away too."

3. (If person is not home) "I just need some basic information. Could you help me?"

4. "I'm a member of a group of adults at All Saints Church who are concerned about young adults, and we are gathering some information at this point."

5. "What is his or her current address? Also, what is the phone number?"

6. (If response from a parent is, "They're not interested." Don't take "no" for an answer the first time. Parents don't always know about their children.) "We know that many young adults are not interested, but it would help us to have a current address."

7. (At some point, we would like to know their status.) "Are you working full-time or going to school?"

8. If there is negative feedback about the church, try not to be defensive, but listen to it and make a note of it. Parents may be defensive about the fact that their children are not interested in the church. You might want to assure them that they are not alone. Any comments about the status of the young adults may be of importance, and it would be useful to make a note of it.

9. Thank them for their time.

The important point is relatively simple: The very first programming step is getting to know the young adults in your church. One advantage to taking an annual survey is that it is unwise to do ministry programming by assumption. Another advantage is that continual feedback helps to break down wrong assumptions or unhelpful stereotypes.

STEP TWO: BEGIN A LEADERSHIP DEVELOPMENT GROUP

Many great ideas have failed for want of effective leadership. Effective leadership must be developed. A leadership development group is a small group of individuals who can be trained, encouraged and released to do ministry. It is a place where leadership can be defined, leadership skills and spiritual gifts uncovered, and a place where one can receive the permission to risk, even with the possibility of failure. It's the setting in which you build your core group of program leaders.

In Chapter 10 we walked through the practical steps necessary for developing effective leaders and for establishing a leadership development group. Let's review those steps:

•**Practice selective leadership.** Begin to identify a small number of persons that you could approach about meeting weekly with you to discover leadership potential. The "Leadership Potential List" recommended on page 108 is a helpful way to begin the selection process.

•**Set aside six to eight weeks for the group.** Choose a time—and begin.

•**Use the group as an opportunity to begin "plugging people in" to their appropriate niches in the ministry.** Before we do that, we must recognize that not everyone in the leadership development group will be suitable, ready or interested in a formal leadership commitment. That's okay. For above all else, the leadership development group is for development as a Christian, not recruitment as a leader. And, in the end, leadership breaks down if it is done under compulsion.

As a helpful starting point, I recommend following the agenda found on pages 100-102 for your first leadership development group. You also can cover Mark 1:32-37 and John 15:1-17 and discuss spiritual life—our spiritual and personal development is tied to our "connectedness" with Jesus, and is learned through solitude. Ephesians 6:10-18 highlights the point that life is difficult and until we understand that, we cannot learn the tools such as discipline that are necessary to make choices for a healthy and whole life.

What do we do when six or eight weeks of the first leadership development group are over? Begin putting some of the people to work. Begin the practice of giving away responsibility. The ones who accept leadership roles become your core group (see Step Four.) Then start a new leadership development group, or give the responsibility of leadership development groups to another mature member of the team. This is not a one-time event. Leadership development continues ... and continues ... and continues.

STEP THREE: SPONSOR A DREAM SESSION

Your young adult ministry will experience vitality when people are encouraged to dream. If a young adult program is simply going to be another proram added to the church staff's administration list, then it should not be done. It is a ministry that must be birthed from the heart of the people.

"But the people in our church don't want to dream," is a common statement.

"I understand that," is my reply. "But have you given them an opportunity? Have you looked past the rigid ones—with hardening of the attitudes—to find those who carry inside them dreams that need only permission to be set free?"

A Dream Session can be done in a variety of ways. It can be done with the whole church. It can be done just with young adults. It can be done only with the leadership core group. It doesn't matter—only that you at least try it. And, if possible, invite the whole congregation. The specific steps for conducting a Dream Session are given on pages 140-141.

STEP FOUR: ESTABLISH A CORE GROUP

This is the group responsible for program and structure mainte-nance, creative input and overall leadership. Many of the members will come from your leadersip development group. Others may have previously been involved in leadership capacities. And still others may have been leaders in different areas in the church life, but now want to put their energy in the development of a young adult ministry.

The primary purpose of the core will be that of providing a place of nurture for all those with roles of responsibility. Earlier, I referred to this core group as spending time with a few. And that, I believe, is important. If my core group cannot become a place of nurture, no amount of program wizardry will change things. Strong ministry reflects strong relationships. The primary purpose of the core group is to build strong relationships.

If leaders cannot pray together, how will there be any unity of spirit for conducting a program? Many core groups get together for business, but never for nurture. This is unfortunate. *Nurture must be primary.*

The core group is the place where established programs need to begin. It means meeting as a core group at least twice a month apart from business. I recommend the following as a sample schedule for a core group meeting:

CORE GROUP

- Sharing From Activities Over the Last Week   15-20 minutes
  (this can be cone in groups of three or with the entire group)
- Bible Thoughts   15 minutes
  (rotate leadership each meeting, so that all can participate)
- Application Time   15-20 minutes
  (discuss questions such as, "What can I do this week with what I learned?" "Where are the areas of personal growth that need work?")
- Prayer Time   15 minutes
  (groups of three and/or the entire group)

Yes—the core group must do business, but this is not the time. Business meetings can be conducted some other time. But business will not be effective without the foundation of nurture. The first comment to such a strong recommendation is invariably a question, "Where do you get the time?" I believe that if we've got time for business, we've got time for nurture.

No one said this would be easy. But I'm convinced it is worth the price, time and energy that we need to pay.

By now you're asking how those first four steps fit together. Although the steps are not exactly chronological, this time line helps you see how the steps fit together:

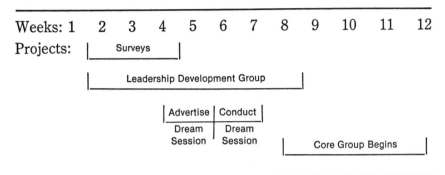

These steps are still appropriate for existing, active young adult ministries. When I began my work at one church, I inherited an established 10-year-old ministry, and we were still able to apply these steps to that situation. We took surveys, gathered fresh information, established a leadership development group, built each other's confidence, sponsored a Dream Session, gave everyone a chance to voice ideas for young adult ministry, and established a core group of leaders.

STEP FIVE: ESTABLISH YOUR PURPOSE STATEMENT

Begin to answer (or re-evaluate your answer to) the question "Why?" Focus on why you're in the business of young adult ministry in the first place.

Purpose statements do not evolve overnight. They take time. I recommend the retreat format described on pages 14-15. Spend particular time going over the material on the program planning arrow in Chapter 8. Don't be afraid to take the necessary time to complete this process.

Once you are confident about the ministry direction you have established, let it be known. Print the purpose statement in brochures, flyers and church bulletins. "This is why we're here!" "This is what we're committed to!"

STEP SIX: TRY SOMETHING

In other words, sponsor an event. Put one of the program dreams to work. Don't try everything, but what you do try, go for it with enthusiasm. Don't be intimidated by those who tell you that there are other programs you "should be trying." There will always be opportunities to get sidetracked. Right now, the program ideas you are attempting are coming from a strong foundational process. And that makes a difference.

The first idea you implement may not be a program specifically for young adults. You may think your church needs to begin with an intergenerational retreat focusing on everyone's similarities as children of God. Or you may begin with a series of sermons on young adult development, or a topical Sunday school class on young adults and the church. Whatever program you choose, go for it with gusto.

STEP SEVEN: ANNOUNCE THAT YOU'RE IN THE BUSINESS

Hang out your shingle. Let it be known that young adult ministry is an essential focus at your church. Let it be known that this is an area of ministry you are committed to.

The purpose of announcing that you are in the business is not to impress others. We're not interested in creating hype. We *are* interested in communicating the areas of focus that are important to our church. In other words, young adult ministry is a part of who we are, it is not an add-on program. It is important for the pastor to declare that your church is "in the business." The heart of the church is communicated from the pulpit, and contradictions between pulpit and programs can be glaring.

STEP EIGHT: START SLOWLY ... START SMALL ... START ON A SOLID FOUNDATION

No one said you had to be the biggest overnight. The following chapter discusses burnout. Attempting to do too much too soon is a guarantee to an early grave.

Consistency takes time, but is the key to ministry. There will be innumerable temptations to take a shortcut. Ideas to "double the group size," parties that are "guaranteed to break down barriers," and Bible study topics that "definitely draw big crowds" all have their place. But they must be incidental. Growth must be a consequence of our ministry, not our main focus.

I failed to realize this point when I was waiting for the big crowds to come. I was ignoring the golden opportunities I had to minister with a smaller group. My inattention communicated loudly and clearly that I was interested in numbers only.

Perseverence is the key. You may not see any immediate fruit or results for your labors. That is not easy to understand, but it is okay. Keep on the right track, for the foundation you are building will see results that you could not have imagined.

Remember—slow, small and solid.

STEP NINE: BE FLEXIBLE

Just when you think you've got all the right ingredients, the picture changes. Welcome to young adult ministry. If change intimidates you, you're in the wrong business. If you're spending much of your energy hoping that solving such-and-such problems will free you to devote more time to "the ministry," you are in for even more anxiety.

When I left seminary I was idealistic about ministry. I thought it could be done just like I'd drawn it up on paper. Eliminate this problem, fine-tune that program, adjust this emphasis, "There, I'm ready to minister."

I was wrong. Ministry does not take place in a vacuum. It takes place with real people and real problems. Where there can be real messes. With real interruptions. With real conflicts. Ministry is what happens in the middle of that "realness." Ministry is what happens when we are making other program plans.

Flexibility is essential. You cannot be intimidated by change. Your best plans may be interrupted. Your best ideas may be vetoed. But ministry is not waiting to begin when everything is perfect. Ministry happens when a sincere heart touches a needy world.

STEP TEN: JOIN A NETWORK

Ministry in isolation is dangerous. Isolation distorts our perspective. It exaggerates our anxiety and spirit of competition. It encourages rushed decision making. And it creates ministry myopia. I soon begin to believe that I'm the only person experiencing the things I am experiencing. In truth, I need others to make my ministry more effective.

Networks are intimidating and threatening to many. "What if someone else learns my secrets?" "What if their church steals some of our people?" "What if I feel inadequate in comparison to their programs?"

Those are all normal reactions. But to give in to them is sure death. Such paranoia and myopia begin to choke off the flow of life itself.

And there is only one way to overcome such reactions. Make the choice to build supportive networks with phone calls, lunches, group brainstorming and note-swapping. They are all important. They begin to communicate that we are in this together. We need each other for encouragement, support, affirmation and motivation. For how can we presume to win the world to Christ, if we spend all our energy competing among ourselves?

Where do we begin? That's the question we started with. There are 10 steps. Some apply to your situation. Some may not. But the key is simple. Do something. Talking about what we need to do is ultimately empty. Take a step. And remember, each step is an important step. Just because you're not as far along as another, is no reason to stop. Why? Because ministry is not how far along you are. Ministry is a sincere heart in a needy world.

KEY POINTS

1. Find out who your young adults are—take a survey. Effective ministry and programming begin with effective homework.
2. Begin a leadership development group.
3. Sponsor a Dream Session.
4. Establish a core group.
5. Establish your purpose statement.
6. Try something.
7. Announce that you're in the business.
8. Start slowly. Start small. Start on a solid foundation.
9. Be flexible.
10. Join a network.

REVIEW QUESTIONS

1. Have you ever taken a survey in your church? Do you think it's a good idea? Are there questions you would add to the samples given?

2. Have you set aside time for a leadership development group? When will you begin? What will you study?
3. Sponsor a Dream Session. Have you tried one? How did it go? If you have not, when would you like to try one?
4. What do you think of the core group principle that says nurture comes before business?
5. Review your purpose statement.
6. Which of the 10 steps mentioned are most applicable to you in your situation now? Why?

CHAPTER 14

Avoiding Burnout

Some stories seem to reflect recurring themes. In my travels, there is a story that has become all too familiar. I often ask, "Does your church have a ministry program with young adults?" And too often the answer is not one I enjoy hearing. "We used to. It grew for a while, then fell off to a little group and finally dwindled to nothing. I guess there's no real need." Or some add, "I guess we don't have a big enough church." Or, "I guess it wasn't the right time." Or, "I guess it was never meant to be."

Burnout. We have all encountered someone or some program that has burned out. Maybe that someone was you. Is burnout a requirement? a necessary rite of passage? Can we avoid burnout? Are there red flags which will tell us if our programming is unbalanced, or on the wrong course? The answer is yes. Following are some red flags that warn us to regain a balance and get on the right course.

GOING TOO FAST

"We're going to have the biggest and best young adult group in this state," boasted one church bulletin.

Interesting, I thought. So I inquired, "How long has your program been in existence?"

"Two months," was the reply.

"When do you expect to reach your goal?" I asked.

"Within four to six months," was the answer.

Is that a realistic way to approach ministry and programming? I think not.

We have a tendency to think we must compete with the consumer mentality of our culture. We must offer the best product, be "the fastest growing," "the biggest" or "the most appealing." There's nothing wrong with a big group; but size can be a fickle measurement for young adult ministry. Numbers in attendance is relative and very cultural.

Impact. Integrity. Longevity. Those are the goals that make young adults relevant and alive. Not numbers. And all three take time.

I was raised with the mentality that Jesus is coming soon, so I'd better get about the business of saving the world in preparation. I've since learned that I'm not the Messiah and you're not the Messiah. I have a coffee cup that helps remind me of that. It asks the question, "Have you saved the world yet today?" We are called to faithfulness. And we must be willing to let that take time.

Slow down. That goes against our American mentality. One of our fears is that we will not see any "fruit." We want an immediate "payoff." We're troubled that change and growth in young adults may be imperceptible, and that ministry is the planting of seeds which may not be harvested for months or years. Again Robert Gribbon is helpful with his insight:

> Responsible young adult ministries will not 'pay off' in terms of greatly increased attendance or giving. Motivation for such ministries must therefore be found in long-range institutional goals, in our own need to share our lives, and in concern for the next generation.
>
> The first part of this principle is deliberately overstated to highlight a continuing problem with young adult ministries. Programs for young adults frequently begin with great enthusiasm but falter when there is no immediate 'payoff' in terms of increased institutional loyalty on the part of young adults. When problems or conflicts with the program arise it is often found that there is little congregational support and an underlying resentment about doing things for young adults when they do not reciprocate with institutional support.
>
> Because young adults are in a period of independence, the expectations of loyal affiliation or mutual interdependent support are unrealistic. Our ministries need to have more of the characteristics of outreach or missionary endeavors, and we need to find our motivation and 'payoff' in our own need to be doing what we are doing and in the inherent satisfactions.[1]

Gribbon's approach takes a lot of time. It cannot be overstated. And it is important that we communicate this fact clearly to our church leaders: "If we're expecting miracles and big crowds, then we will continually be planting the seeds for disappointment and resentment, because those young adults are not responding. Granted, we may get a big crowd, but that cannot be the primary reason why we're here."

The issues for persons in their twenties are developmental. By their very nature, developmental issues take time and a lot of care. One-on-one dialogue between the old and the young will go miles in establishing an environment for development. Relationships take time. What are we doing in our churches to increase opportunities for intergenerational dialogue?

For churches starting a young adult ministry from scratch, I recommend that they feel free to wait three to six months before initiating any program. Take that time to talk to the young adults in your church, to establish a foundation and to develop leaders. A healthy program must be built on healthy relationships.

There is no replacement for time.

No Foundation

A crop grows healthy when the soil is good. Jesus' parable of the sower graphically illustrates that point. We need to understand that the condition of the soil for young adult ministry is not a given. We must prepare it. And for ministry, like farming, soil preparation is as important as planting and harvesting the crop. And we will be destined for burnout if we attempt to erect young adult programming on top of a foundation that either is not yet ready, or is not open to discussing young adult integration into the church body.

This is why the first two sections of this book are so important. They encourage us, as well as provide practical tools, toward "soil preparation." Foundation building. That's the task before us.

Many of you don't have the luxury of starting from scratch. Many have inherited a program—with its negatives and positives all rolled together. You may ask, "What if I inherited a weak or inadequate foundation?" A weak foundation is one that does not incorporate the keys to effective ministry as outlined earlier.

A church with a weak foundation:

•does not give away responsibility

•does not focus on developmental (or searching) faith, but rather on dependent faith

•does not create opportunities for integration or belonging into the entire church body

•is not linked to the community, but practices separationist attitudes

•is intolerant of diversity

As we have said before, you can tell a church's theology not by the creedal statement in the narthex, but by the theology practiced in their programs and personal relationships.

Our temptation is to try and compensate for a weak foundation by developing a plethora of new programs. That's the way I approached it in one church. In the long run, it doesn't pay off. The weak foundation eventually gives way. "Wisdom programming" says that "it is okay to take the time necessary to work on foundation repair, at the expense of big programs."

In fact, when I began to take the time to work on the foundation, my young adult group attendance went down. What I discovered was young adults becoming involved in other areas of church life, finding integration possible, and not necessarily needing a sole tie-in to the young adult group.

How is the foundation at your church? Where does it require repair work? Where can you begin?

NO OWNERSHIP

A young adult pastor of a mid-size (approximately 800 to 1,200) congregation recently asked me why his young adult program was not getting off the ground. He said, "I've tried this program idea and that program idea, and nothing seems to work."

"How's your leadership team feel about it?" I asked.

"We don't have one," was his reply.

That is a red flag for burnout. Where there is no ownership, the program is destined to fail. Young adult ministry must be their ministry.

The questions are common ones: "But what if we don't have any leaders?" "But what if they don't want to take responsibility?" "But what if they don't stick with it?" The questions don't negate the point: *Ownership is essential.*

You don't have any leaders? Then develop some. Very few leaders come ready-made. For the young pastor in the previous illustration, ministry will mean delaying his attempts at programming in favor of a two- or three-month leadership development group. I encouraged him to use the material outlined on pages 100-102.

So young adults don't take responsibility? Then give it to them. Why would anyone take responsibility if I continue to take it away or hoard it? This means giving people the freedom to try and the freedom to fail. It means recognizing that some may not do nearly "as good a job as I could have done" and that many will exceed what you are able to do. But the nature of ministry is that "we" do it, not "I" do it.

Ownership—where can you begin to spread it around?

NO GOALS

An informative question I ask groups it, "Where do you want to be in 12 months?" In other words, "What are your goals?" "Do you have a purpose statement?" "Are there any objectives that you are aiming to accomplish?" If a group is not aimed at specific goals, the leaders are headed for burnout and the group is headed for failure.

The following chart allows you to do some long-range planning. By targeting specific goals and programs throughout the year, you will avoid the burnout that comes from trying to be all things to all people.

GOAL SETTING

	Spiritual Life	Social Life	Teaching Ministry	Special Projects
	PURPOSE STATEMENT			
January				
February				
March				
April				
May				
June				
July				
August				
September				
October				
November				
December				

Effective ministry is an intentional ministry. Therefore, a fresh and lively ministry is built on intentional programming. "Without vision the people perish," the Old Testament warns. Without direction, the young adult ministry will experience burnout. It is not enough to be locked into a maintenance mode, perpetuating a busy calendar and a full counseling load.

Avoiding burnout means a willingness to dream dreams, to set goals, to believe in a vision. It means asking the "why" question. If you know who owns you and why you are here, the pressure is off. You don't need to prove anything to anyone; you don't need to impress anyone; you don't need to see programming as a competitive sport. You're free to minister.

In the same way, "intentional programming" is zero-based programming. The program must justify its existence by answering the "why" question. Each program aims at specific needs.

No SUPPORT STRUCTURE FOR THE LEADER

I have a fundamental principle: *A leader must not lead in isolation.* A support structure is a non-negotiable. Without it, burnout is not far behind. In isolation we can make inadequate, ill-informed and unbalanced decisions. We assume we're responsible for the total success or failure of the group. We assume we're responsible to be present at every function, every committee meeting and every activity. We assume that program time takes priority over Sabbath time. And we assume that saying "no" will have negative repercussions on the ministry.

The role of the central leader is to provide direction, to make sure the train is staying on the track, and to provide an environment where all the other lay leaders can take effective responsibility for their areas of ministry. That job cannot be done effectively if the leader is on the edge of burnout. How many of us are just hanging on, waiting for a "break" in the action?

Renewal does not happen spontaneously. It requires choices and discipline. It means saying "no." "No, I cannot be at Saturday night's party; I need time alone." "No, I don't need to run the Social Concerns committee. Susan is doing quite well—and no, it will not collapse without me."

Renewal also means saying "yes." "Yes" to our need for a mentor or spiritual director. A spiritual director is a mature Christian whose task is to help us stay balanced in our spiritual journey, to provide feedback, to help us focus, and to be a sounding board and guide on our ongoing walk through spiritual disciplines.

Renewal also means saying "yes" to our need for a support group or an accountability group. I do not mean job accountability, but personal accountability for which peers get together regularly for the purpose of encouragement, support and admonition. It means saying "yes" to a regular calendar inventory (see pages 77-78). For more information on a spiritual director, I recommend that you read **Soul Friend: The Practice of Christian Spirituality** by Kenneth Leech.[2]

My task at a recent leadership conference was to address the issue, "How to Stay Fresh in a Stale World." I was grateful for the opportunity. That is where my heart is. I told the conferees, "It will not be enough to return to this place in two to five years only to compare notes on the percentage of program growth each of us has experienced. Sure, that will be encouraging news. But the great news will be in our ability to say, 'I'm still fresh, I've not gone stale!' We cannot afford more casualties in leadership and staying fresh begins with personal renewal. How are you being renewed? How are you plugged into a support structure?"

"But what if I don't have time for a support group?" many will ask. "Make time," is my reply. "Your life and ministry depend upon it."

AN INADEQUATE VIEW OF FAILURE

Nothing can send you to burnout faster than a distorted perspective of success. And a distorted perspective of success is one in which closure and death are enemies to ministry. Because of our fear of closure, we perpetuate many programs "because we've always done it that way."

Intentional programming is automatically selective programming. Because we are aiming at specific needs, we cannot do everything, and therefore must say "no" to certain programs. This is not to say they are "bad program ideas," but that they are not right for the direction we are headed. To maintain a program despite its incongruence with your ministry direction is preparing the way for burnout.

At one church where I ministered, one of the first tasks was to "kill" the existing young adult group. After several months of observation, I discovered that the purposes of our young adult ministry could not be met by the objectives of the existing group. In fact, the group had cancerous characteristics—ingrown, withdrawn, antagonistic—which prevented successful programming. As an organized group, it needed to be given a proper burial. Of course, that is one thing to say and quite another to carry out. I was tempted not to "rock the boat," and maintain programs that covered our inadequate foundation.

After full disclosure and dialogue with the members of the group and the other church staff members, the decision was made. And my popularity decreased sharply. In isolation, such a blow to my ego would have been too much to handle. That is why my support group was invaluable in the encouragement necessary to go through with the decision.

I immediately wanted to second-guess the decision, convinced that such a decision was surely a reflection of failure. That's where I needed this helpful advice: *Closure is not always failure.* In fact, closure is often very essential to the growth process. We need to know when to begin, and we need to know when to shut down and reconstruct. Closure of the group is as essential to group health as the initiation of the group.

Does this mean that all of us need to begin a "campaign of closure"? No. It simply means that closure is not an enemy. It is not always an indication of failure. And to see closure as an enemy, is to pave the way for burnout.

Burnout. We've looked at six red flags. Remember them. And if any of them are visible in your programming now, take the necessary steps to eliminate them. Don't wait. You and your ministry depend upon programming that stays fresh, vibrant and relevant.

KEY POINTS

1. Going too fast causes burnout.
2. No foundation causes burnout.
3. No ownership causes burnout.
4. No goals causes burnout.
5. No support structure for the leader causes burnout.
6. An inadequate view of failure causes burnout.

REVIEW QUESTIONS

1. Do you agree or disagree with the quote from Robert Gribbon? How does this element of time apply to your particular young adult program? Are there any areas where you need to slow down?
2. Review the characteristics of a weak foundation. Do any of those areas need any work in your church or program? What steps can you take to strengthen the foundation?
3. Rank your current programs for young adults on the scale of one to 10. Indicate whether or not the young adults have ownership for the program and the ministry involved.

Program	No Ownership					Complete Ownership				
1.	1	2	3	4	5	6	7	8	9	10
2.	1	2	3	4	5	6	7	8	9	10
3.	1	2	3	4	5	6	7	8	9	10
4.	1	2	3	4	5	6	7	8	9	10
5.	1	2	3	4	5	6	7	8	9	10

4. Review your planning arrow from the second section. Are your program objectives clear?
5. Where do you go for support? Is your support group a non-negotiable? If you have none, what steps can you take to begin today?
6. Is a proper view of closure necessary for avoiding burnout? Why or why not? Does the principle apply to your situation at this time? Explain.

CHAPTER 15

Practical Program Ideas

Programming for young adults is never easy. It's an ongoing journey that requires time, effort and a good deal of flexibility. Change is a necessary part of the learning process. And when it comes to the "nuts and bolts" of making a program work, there is nothing better than the trial-and-error method. However, if there's no need to reinvent the wheel, why do it? This chapter could have been titled, "Helpful Hints I Wish I Had Known When I Started!"

We've made it clear that the ministry does not start with nuts and bolts. Programs make sense only when they are applied to an adequate foundation. You will only be frustrated if you hope that by imitating another's program you will have an adequate foundation for your ministry.

The following program ideas are not listed in order of importance. After most of the ideas there are contact persons and addresses to write to for further details. Several of the activities have been adapted from SALT Newsletters.

NEW MEMBER HOSTS AND GREETERS

This idea is a structured way of creating a welcome environment for newcomers. It is an opportunity for those members who feel the calling to reach out and minister to newcomers. All young adults are welcome to minister as a host or greeter whenever and as often as they feel the desire. Following is a list of responsibilities:

RESPONSIBILITIES OF HOSTS

1. Meet 20 minutes before starting time at the membership table,

and pick up a "Host" badge. Remember, your participation is wanted even if you are not early. This is a responsibility of *all* members. Try it, you might like it.

2. Smile as you greet and introduce yourself to newcomers (newcomers will have on a red name tag). Ask them if they would like a friend for the event.

3. Make them feel welcome and comfortable in as short a time as possible. Introduce them to your friends.

4. Answer questions and discuss the activities calendar. Briefly describe the different events. Encourage their attendance and participation.

5. Mix and introduce yourself to as many newcomers as possible. Make a point to follow up your friendship in future meetings. Especially watch for the new people in the social events.

Note: Encourage the hosts to use same-sex pairings with newcomers. In that way you can avoid the level of threat, and the possibility of someone using this opportunity for advantage.

Along with the hosts, greeters insure that new members are welcome. Here are their responsibilities:

RESPONSIBILITIES OF GREETERS

1. Pick up badge at membership table.

2. Greet all people with a warm smile and positive attitude. Reflect a friendly atmosphere.

3. Give directions and answer questions.

4. Help newcomers—direct them to the membership table, introduce them to a New Member Host.

5. Give current members their name tag.

MARRIAGE ENCOUNTER

Thousands of married couples from all denominations have participated in the Catholic church's Marriage Encounter, or some other marriage-growth weekend based on the encounter concept. But the effectiveness of this concept is not limited to married couples. It has also been proven to be very valuable for engaged couples. Since 1969, Catholic Engaged Encounter has slowly spread to every state. As with its predecessor, couples from many faiths have participated.

Whether you choose to encourage your engaged (or seriously dating) couples to participate with an already established encounter group, or whether you choose to begin one of your own, the idea—helping couples make a lifetime commitment—seems most valid for those in young adult ministry.

Here's how the encounter works: Engaged couples spend a weekend (Friday evening through Sunday afternoon) in a retreat or camp setting. The weekend is usually led by two married couples plus a priest or pastor. (One of the leader couples has been married more than 10 years; the other couple less than 10.)

About one-third of the weekend is spent as a group discussing every aspect of marriage: money, sex, children, in-laws, etc. The participants are encouraged to ask questions during this time. The remainder of the time is set aside so that each couple can talk (privately) about the group discussion, plus complete specific assignments provided by the leaders. (The assignments are usually a series of questions designed to open up lines of communication.)

According to Jan Lynk, Oregon State Engaged Encounter coordinator, "One of the rewards of this weekend is to have couples decide to postpone their marriage, or even sometimes realize they should not get married at all. We want to do everything we can to help the couple seriously think through this commitment. One of our slogans says it well: 'A wedding is a day. A marriage is a lifetime!' "

For information about Engaged Encounter in your area, contact Jan Lynk, 2313 Blackburn, Eugene, OR 97405 or call (503) 484-9029.[1]

STARTING A YOUNG ADULT NEWSLETTER

Effective communication is vital to a successful young adult ministry. And a good newsletter can be an integral part of that communication.

Lana Wilkinson is editor of "Growing Together," a publication for adult singles published by First Baptist Church, Woodlands, Texas. Here are some suggestions she gives about starting your newsletter.

REASONS FOR HAVING A NEWSLETTER

1. Many people do not attend activities regularly. A newsletter helps remind them of your young adult ministry, plus it keeps them informed about your calendar of events.

2. It can be a regular, consistent way of saying "God loves you" and can exhort, encourage, entertain and challenge.

HOW TO GET STARTED

1. Meet with your pastor or other church staff member responsible for young adult ministry. Together, determine a budget, newsletter size and method of printing. (If no church budget exists, there may be several persons in your group who would be willing to underwrite this ministry project.)

2. Select an editor. This person must understand and be committed to the ministry, have good writing skills and be able to meet deadlines. (The editor should meet with the printer to learn the process and deadlines for timely delivery.)

3. Determine content and format. Glean ideas from other publications. Brainstorm with your young adults. Will your pastor write a monthly column? Will your activities coordinator describe events? Are members of your group interested in writing? Can someone in your group or community provide regular tips on career development, relational Christianity or other pertinent issues? Will you feature one of your young adults in each issue? How many pages will the newsletter have? How many columns will there be per page? Approximately how many words will each article have? Will your calendar have artwork? If so, who will do it? Can you print photos?

HOW TO PUT IT TOGETHER

1. Selecting a typist with good spelling and grammar skills is a must. Work out the schedule so your typist has a reasonable amount of time to get all the material typed and proofread.

2. Design an attractive masthead to add interest. Visit a local graphic supply store to purchase some rub-on lettering and decorative border tape. Explore buying some clip art books for cut-out pictures and graphics. This always adds visual appeal when done with creativity.

3. Keep a file of jokes, poetry, scriptures, cartoons and one-liners for fillers.

4. Assign the articles in advance. Allow at least three to five weeks for the writers to complete their assignments. Keep the articles short and to the point.

5. Paste up the newsletter so it doesn't look too cluttered and hard to read.

6. Allow space for your return address, stamp and address labels. Get mailing rates from your local post office.

7. Select a mailing person who will be responsible for labeling and mailing the newsletters. Many groups make a party of this. Just invite

several people over some evening for labeling and snacks!

A newsletter can be a lot of work, but well worth it when your young adults eagerly anticipate receiving their newsletter and proudly pass it on to friends.

For examples or more information, send a self-addressed, stamped business-size envelope to the following addresses:

Growing Together, Lana Wilkinson, P.O. Box 7823, Woodlands, TX 77387.

The Single Scoop, Ward Church, 17000 Farmington Road, Livonia, MI 48154.

BEACH HOUSE MINISTRY

For the past 10 years, the single young adults of Fourth Presbyterian Church, Washington, D.C., have corporately sponsored a unique ministry for their members and friends.

Here's how it works: Several young adults put up money to pay rent on the spacious beach house for the entire summer season. (Their beach house is less than a three-hour drive from D.C.) These "investors" are considered shareholders. The shareholders have the privilege of making reservations ahead of non-shareholders; they receive their rent money back at summer's end plus any profit that may be realized; and they are responsible for the organization and upkeep of the house during the rental period.

One person, usually a school teacher or someone between jobs, is designated the house manager and lives at the house full time during the summer. He or she coordinates use of the house facilities, helps maintain the house rules, plans a Saturday evening family-style meal, and helps plan and lead other corporate activities such as Sunday morning worship on the beach.

During the summer any young adults from the church group (shareholders or not) have the privilege of staying at the house on a first-come, first-served basis. The fee is usually half to a third of the going rate for other comparable accommodations.

According to leaders in the group, "The purpose of the house is to provide an inexpensive opportunity for young adults to get to the beach where the accommodations are comfortable and the atmosphere is Christ-centered. The shareholders work to make this a ministry—not just a business—so that Christian young adults can share and fellowship together as their schedules allow."

Many of the young adults at Fourth Presbyterian consider this a highlight of their summer. The same concept could easily be tailored to other areas of the country with different resort or vacation environments. For more information contact Ambassador Singles Ministry, 5500 River Road, Bethesda, MD 20816, (301) 320-3600.[2]

BAKE OFF: A FUN, FATTENING EVENT

A special event that has been popular with the Single Point Ministries of Ward Church is an annual bake off. The theme is desserts. (Yum!)

Here's how it works: The young adults participating may enter the category which best suits them: beginners (those who have only been cooking for a year or less), most exotic, female, male, and fanciest. Those making an entry are encouraged to notify the organizers in advance. This helps with planning and also insures an adequate number of entries for the evening.

All participants make their dessert in advance, then bring it "ready-to-eat" on the designated evening of the bake off. Judges are selected in advance. Ward Church young adults use their imagination on finding interesting judges such as state fair judges, local radio or television personalities, etc.

During the actual event, while the judges are selecting the winners, there is a program, a comedy skit or film to keep everyone occupied—and away from the goodies. This can be a great time of fellowship and interaction in a festive atmosphere.

The judges are supplied with clipboards and sheets for each category. Each entry is assigned a number to keep the contestants unknown. Pitchers of water and cups are placed at each table so the judges may regularly wash their palates.

After the judges are finished, they tally up their choices, provide the results to the emcee who then announces the winners. Each winner receives a nice gift.

After the prizes have been awarded, the highlight of the bake off begins as the evening becomes a dessert potluck.

The young adult pastor feels that special events like this can be a vital part of a healthy, growing young adult ministry. Not only do they help members bring unchurched friends, but they also provide a great evening of fun and fellowship for the regulars. For more information, contact Ward Church, 17000 Farmington Road, Livonia, MI 48154, (313) 422-1150.[3]

PAINTING UP THE TOWN

Here is one illustration of how you don't have to be a large young adult ministry to help make a difference in your community. The First Presbyterian Church of River Forest, Illinois has around 15 people in its young adult ministry. But when they learned that a community center in the Chicago inner city was needing help in refurbishing some old apartment buildings, they enthusiastically volunteered. They committed three Saturdays to scraping and painting all the stairwells, hallways and entries in a 30-unit apartment building. They also contacted several people in their church and community and were able to get all the paint donated.

According to the assistant pastor, "The three Saturdays turned out to be lots of fun—laughter, paint fights and deepening friendships. But more than that, there was a contagious sense of feeling good about doing something for others that they were unable to do for themselves. It was a sense of accomplishment. And it was a very practical way to live out our Christian faith in the real world. Our young adults plan to do it again."

Most cities across the country have community or city agencies which desperately need short-term volunteer help, especially in the inner city or lower-income areas. This may be an excellent way for many of your young adults to give of themselves in practical, meaningful ways. For more information, contact First Presbyterian Church, 7551 Quick, River Forest, IL 60305, (312) 366-5822.[4]

LUNCH CLUB FOR CAREER SINGLES

The singles ministry of University Presbyterian Church, Seattle, Washington, provides a special opportunity for singles who work in the downtown area to meet monthly for sharing and building relationships. The flyer says, "Bring a sack lunch and discover how a growing body of Christians are discovering new opportunities to apply their faith in the everyday work environment."

The Seattle Lunch Club meets at noon on the third Wednesday of each month. The hour is highlighted by a keynote speaker who addresses pertinent issues in the marketplace from a Christian perspective. Past speakers have included the Seattle Chief of Police, the general manager of the SuperSonics, the KIRO TV news anchorwoman and the "Galloping Gourmet," Graham Kerr.

In addition to the monthly gatherings, the Lunch Club encourages weekly lunch hour small group Bible studies for mutual support and prayer. These groups meet throughout downtown in restaurants and offices for an agreed-upon period of several weeks, after which the groups may choose to continue meeting or its members may join new groups being formed. The focus of these groups varies from Bible study to job-related issues.

The Lunch Club has proven to be a catalyst for new friendships and Christian networking.

For more information, contact John Westfall, University Presbyterian Church, 4540 15th N.E., Seattle, WA 98105, (206) 524-7300.[5]

TWO CREATIVE FLYERS THAT HELP REACH OUT

Russ Carroll of South Coast Community Church, along with Dave Papjohn (a member of the young adult group), decided they needed a leaflet to distribute to non-Christian young adults in their community. As Russ explains it, "They create interest, and they help young adults see we are fun, enjoyable people to be around. Periodically, we have people come to our group just because they saw the flyer someplace."

In addition to exhibits, the flyers are also given to the church young adults to place on office bulletin boards, doctor's offices, etc.

The "Walk on Water" flyer (a play on increasing one's faith) is primarily geared to younger career singles. The "For a Free Lift" flyer is geared more to those singles who might be hurting and struggling.

For more information, contact Russ Carroll, South

FOR A FREE LIFT

Call 854-7600

Or better yet come Wednesday evenings to the

SINGLES CONNECTION

A single adult group designed for:
- Fun, Interaction, Activities
- Singles in their 30's & 40's
- Singles interested in pursuing the spiritual parts of their lives.

Currently 125 singles are getting a lift on Wednesday night at 7:30 p.m. Come and join us.

South Coast Singles

SOUTH COAST COMMUNITY CHURCH
5120 BONITA CANYON DR., IRVINE, CA. 92715

Coast Community Church, 5120 Bonita Canyon Drive, Irvine, CA 92715, (714) 854-7600.[6]

JOB CLUB

The flyer reads, "Job club is a no-nonsense approach to getting a job and an opportunity to be with others who seek employment or who wish to develop job-search skills appropriate to today's job market."

The Job Club was organized by the Arcadia Presbyterian Church's ministry with single adults for the purpose of providing Christian support and encouragement to unemployed and underemployed members of their church and community. Specific goals include:

- communicating and teaching job-search skills and techniques;
- sharing information about today's job market and how to get a job;
- facilitating open discussion by club members about their job-search concerns and their successes; and
- providing material resources useful for supporting each member's job-search campaign.

Additionally, three high quality videotapes were produced demonstrating effective interviewing procedures. A notebook with detailed lesson plans for future club sessions has also been completed.

During each club term (which lasts two to five months) the club meets each Monday evening. More than 40 people attend the workshops on such subjects as writing resumes, developing interviewing skills, how to market oneself to an employer, and the use of networking and personal contacts for job referrals and career planning. During the most recent club term, at least eight members reported back to the group that they had found employment and that the club had been instrumental in their successful job search. Many others found regular encouragement for updating their resumes and for continued searching and evaluation.

For more information, contact Single Adult Fellowship, Arcadia Presbyterian Church, 121 Alice Street, Arcadia, CA 91006, (818) 445-7470.[7]

YOUNG ADULT JOB FAIR

The idea for this free Saturday fair started with David Short, outreach coordinator for the single adult ministry of First Southern Baptist Church, Del City (an Oklahoma City suburb). According to Mike Clayton, young adult minister, "We are always seeking ways to let the young adults in our community know we care about the total person. Since there are many people looking for jobs these days, we felt this job fair could be one of those ways. It was an excellent opportunity for unchurched young adults to walk through our doors without sensing heavy religious overtones."

1. Budget: Since the ministry had no money for this project, they presented the idea to one of the larger banks in the area. The bank's community relations office liked the idea, agreed to co-sponsor the fair and provided all the workshop speakers.

Next, the church mailed out 2,000 announcements to area businesses, inviting them to rent a booth for $75. Twenty businesses responded. They included companies like McDonald's Corporation and the Armed Forces as well as employment agencies and resume-writing services.

This booth rental income covered all the out-of-pocket expenses for posters, mailings and other miscellaneous items.

2. Advertising: They spread the word by distributing posters in many key locations, through free public service announcements on radio, through news coverage in the paper and by sending a flyer to their mailing list.

3. Program: The six workshops were scheduled so that each person could attend three. The workshops included: "Applying to the Work Force," "Women Returning to the Work Force" and "Passing the Employment Interview."

McDonald's served free refreshments. And the church young adults offered additional information about their ministry and services.

4. Response: Even with five inches of rain the morning of the fair, 300 young adults attended.

5. Results: Of those attending, five percent were from the church, 15 percent had been in previous contact (visitor, mailing list, etc.), and 80 percent had never been in contact with the church before. Several of the young adults came back on the following day to attend Sunday school for the first time. According to Mike, "We gleaned 250 new prospects, plus raised the community's awareness that we exist and that we care about young adults."[8]

CO-ED CHRISTIAN COMPETITION

According to the single young adult leaders at Eastside Christian Church, Mercer Island, Washington, here's a fun party idea for your group. Remember the TV show "Challenge of the Stars"? Although this church retitled it, "Co-ed Christian Competition" they kept it challenging. They had over 25 events including volleyball, softball tournaments, sack races, wheelbarrow races, egg toss, pie-eating contest, and much more. Their only requirement was that each participant have a partner of the opposite sex. For more information, contact Eastside Christian Singles Fellowship, 3200 78th Ave. S.E., Mercer Island, WA 98040, (206) 232-1015.[9]

NEW YEAR'S EVE PARTY

One year, Eastside single young adults rented an entire fitness center for an "All City Singles New Year's Eve Party." It was scheduled from 8:00 p.m. to 1:00 a.m. Nearly 1,000 young adults participated in swimming, racquetball, basketball, volleyball, table games, aerobic exercise, movies and party favorites. They also had one of the Seattle Seahawks football players speak.

The event was co-sponsored by two other churches and The Family Fitness Center. They emphasized the no-alcohol rule by stating on their promotion, "No Alcohol = No Hangovers = No Tickets = No Accidents = No Regrets." The leaders felt it turned out to be one of their most successful events.[10]

DINNERS FOR EIGHT

One creative way to meet new people is to provide informal opportunities in homes. What better way than through food?

Dinners for Eight runs for four to six months. Once a month is a dinner party night. Here are the steps:

1. Have a sign-up for all interested. It works best with 32 to 48 persons.

2. Announce that each month people will be rotated to a different home and will have dinner with seven different persons each month.

3. The home hosts are responsible for planning the menu and contacting the seven persons assigned to their house. (We recommend team hosts.) The dinner can be provided by the team hosts (with others pitching in money) or can be potluck.

4. The evening can conclude with entertainment or music—or even the game "Baby Boomer Trivial Pursuit."

5. The next month, each person is invited to a new home for Dinners for Eight.

This program provides an informal environment for making friendships; allows for one to meet new friends in a non-threatening way; and it creates an opportunity for informal group interaction.

FIVE KEYS TO PLANNING A SUCCESSFUL WEEKEND CONFERENCE

More and more young adult conferences are being held across the country each year. This is exciting as more and more leaders realize the potential growth and outreach that a local conference can have in their ministry.

There are five big keys to having a successful young adult conference in your city or area.

1. Content: What do you want to say to the young adults who will attend your conference? Young adults have different needs and it is wrong to simply let any speaker come to your group and speak on anything he or she wants. Get a reading on your people. Ask them what topics they would like to hear covered in your conference. Many conference planners never think of the content. They simply book a speaker, find a place, think up a catchy slogan and let it happen. Content is the key to a good, growth-producing conference.

2. Staffing: Who do you want to communicate the content you have decided upon? There are two kinds of staff in any young adults conference—local and imported. Often, the specialists who live in your own city can do a super job in delivering the content you want in your conference. You don't always have to fly a person in from the ends of the earth. A nationally known speaker does add snap and appeal to any conference but it is not always a necessity.

When you look for speakers, look for the ones who are warm, loving and sensitive to the areas you want covered. Have they worked with young adults? Do they understand them? Will they speak in a language your young adults understand?

3. Promotion: How will you tell the world about your conference? Many groups just seem to hope it will happen. Promotion has to be planned and carefully prepared *well in advance.* Flyers, brochures, posters, news releases, radio and TV coverage have to be planned. In my own travels across the country, I have come to the conclusion that only about 20 percent of the places I speak have done a top job in promotion.

Much of the publicity material floating around the country looks like it was done by a third-grade artist. Have your major promotional pieces done by a professional. Your flyers either breathe quality and content or second class and amateur.

4. Finances: How will you pay for your conference? Many groups are afraid to plan a major conference because they fear that they will not meet their financial goals. *Plan a budget and stick to it!* A careful, prayerful budget will make for a good conference that finishes in the black.

Expect the unexpected in your budget. It usually happens. Get all your costs down, set a *realistic* attendance figure, and set a per-head fee. Many groups will raise a lump sum in advance aside from what they need from individual fees. Conferences do cost money. Speakers and talent cost money. There are a million details and all of them seem to have a dollar sign in front of them so *be realistic.*

5. The place: Where will you hold your conference? your church? a school? a church camp? a hotel complex? Take your time well in advance and find the right place. Ask yourself, "If we put 400 young adults in this place for three days, how would it do?" Decide the kind of facility you want, then go find it. Check the rates, package deals, etc. Some motels in the off-season will be cheaper than some church-owned facilities. The place you choose can often make or break the spirit of the conference. Good housing and good food add a great deal to a well-programmed young adult conference.

One last word. Don't try to do it all your first time. Start small and grow big. Don't watch all the conference ads and try to outdo everyone. Most conferences billed as "national" won't attract any more people than yours will. And start at least eight to 10 months in advance in your planning![11]

SEMINARS AND WORKSHOPS

Find the issues that are the "hot buttons" with your young adults, and sponsor a one- or two-day seminar. Day-long seminars can be a helpful way to provide a concentrated focus on a particular issue, as well as offer opportunity for some integration of learning through small-group discussion. Seminars should be "hands-on" experiences. A four- or five-hour lecture is not sufficient. Learning takes place as we "speak back" what we are trying to digest.

For a successful seminar, use the following tips.

1. Allow the ideas for such events to come from the young adult group (for example, through the Dream Session). Be intentional.

2. Plan the event six to 12 months ahead of time. To help in the planning and to alleviate hassles, use the following event planning guides.

3. Remember in planning that "assumption is the parent of mess-up."

4. Delegate the planning to a team of young adults.

5. Make sure your seminars are opportunities to unify and encourage your young adults, not isolate them.

6. Don't be afraid of too much publicity.

7. Follow up the seminar with weekly growth groups for those who wish to "go deeper" into the material.

8. Get adequate feedback from the event. Use an evaluation that helps provide an accurate picture.

Ideas for seminars can include:

- Understanding Sexuality—Sexual Ethics
- Making Moral Choices
- Intimacy
- Career Directions
- Dating and Relating
- Lifestyle Evangelism
- Living Life From the Inside Out
- Effective Communication

Following are sample publicity flyers and planning checklists for seminars or workshops. Use these ideas to help you organize and publicize your own event.

INTIMACY . . .

Where do I go to find love?
with TERRY HERSHEY

A workshop on building relationships that work . . .

Whether it be marriage, friendship, dating or parenting . . . our relationships can be healthy.

- What is the elusive thing called "intimacy"?
  - Why is it so hard for me to be intimate with another person?
  - Is intimacy even worth the risk involved?
- What will it cost me to build an intimate relationship?
- Why does my sexuality end up being a barrier to intimacy?
  - What are the practical steps in nurturing a significant relationship?

When God created us, he knew that it was not good for us to be alone. He created us to be in a relationship with him and with each other. We all have the desire to know and to be known, to love and to be loved. Each of us craves this kind of closeness, yet few ever experience it.

February 8-9, 19___
Friday evening and Saturday

Christian Focus • P.O. Box 17134
Irvine, CA 92714 • (714) 756-1911

WHERE:
Irvine Presbyterian Church
5 Meadowbrook
Irvine, CA

COST:
$15.00 Pre-registration
$18.00 at the door.
(Includes refreshments)
$12.00 Saturday ONLY

SCHEDULE:
FRIDAY
6:30 p.m. Registration
7:00 p.m. Seminar Begins

SATURDAY
9:00 a.m. Seminar Begins
12:00 p.m. Lunch (on your own)
1:15 p.m. Seminar Resumes
4:00 p.m. Closing Statements

Yes, I'd like to attend "INTIMACY: WHERE DO I GO TO FIND LOVE?"

Fill out and mail check made payable to:

Christian Focus
P.O. Box 17134 • Irvine, CA 92714
(714) 756-1911

The registration fee must accompany this form.

Name _____
Address _____
City _____
State _____ Zip _____
Phone: (_____) _____

BUILDING A BETTER BODY
-or-
Adding Muscle to Your Ministry

Singles Life Seminar
Saturday, April 13, 19____

You are invited to participate in a seminar designed to challenge and inspire you to action in ministry and adventure in your Christian life.

The theme of this year's seminar deals with equipping and enabling singles for more effective service. Paul wrote to the Corinthians (1 Cor. 12:12) explaining that the church is to be considered Christ's body and that we, as members of that body, are given different functions to perform. We need to discover our role and responsibility.

The Singles Life Seminar will help you to gain perspective on how to more effectively serve in the following areas: Discipleship, Evangelism, Missions, Spiritual Gifts, Music and Arts, and Teaching. Throughout the conference you will attend different workshops and interact with many other singles. Each session will motivate and stimulate your Christian walk.

Bring a notebook or tape recorder. Prepare to be challenged; it promises to be a most productive and enjoyable day. One day can make a difference!

SCHEDULE

8:00- 9:00 a.m.	Registration
9:00-10:00 a.m.	Intro & Welcome . . . Doug Fagerstrom Plenary Session . . . Vernon Grounds
10:00-10:30 a.m.	Coffee Break
10:30-11:30 a.m.	Workshop 1 . . . Seminar leaders (choose from 6)
11:30 a.m.-12:30 p.m.	Lunch (PROVIDED)
12:30- 1:30 p.m.	Plenary Session . . . Vernon Grounds
1:30- 1:45 p.m.	Break
1:45- 2:45 p.m.	Workshop 2 . . . Seminar leaders
2:45- 3:00 p.m.	Coffee Break
3:00- 4:30 p.m.	Wrap-up . . . Vernon Grounds Concert . . . Steve Gamble

The seminar will be held at Wooddale Church, 6630 Shady Oak Road, in Eden Prairie, MN.

REGISTRATION

Please complete the form below and make checks payable to Wooddale Church in the amount of $10.00 (before April 1), or $15.00 (after April 1). Anticipate a confirmation letter with additional information after we receive your registration. Contact Kris Ritmire at 944-6300 if you have any questions regarding registration.

Name _____

Address _____

Phone (home)_____(work)_____

You will be attending two workshops; to help us plan accurately, please indicate on the reply card your first three preferences:

☐ Spiritual Gifts   ☐ Teaching   ☐ Disciplemaking

☐ Evangelism   ☐ Missions   ☐ Music & Arts

Mail with remittance to: Wooddale Church, 6630 Shady Oak Rd., Eden Prairie, MN 55344.

SEMINAR MASTER PROCEDURE LIST

Date Needed	Item	Person Responsible	Confirmation
	1. Confirm Speaker •Contact speaker •Telephone speaker 2. Confirm Musician		
	3. Confirm Room •Technical services (use of property) •Musician to accompany •Monitor •Recording sessions •Confirm time		
	4. Flyer •Picture and press releases from speaker •Write copy and art •Print •Distribution		
	5. Publicity •Write news release •Send releases to newspaper and radio •Church bulletin •Group newsletter and calendar •Announcements in church		
	6. Food Service •Meals •Refreshments •Assign persons responsible		
	7. Personnel •Master of ceremony •Small group leaders		
	8. Materials •For attendees •For registration •Handouts •Equipment for speaker		
	9. Volunteers •Registration •Miscellaneous 10. Relax 11. Event 12. Follow-Up •Letters sent •Check sent •Thank yous sent •Event report		

SEMINAR PLANNING CHECKLIST

Publicity

____Flyers (have ready for distribution one month in advance of event).

____Articles in church bulletin (should be in the bulletin at least three Sundays prior to the event).

___Articles in program newsletter.

___Bulletin stuffer (two to three weeks prior).

___Press releases in local newspapers.

___Note on monthly program calendar.

___Radio public service announcements (two to three weeks prior to event).

___Announcements (Sunday school classes, from the pulpit, leadership meetings at least three weeks prior to event).

Volunteers	**Names and Phone Numbers**
_Registration—three people	1.
	2.
	3.
_Refreshments—three people	1.
	2.
	3.
_Sound equipment—two people	1.
	2.
	3.
_Book and tape table—one person	1.

Note: You need to know who your volunteers are going to be no less than one week prior to the event so that you can explain their duties and they will have time to make the necessary arrangements.

Materials

___Registration materials: badges, markers, etc.

___Material for attendees: paper, pen or pencil, handouts.

___Equipment for speaker(s):

- lecturn
- blackboard
- chalk and eraser
- visual equipment
- stool
- microphone

Facilities

___Reserve a room and arrange for it to be set up with an appropriate number of chairs and tables.

- Heating or air conditioning—as required.
- Be sure restrooms are unlocked.
- Have signs or posters painted and placed outside the room or building so attendees can find their way.
- If necessary, furnish a map of the event area.

___Refreshments

___Do you need to arrange for child care?

Follow-Up

___Honorarium. Be sure you have made arrangements for the

speaker's honorarium. It is a matter of courtesy that you present the check to the speaker so that he or she does not have to ask for it!

____Thank-you letters sent.

____Event report.

MATERIALS EQUIPMENT CHECKLIST

____Coffee/coffee pot(s)

____Tea/tea pots

____Punch/punch bowl(s)/ladle(s)

____Other beverages

____Sugar

____Cream

____Sweeteners

____Cups

____Stirrers

____Napkins

____Ice and ice bucket

____Refreshments (fresh fruit, fresh vegetables are preferred)

____Plates (large and/or small)

____Plastic ware

____knives

____forks

____spoons

____serving tray(s)

____serving instruments

____Paper towels or rags (for cleaning up)

____Soap (for same)

____Tablecloth(s)

____Bowl(s)

____Hot pads

____Toothpicks

If food is being served then you will need: salt, pepper, catsup, mustard, mayonnaise and a host of other condiments.

EVENT REPORT

Event: _____

Date of Event: _____

Place Held: _____

Number in Attendance: _____

Sponsoring Group:_____

Person(s) in Charge: _____

Speaker(s): _____

Receipts _____ Account # _____ Amount _____

_____

Total $ _____

Disbursements _____ Account # ____ Amount ____

_____

_____

Total $_____

Net Proceeds $_____

_____

TALK-IT-OVER

Talk-It-Overs (TIOs) are discussion groups. They are designed to create a non-threatening environment for dialogue. A TIO can be held on any given weeknight. Persons are divided into groups of six to eight. Each group is led by an enabler—an individual trained to lead a TIO group. The training consists of group dynamics, group discussion skills and handling conflict situations. Each evening is dedicated to a topic of relevance to the young adult lifestyle. Sample questions are shown on the next pages.[12]

The success of a TIO group depends upon the group members observing the following guidelines. These guidelines are read at the beginning of the discussion.

GUIDELINES

1. If you don't want to talk you don't have to.

2. If you want to talk the entire time, you can't.

3. We're not here to give advice. We make "I" sentences, not "you" sentences.

4. If you want to use the Bible, you must use it as a personal reference. This is not the place to begin applying the Bible to other's lives.

5. What is said here is meant to stay here.

6. We will not discourage emotions.

7. We begin by making our circle as tight as we can.

Because the TIO questions are not specifically related to the Bible (though they certainly have a biblical base), this is a good opportunity to bring friends who would be turned off by a "church function."

TALK-IT-OVER GUIDE SHEET

(Before the first four sessions, enablers should read Chapter 6 of John Powell's book **Fully Human, Fully Alive.**)

Session One: Life Is ...

1. Life is a pleasant experience when ...

2. Life is a struggle when ...

3. Life is important when ...

4. Life is an adventure when ...

5. Life is defeating when ...

6. Life is too short when ...

7. Life is dissatisfying when ...

8. Life is a time for giving when ...

Session Two: I Am ...

1. I am compassionate when ...

2. I am undependable when ...

3. I am hardworking when ...

4. I am indecisive when ...

5. I am loyal when ...

6. I am unlovable when ...

7. I am consistent when ...

8. I am needed when ...

Session Three: Other People in My Life Are ...

1. People are usually hostile when ...

2. People are usually trustworthy when ...

3. People are usually loving when ...

4. People are usually greedy when ...

5. People are usually honest when ...

6. People are usually unfeeling when ...

7. People are usually cooperative when ...

8. People are usually authentic when ...

Session Four: Agree or Disagree ... Why?

1. I cannot be angry with anyone but myself.

2. Loving yourself or admitting your talents is not egotistical and conceited.

3. Self-forgiveness is self-indulgence.

4. People make me mad or afraid.

5. I don't have to bury forever many of my memories because they would make me too angry or sad.

6. My thoughts and feelings would really shock you.

7. Keeping peace in a relationship is not the most important thing.

8. You can't say what you really think and feel.

Session Five: Your Emotions

1. How do you know when you are growing in emotional stability and maturity?

2. How do you relate to people who are on different emotional levels than you?

3. To what extent are your actions guided or controlled by your

emotions?

4. What can we do to bring about emotional growth for ourselves?

5. How do you identify your own emotional growth?

6. How do you recognize areas that you need to work on?

7. In what ways can taking responsibility for our emotions help us to love our neighbor as ourself?

Session Six: Letting Go

1. What is one area of your life where you need to let go?

2. How would you know if you were really releasing this problem area?

3. Once you have "let go," what do you do next?

4. How do you avoid a rebound situation?

5. How does faith play a part in letting go?

6. Share one small thing that you could practice letting go.

Session Seven: Dating Relationships

1. How do you find out where to go to meet people?

2. Why do people avoid taking time to know others and establish friendships?

3. How do you go about beginning new friendships?

4. What is the difference between a casual friend and a good friend?

5. If you are interested in someone of the opposite sex, how do you show that you care without seeming pushy or aggressive?

Session Eight: Fighting Friends

1. What traits attract men and women to each other?

2. How do you know what you should improve in yourself to make you more attractive to others?

3. What situations create conflict in a relationship?

4. How do you handle relationships in an adult manner when you disagree?

5. How do you end a relationship?

GROWTH GROUPS

Growth groups are small groups designed around a six- to 12-week curriculum. They are different from home Bible studies which last one to two years. Growth groups have two specific purposes:

•to place people in a small group environment where they realize the necessity of the interaction, support, encouragement and accountability of others in the growth process;

•to create a place of learning other than the "lecture" environment—through dialogue and building relationships.

Through growth groups people can begin to take seriously the reality that it is impossible to be a Christian in isolation.

The groups are led by lay persons who have been trained as small-group facilitators. The training covers areas such as group communication, group dynamics, principles for effective discussion and effective use of curriculum. Ideally, growth groups can be held twice in the fall, and two or three times in the spring. Sign-ups can be encouraged through flyers (see the following sample), or through a special "sign-up" Sunday.

GROWTH GROUPS
(SPONSORED BY SMALL GROUP MINISTRY)

WHAT IS A GROWTH GROUP?

1. A bible and prayer group
2. A healing fellowship
3. A caring community
4. An extended family
5. A base for reaching out to others

YES! COUNT ME IN!
(Please check the option of your choice.)

☐ **SPECIAL INTEREST GROWTH GROUPS.** Designed to address specific needs and provide a group environment which will promote growth in those areas. Groups meet for six weeks from 8:15 to 9:15 p.m. on days indicated.

  ☐ RELATIONSHIPS—A group for non-married couples—Thursday nights
  ☐ MAN TO MAN—Tuesday nights
  ☐ WOMAN TO WOMAN—Tuesday nights

☐ **BIBLE STUDY SMALL GROUPS.** Designed to meet the needs of the Christian who desires to grow in his faith and Christian walk. Group time involves Bible study, prayer, goal setting/accountability, scripture memory, outreach. Groups meet any/every weeknight for one year in homes around the southern California area.

Which day do you prefer? (Circle one):
Mon.   Tues.   Wed.   Thurs.   Fri.   Sat.   Sun.

☐ **DISCOVERY GROUPS.** Covers basic issues of the Christian faith for new believers and new members of the congregation. (Examples: I Believe in God and Jesus Christ, Prayer, Role of Holy Spirit, Christian Growth.) Meets Sunday morning for six weeks on campus.

Name _____

Address _____ City, State, Zip _____

Phone (Day) _____ (Evening) _____

—PLEASE TURN ENTIRE FORM IN TO THE MEMBERSHIP TABLE— OR SEND TO:
Small Group Ministry
12141 Lewis Street, Garden Grove, California 92640 • (714) 971-4073

Persons who enroll are aware that they have made a minimum six-week commitment. Each member signs a "Small Group Covenant" (see the following sample). Groups can meet in homes or on the church campus. If held at the church, it is important that the room be small and comfortable—offices with couches are recommended.

SMALL GROUP COVENANT

1. The *purpose* of our group is _____
   _____
   _____
   _____

2. Our meetings will he held _____
   _____

3. Our meeting place will be _____
   _____

4. The meeting will begin at _____ and close by _____ with the following schedule _____
   _____

5. The group shall consist of_____people. The group will be an open group accepting new members as the space allows ____
   _____our group will not accept any new members until we have completed one year of fellowship together with the original group _____

6. The leader shall be _____

7. Our group agrees to the following disciplines:
   a. _____
   b. _____ ____
   c. _____
   d. _____
   e. _____
   f. _____

8. Additional decisions agreed upon:
   a. _____
   b. _____
   c. _____
   d. _____
   e. _____
   f. _____

DATED _____
GROUP MEMBER'S SIGNATURE _____

CHAPTER 16

Group Study Material

This chapter is filled with material that you can implement within small groups. Feel free to adapt the ideas to fit your group's needs. Included is material for sessions on intimacy, relationships, loneliness, discipleship, rejection, identity, "catching tears" and forgiveness.

INTIMACY

These sessions include quotes, principles, and "price tags" (costs of intimacy) that I present in seminars and in my book **Intimacy: Where Do I Go to Find Love?**[1] The purpose of these sessions is to create a better understanding of our need for healthy relationships.

SESSION ONE

Begin this session by having the participants each get with somebody they don't know. Have the partners guess the following four things about each other:
- •Where were they born?
- •What type of car do they drive?
- •What type of music do they listen to on the car radio?
- •What is the average speed they drive?

Ask who had the most correct guesses. Then highlight in lecture format the following principles and characteristics of intimacy.

•**PRINCIPLE ONE:** *Everybody's looking for healthy relationships.*

Everyone has a need to belong and everyone has a need for significance.

•**PRINCIPLE TWO:** *We make choices and decisions which lead away from the life we desire.*

> And they heard the sound of the Lord God walking in the garden in the cool of the day, and the man and his wife hid themselves from the presence of the Lord God among the trees of the garden. But the Lord God called to the man, and said to him, 'Where are you?'
> And he said, 'I heard the sound of thee in the garden, and I was afraid, because I was naked; and I hid myself!' (Genesis 3:8-10).

"The task we face is to live a fulfilled life in spite of many unfulfilled desires."—Walter Trobisch

•**PRINCIPLE THREE:** *The first step of growth is my honesty or confession.*

I cannot go anywhere until I admit where I am. So I need to be honest about the myths that tempt me. The following are myths about intimacy:

1. There is a magic wand. We live in a microwave culture, and we want our relationships microwave. We want magic dust.

2. Intimacy is ecstasy. Culture worships "erotic" encounters. We mistake our hormones for intimacy. We assume that if we are living life right we're in ecstasy most of the time.

3. Intimacy is romance. We live with the fantasy that all our needs can be met by one person. And God knows who that person is—it's my job to find that person, and God seems to be playing "hide 'n seek." When romance dies, we seek greener pastures or settle for less than "real intimacy."

4. Intimacy is a status.

•Marriage. People become objects on the road to my goal called intimacy.

•Sexual encounter. (For example, "Last night we were intimate.") Rollo May says, "We've taken the fig leaf off our genitals and covered our faces."

5. Intimacy begins "out there" somewhere.

•with the "right" person
•with the "right" circumstances
•with the "right" mood

We live life with the perpetual "if only ..."

"We spend our entire life indefinitely preparing to live."—Paul Tournier

•**PRINCIPLE FOUR:** *Intimacy is intentional. It is an aerobic sport.*

It is impossible to do aerobics for only one day. Intimacy is not spontaneous. It is not a plateau. It is not a possession. It is not where you arrive.

It is the direction you are going. It is jumping hurdles. It is not "crossing the finish line," it is a lifestyle of behaviors and choices made in running the race. Intimacy is a journey.

It would be easy to give a one- or two-sentence definition for intimacy. But we cannot do that. With a definition neatly typed on paper, people see intimacy as a possession, "So that's what intimacy is." Instead, we will give four characteristics:

Four Characteristics of Intimacy as a Lifestyle

1. Intimacy is willful. It is a choice, a decision. It is something I do, not just something I talk about. Intimacy begins with me. It will not spontaneously descend from above or from another. We believe in "victim intimacy" —we wait for it to happen and we react.

2. Intimacy is an aerobic sport. It is something I do regardless of the way I feel. It takes time, practice, effort. The absence of positive emotions do not negate the possibility of intimacy.

3. Intimacy is "grunt work." "Love in practice is a harsh and dreadful thing compared to love in dreams."[2]

"One thing that bothers me about life, it is so daily!" We need a new understanding of boredom.

4. Intimacy is the journey of becoming real. It is not a possession. It is never a campground, but always a bridge.

Divide into small groups of two to three people. Have them discuss these questions.

1. What are the characteristics you want in a healthy relationship? Make a list.

2. Why are we afraid of the things we just put on that list? (For example, honesty, vulnerability, etc.)

3. Why is honesty necessary?

4. Which myth tempts you the most? Why?

5. Make a list of "if onlys" that occupy your mind and time.

6. Why is intimacy an aerobic sport?

7. Which of the four characteristics are most appropriate for your life right now? Why?

Close this first session by reading the **Velveteen Rabbit.**[3] In this book, a toy rabbit is searching for the meaning of "real."

SESSION TWO

Begin this session by dividing into groups of threes. Give each small group a book of matches. Tell each person to, one at a time, strike a match and tell as many things about who he or she is before the match burns out.[4]

Highlight the following information in lecture format.

•**PRINCIPLE FIVE:** *Intimacy is costly and few are willing to pay the price.*

Many of us "willingly" take out the loan, and then act shocked when it comes time for the balloon payment.

So, having said a hearty "amen," we plunge headlong into a relationship we call intimacy. In a few weeks or months (or minutes) we come back home to "lick our wounds," and we assume a new battle slogan and increase our defense budget. Having secured our fortress—"unpenetrable," we say confidently—we are surprised (or are we?) to see ourselves once again licking wounds and crying to the tune of "Alone Again, Naturally." "Who needs it?" we ask.

PRICE TAG ONE: An Honest Self-Image

We assume that we walk in a vacuum and that we are responsible for our own identity.

Intimacy is difficult because it confronts our desire to be in control, to be the "caretakers of our own souls" for belonging and significance. What are the consequences?

•People become objects to be used for my advantage.

•I begin to sabotage relationships from the start (approach-avoidance).

•**PRINCIPLE SIX:** *Healthy relationships are built on healthy identities. It's who owns us that makes us important.*

All relational problems are ultimately identity problems. (See page 235 for the study on "Identity.") Although it is easier to blame "you," the first step to understanding intimacy is coming face to face with "me."

"Most people don't know what they want, but they're sure they haven't got it."—Alfred E. Neuman

A healthy identity is not striving to be free, but learning service under the best master. Why? Because we need a purpose greater than ourselves to give significance to our relationships.

What is the solution?

That evening, at sundown, they brought to him all who were sick or possessed with demons. And the whole city was gathered together about the door. And he healed many who were sick with various diseases, and cast out many demons; and he would not permit the demons to speak, because they knew him.

And in the morning, a great while before day, he rose and went out to a lonely place, and there he prayed. And Simon and those who were with him pursued him, and they found him and said to him, 'Every one is searching for you.'

And he said to them, 'Let us go on to the next towns, that I may preach there also; for that is why I came out.' And he went throughout all Galilee, preaching in their synagogues and casting out demons (Mark 1:32-39).

The solution to a healthy identity is solitude. Silence. The step to break the tyranny of our temptation to be caretaker and king. In silence we can hear our true master. "Be *still* and know that I am God." We need to hear God say, "When I created you I made you special. When I came to earth I gave you dignity and worth."

"You know that your were ransomed from the futile ways inherited from your fathers, not with perishable things such as silver or gold, but with the precious blood of Christ, like that of a lamb without blemish or spot" (1 Peter 1:18-19). I love you for no good reason!

You can be content with who you are. "I can do all things in him who strengthens me" (Philippians 4:13). You may give and receive ... not take and protect. Get rid of mistrust, fear and jealousy.

Divide into small groups of two to three people. Have them discuss these questions.

1. Why do we want to avoid all costs involved in intimacy?

2. Do you agree that healthy relationships are built on healthy identities? How does that apply to you today?

3. Is it true that we can never do enough to be okay? How does that manifest itself in you?

4. What do you think of the statement, "A healthy identity is learning service under the best master"? How does that fit where your life is today?

5. Are solitude and silence necessary? Explain.

6. What difference would it make in our relationships if we believed what God said about us?

7. Why is it difficult to believe God loves us for "no good reason"?

Close this session by forming a large circle (or smaller circles depending on the size of the group). Encourage everyone to be a part of the prayer by each adding one word. Begin the prayer with, "Dear God, please hear us as we ask for these things in our lives." Each person can add one-word petitions such as "forgiveness," "significance," "identity," "freedom," etc.

SESSION THREE

As the young adults enter the meeting room, divide them into small groups. Give each small group a ball of yarn and scissors. Ask everyone to cut a piece from one to 12 inches. One at a time, each person wraps the yarn around his or her finger. For each "wrap," the person tells one thing about himself or herself.[5]

Highlight the following information in lecture format.

PRICE TAG TWO: A New Understanding of Love Received

"Person"—real me; real emotions.

"Personage"—masks I wear to protect the real me, so that you will like me or accept me.

Consequence? Dependence. We are caught in the dilemma that we need the other person to make us okay. Many of us don't have relationships, we take hostages!

What is the solution? Do we tear off our masks with anyone?

"A person who strives after intimacy with everyone, experiences it with no one."—Donald Goergan

No, in fact, it is impossible and unnecessary to tear off all our masks. But we need to learn the difference. And we need the freedom to peel back one corner at a time on the journey of self-revelation.

Where do we begin? We begin with confession: I am not God, and furthermore, I do not want to apply for the job.

The more we play God, the more we depend upon our masks. But, if my identity is intact in the hands of a loving and faithful God, the pressure is off. I do not need to perform. I don't need to impress anyone. I am free to peel back one corner of my mask. It's not an issue of "know thyself" but "know thy Lord."

Now before the feast of the Passover, when Jesus knew that his hour had come to depart out of this world to the Father, having loved his own who were in the world, he loved them to the end. And during supper, when the devil had already put it into the heart of Judas Iscariot, Simon's son, to betray him, Jesus, knowing that the Father had given all things into his hands, and that he had come from God and was going to God, rose from supper, laid aside his garments, and girded himself with a towel. Then he poured water into a basin, and began to wash the disciples' feet, and to wipe them with the towel with which he was girded (John 13:1-5).

Jesus was free to risk, because he knew who owned him.
Divide into small groups and have them answer these questions.
1. What are some of the masks we wear?
2. Why do we wear masks? When are masks ever appropriate?
3. Do you agree that many of us take hostages? In what way?
4. What do you think of Donald Goergan's comment?
5. How do we play God in our relationships?
6. If we are free to be loved by God, how does this set us free to love (and risk with) another? How is the "pressure off"?
7. How does John 13:1-5 apply to your life now?
Close the session by giving everyone a pencil and 3x5 card. On the cards, have the participants write prayer concerns (can be anonymous). Form a circle. (If you have a large group, divide into smaller groups and form several circles.) Have everyone fold the cards and place them in the center of the circle. Ask one person to mix the cards and redistribute them. Allow time for a silent prayer. Each person prays for the concern on his or her new card. Ask the participants to keep the cards and pray for the concerns during the next week.

SESSION FOUR

Before this session, draw a large jean pocket on an 8½x11 piece of paper and make copies for the participants. Open the session by giving each person a copy of this pocket and a pencil. Tell the participants to write their name on the pocket and then describe the kind of person that would wear these jeans. For example, Mary Jones ... likes summer more than winter, has long talks with old friends, enjoys the sunrise.[6]
Gather in small groups and share the descriptions.
Highlight the following information in lecture format.

PRICE TAG THREE: Risk and Honesty ... With Pain
Risk = moving beyond one's comfort zone. To risk being hurt is to be vulnerable.

To love at all is to be vulnerable. Love anything, and your heart will certainly be wrung and possibly be broken. If you want to make sure of keeping it intact, you must give your heart to no one, not even to an animal. Wrap it carefully round with hobbies and little luxuries; avoid all entanglements; lock it up safe in the casket or coffin of your selfishness. But in that casket—safe, dark, motionless, airless—it will change. It will not be broken; it will become unbreakable, impenetrable, irredeemable. The alternative to tragedy, or at least to the risk of tragedy, is damnation. The only place outside Heaven where you can be perfectly safe from all the dangers and perturbations of love is Hell.—C.S. Lewis[7]

"Sign up for this risk-free account" is the wish of our generation. We want the same thing for everything we do. Sign up for risk-free relationships, risk-free social encounters, risk-free lives. We assume risk produces opportunity for loss.

Applying that definition to relationships, we end up with malnourished, poverty-stricken relationships. In relationships and growth:

•Risk = opportunity
•Opportunity = soil for caring behavior, big dreams, adventure
•Caring behavior, etc. = expanded world
•Expanded world = open doors for a critic ("I reject you. Therefore your choice to risk was foolish.")

We want a "Bayer Aspirin God"—take three times a day and no pain.

But the inevitability of discovering what we want is also discovering what we don't want: sun/clouds, health/sickness, love/hurt. We assume that intimacy comes when there is an absence of pain.

The issue here is not choosing rejection and pain. But facing the reality of it. There are two pains: the pain of risk; or the pain of regret.

•**PRINCIPLE SEVEN:** *Love that is guaranteed is not love.*

Only if you are free to leave are you free to stay. To seek a guarantee is to remove the heart of freedom.

Question: What is the difference between guarantee and commitment?

Result: I need not fear pain. It is not an enemy to my ability to be intimate. I can be thankful for my pain. (There is a difference between thankfulness and enjoyment.)

Pain is inevitable. Misery is an option.

Divide into small groups and discuss the following questions.

1. What is your response to the C.S. Lewis quote?
2. Are we afraid of risk? Why?

3. Is pain an inevitable part of life? How does that apply to your intimacy journey?

4. "Love that is guaranteed is not love." Do you agree or disagree? Explain.

5. What is the difference between guarantee and commitment?

6. Is it helpful to know that pain need not be an enemy to our ability to be intimate? Does it apply to where you are today?

Close the session with partner prayers. Divide into pairs and take turns sharing a need concerning the topic of this session. Ask the partners to join hands and pray for each other's needs.

SESSION FIVE

Begin this session by dividing into pairs. Give each of the partners one minute to share about themselves. They can tell anything they wish. Encourage the participants to tell things which few, if any, of the people know. General topics include family, hobbies, favorite sports, friends, thoughts about God, thoughts about relationships, etc. If time permits, have each person introduce his or her partner to the entire group stating the most interesting fact that was shared.[8]

Highlight the following information in lecture format.

PRICE TAG FOUR: Accountability

Everyone enters relationships with expectations. Unfortunately, few are ever verbalized, and many are subconscious. Perhaps we are afraid to verbalize expectations, for in doing so, we may be disappointed, even rejected. "So," we assume, "it's better to say nothing and hope for the best."

"But expectations connote 'strings attached,'" suggested one young man at a recent seminar, "and I want to love with no strings attached."

That sounds noble. But, in fact, such is not possible by pretending that we carry with us no expectations for a relationship. Our need for comfort and security prevents us from being open with our expectations for fear that we may "drive the other person away." So we opt for silence—or dishonesty. John Powell observes that most of us feel that others will not tolerate such emotional honesty and communication. Consequently, we would rather defend our dishonesty on the grounds that it "might hurt them" if we are honest. Having rationalized our phoniness into nobility, we settle for superficial relationships.

Interestingly enough, our silence (or inability to be up front with our expectations) comes back to hurt us. For, as the relationship goes on, we realize that we are needing to sacrifice many of our expectations (some of which may be legitimate!) not desiring to express them for fear of hurting the other. The more we sacrifice, however, the more we begin to resent the other, blaming him or her for our "losses."

We have been conned into believing that obstacles, conflict, frustration, expectation and suffering are all of necessity enemies to intimacy. Believing that myth, we avoid contact with any sign of their occurrence. The price tag called accountability says, "I do not have to allow conflict and obstacles to become a threat to my ability to be intimate." Accountability says, "I am putting myself on the line and am honest enough to ask you to do the same."

> One of the ways in which love grows is by conflict. Such a statement obviously runs against much of the romanticism about love. An "ideal marriage" is one in which the lovers never fight, but beware of the couple who proudly proclaims that they have never quarreled, for either their relationship involves immense amounts of repression or they are archangels.
>
> Lovers must fight. They can only love if they fight; it enhances the quality of their love. Love without conflict is tame, passionless, dull.
>
> One can take it as axiomatic that the longer the conflict is put off, the more likely it is that the pain, anger, and resentment will blind lovers to the self-revelation in a conflict situation.
>
> Conflict should be an ongoing part of the relationship. Lovers must confront each other constantly in the process of self-revelation and self-disclosure.
>
> A confrontation is a demand for the best in the other. It says in effect, 'I chose you for a spouse (or a friend) because I saw in you certain admirable qualities. I will not settle for anything less than those qualities. You are a person who is capable of excellence, and it is excellence that I want and nothing else.'[9]

Accountability = the ability to be mutually honest regarding clear and just expectations. Intimacy is ultimately a two-person sport.

Observations:

• Intimate behavior must begin with me. If I wait for you, I resent you.

• I must not assume you see the relationship the same way I do, until I ask.

Divide into smaller groups and discuss these questions.

1. Do we all enter relationships with expectations? Why or why not?

2. Why are we afraid to express our expectations?

3. Are expectations necessarily wrong? Explain.

4. What are some positive ways to express expectations to those with whom we are in relationship?

5. "Conflict is necessary for intimacy." Do you agree or disagree? Why or why not?

6. "Lovers must fight." What does that mean to you?

7. What are some positive ways to resolve conflict?

Distribute a piece of paper and pencil to each person. Ask the participants to write down positive ways to resolve conflict. Have them take the paper home with them and keep it in a prominent place as a daily reminder.

SESSION SIX

Open this session by gathering everyone in small circles of six to eight people. One person begins by answering one of the following questions about the person seated to his or her right. The person must answer the question as he or she thinks his or her neighbor would answer it. (The point of this exercise is not to have the person necessarily know the right answer, but to have fun guessing.)

Once the person has guessed, allow the neighbor to give the correct answer. Go around the circle in this manner twice, asking different questions of each individual.

• What was the best vacation he or she ever had?

• What is his or her favorite sport?

• Given an afternoon totally unplanned, what would he or she do?

• What is something that really bores him or her?

• What present would he or she like to receive?[10]

Highlight the following information in lecture format.

PRICE TAG FIVE: Humility

"Life contains no guarantees."

"Yesterday's roses are never fresh enough to fill today's vases."

It costs so much to be a full human being that there are very few who have the enlightenment or the courage, to pay the price ... One has to abandon altogether the search for security, and reach out to the risk of living with both arms. One has to embrace the world like a lover.

One has to accept pain as a condition of existence. One has to court doubt and darkness as the cost of knowing. One needs a stubborn will in conflict, but apt always to total acceptance of every consequence of living and dying.[11]—Morris West

●**PRINCIPLE EIGHT:** *Today is the only currency intimacy is able to spend.*

It is a myth to assume we can wait until a time when life will be better or easier. "Life is what happens when you're making other plans."—John Lennon

PRICE TAG SIX: Thankfulness

We must begin with being thankful for who we are today. If I have to move 10 inches to be okay, I'll never be okay. My "okayness" is something that happens inside, not outside. "Happiness" is relative to externals. "Joy" is the presence of self-confidence and peace in the midst of pain and the real world.

If we're not thankful, we become resentful. People never seem to do enough. Did you ever try catching others doing something right?

Thankfulness involves the ability to laugh at ourselves. Humor is the great exorcist.

Divide into small groups and discuss the following questions.

1. How does Morris West's quote apply to you today?

2. If today is the only currency you have, what would you like to do about it?

3. "Life is what happens when you're making other plans." Can you relate? If so, how?

4. Why is thankfulness necessary?

5. Is there a necessary difference between happiness and joy? Where does joy come from?

6. What are you thankful for about you?

7. "Humor is the great exorcist." Give an illustration or personal story where that has been true.

Distribute a paper and pencil to each person. Give the group members 10 minutes to do the following: List five things for which you are thankful. Ask each person to share his or her answers in a small group.[12]

As a large group, pray this prayer of commitment:

God, I'm afraid to commit myself to you, to be known by you. But even though I'm afraid, I would like to commit as much of myself to you as I can—to as much of you as I can grasp. I would like to give you permission to teach me about yourself and to lead me on the journey toward an honest, open kind of intimacy with yourself and with other people. Amen.

RELATIONSHIPS: WORKING WITH PEOPLE; HANDLE WITH CARE

"I love humanity. It's people I can't stand."—Linus

This material highlights three foundational assumptions:

•We are creatures in relationships. There is no such thing as Christianity in isolation. Working with people cannot be avoided.

•We are creatures with relationship problems. Read Genesis 3:7-13.

•We are called to be a part of a kingdom of right relationships. Read Ephesians.

SESSION ONE: THINK OF YOURSELF WITH SOBER JUDGMENT

Tape newsprint on the meeting room wall and have lots of markers on hand. Ask the participants to write their first and last names on the paper and a one-sentence description. For example, "Tim Jones ... I'm an outgoing person who enjoys hiking, swimming, jogging and reading." Save the newsprint until the end of the meeting.

Use the following information in lecture format. The material is from Christian Focus curriculum.[13]

The process of healthy relationships can only be built on a healthy identity. Because of sin, our identity suffers. We begin this journey with poor self-images. We carry those poor self-images into our relationships and the results are obvious:

•"I'll like you, if you like me first."

•"I like you for what you can do for me."

•"You'll like me when I can earn it."

•"I'll forgive you, when you show sufficient penance."

The people to whom we relate become "objects."

What is thinking of yourself with sober judgment? Read John 13:1-5. *It is knowing who you are and whose you are.* If you know who you are you do not need to impress anyone, prove anything to anyone or manipulate anyone. You're free to give and receive.

Read John 13:34-35; Romans 12:4. Divide into smaller groups and discuss these questions.

1. Are healthy relationships built on a healthy identity? Why or why not?

2. How do we treat people as objects?

3. What difference does John 13:34-35 make in the way we relate to people?

4. What difference does Romans 12:4 make in the way we relate to people?

While the small groups are discussing, ask a few volunteers to cut out each name (with its description) from the newsprint and randomly group them in twos.

After the participants are finished discussing, call out the names of each pair and give them their slips of paper. Give them a few minutes to discuss the descriptions and get to know each other. Tell the pairs that they will be "special friends" for the eight weeks of this study. Their sole task is to do creative, fun things for each other. For example, surprise them with a bouquet, give them a call during the week, pray for them, send them a "Have a happy day" card, etc. Eight weeks to do eight special things.

SESSION TWO: MEMBERS OF ONE ANOTHER

Begin the session by forming circles of six to eight people. Have a person with the longest eyelashes go first and answer this question: What is the nicest thing a friend ever did for you?

Highlight the following information in lecture format.

It is impossible to be a Christian in isolation. Christian growth— or Christlikeness—is produced in mutuality. The Bible is very clear: *I* do not become Christlike; *we* become Christlike. We're all in this together.

Read Romans 12:5; 1 Corinthians 12:12. These verses discuss the unity of the body. There is but one purpose, shared by all the members of the body. If we sever any joint, we not only hurt them, but ourselves as well.

There also is diversity in the body; we are all unique. Two extremes to avoid are:

•assuming that the body doesn't need me,

•assuming that there is a part of the body we can do without.

Divide into smaller groups and discuss these questions.

1. What difference does it make that Christlikeness is a *we* activity?

2. Is diversity a sign of lack of unity? Why or why not?

3. Which of the two extremes is most tempting to you? Explain.

Close with a large group prayer asking God to help us stay away from the two extremes. Ask him to help us remember that we *all* are important in the body of Christ.

SESSION THREE: BE DEVOTED TO ONE ANOTHER

Begin this session by gathering everyone into small groups. Ask the young adults to use their imaginations and answer the following questions:[14]
- If you could be *anybody,* who would you like to be?
- Where would you live?
- What time in history (past, present or future) would you live?
- Who would you have as friends?
- What special characteristics would your friends have?
- What would you do for a favorite hobby?

Highlight the following information in lecture format.

How do we function as members of one another? We are to be devoted. It means putting the interest of "building up" ahead of my need for approval or praise.

An analogy in Psalm 133: We are "precious oil." Listen to Eugene Peterson:

> There are two poetic images in Psalm 133 that are instinct with insights in the work of encouraging and shaping a good and delightful life together in Christ. The first image describes community as 'precious oil upon the head, running down upon the beard, upon the beard of Aaron, running down onto the collar of his robes!'
>
> The picture comes from Exodus 29 where instructions are given for the ordination of Aaron and other priests. After sacrifices were prepared, Aaron was dressed in the priestly vestments. Then this direction is given: 'you shall take the anointing oil, and pour it on his head and anoint him ... Thus you shall ordain Aaron and his sons' (Exodus 29:7-9).
>
> Oil, throughout scripture, is a sign of God's presence, a symbol of the Spirit of God. The oil glistens, picks up the warmth of sunlight, softens the skin, perfumes the person. There is a quality of warmth and ease in God's community which contrasts with the icy coldness and hard surfaces of people who jostle each other in mobs and crowds.
>
> But more particularly here the oil is an anointing oil, marking the person as a priest. Living together means seeing the oil flow over the head, down the face, through the beard, onto the shoulders of the other—and when I see that I know that my brother, my sister, is my priest. When we see the other as God's anointed, our relationships

are profoundly affected.[15]

Read Dietrich Bonhoeffer's **Life Together,** pp. 23-25.
"Love one another with brotherly affection" (Romans 12:10a).
Divide into small groups and discuss these questions.

1. How does the analogy of oil apply to relationships?

2. Are there relationships in your life where there is "precious oil"?

3. What difference does Romans 12:10a make in the way we relate to people?

Ask the young adults to think of one person in their life who is "precious oil." Have them offer a silent prayer of thanks for this relationship.

SESSION FOUR: GIVE PREFERENCE TO ONE ANOTHER

To open this session, play a get-to-know-you game. Tell the young adults you will ask some questions that each have four choices. After you read a question, you will designate one corner of the room for each answer. They are to move to the corner of the room that designates their answer. After each question, allow a few minutes for discussion (within these corners) on why they chose as they did.

1. What is your favorite season?
•Winter
•Spring
•Summer
•Fall

2. What is your favorite color?
•Red
•Yellow
•Green
•Blue

3. What is your favorite food?
•Pizza
•Hamburgers
•Seafood
•Steak

4. What is your favorite exercise?
•Jogging
•Swimming
•Biking
•Dancing

Use the following information in lecture format.

The example here is given of a person who is an accompanist for a musician. His desire, "to make the musician look good." This is the flow of Paul's phrase. We are to make one another look good.

An analogy in Psalm 133: "We are like dew." Listen again to Eugene Peterson:

> In the second image, the community is 'like the dew of Hermon, which falls on the mountains of Zion!' Hermon, the highest mountain in that part of the world, rose to a heighth of over nine thousand feet in the Lebanon range, north of Israel. Anyone who has slept overnight in high alpine regions knows how heavy the dew is at such altitudes. When you wake in the morning, you are drenched. This heavy dew, which was characteristic of each new dawn on the high slopes of Hermon is extended by the imagination to the hills of Zion—a copious dew, fresh and nurturing in the drier barren Judean country. The alpine dew communicates a sense of morning freshness, a feeling of fertility, a clean anticipation of growth.
>
> Important in any community of faith is an ever-renewed sense of expectation in what God is doing with our brothers and sisters in the faith. We refuse to label the others as one thing or another. We refuse to predict our brother's behavior, our sister's growth. Each person in the community is unique, each is specially loved and particularly led by the Spirit of God. How can I presume to make conclusions about anyone? How can I pretend to know your worth or your place? Margaret Mead, who made learned and passionate protests against the ways modern culture flattens out and demoralizes people, wrote, 'No recorded cultural system has ever had enough different expectations to match all the children who were born within it.'
>
> A community of faith flourishes when we view each other with this expectancy, wondering what God will do today in this one, in that one. When we are in a community with those Christ loves and redeems, we are constantly finding out new things about them. They are new persons each morning, endless in their possibilities. We explore the fascinating depths of their friendship, share the secrets of their quest. It is impossible to be bored in such a community, impossible to feel alienated among such people.[16]

Divide into smaller groups and discuss these questions.

1. How do we make others look good?

2. How are we to be like dew?

3. Give some specific ways these principles can be applied to your current relationships.

4. What difference does Romans 12:10b make in the way we relate to people?

Have the young adults think of one thing they can do this week to make another person look good. Ask them to carry out the activity by the next session.

SESSION FIVE: BE OF THE SAME MIND

Before the session, make copies of the "Sign-Up Mixer" list.[17] Add questions of your own.

Sign-Up Mixer

_____ I use mouthwash regularly

_____ I lie about my age

_____ I have a hole in my sock right now

_____ I have no cavities in my teeth

_____ I watch cartoons

_____ I was born 1,000 miles from here

_____ I love Bach

_____ I like to play chess

_____ I like to read Hemingway

_____ I cry at sad movies

_____ I eat raw oysters

_____ I mash the toothpaste in the middle

_____ I refuse to walk under a ladder

_____ I don't tan; I freckle

Distribute the sheets and pencils to the young adults as they enter the room. Ask them to find someone to sign for each item on the list. They can ask a person only one question. If the answer is no, they must go to someone else before returning to this person with another question. If the answer is yes, have the person sign the list next to the item. After 10 minutes, declare the person with the most names the winner.

Highlight the following information in lecture format.

Read Romans 15:5; Ephesians 4:15, 25-27. The necessary emphasis here is on the goal of relationships. In other words, relationships do not exist as separate entities, but as building blocks to a greater reality: _the presence of Christlikeness._

As this is the case, we have a firm foundation for dealing with conflict: "Be of the same mind" does not mean cloned uniformity. As if all Christians were cast in the same mold. Conflict is not anti-

Christian. It is not a sin. *Conflict is natural, normal, neutral and sometimes even delightful.*

Read David Augsburger, **Caring Enough to Confront.**[18] Augsburger says we have five options with conflict.

1. I win you lose (black and white)
2. I'll get out (withdrawal)
3. I'll give in ("whatever you want")
4. I'll meet you halfway (compromise)
5. I'll care enough to confront (I'll be honest with my feelings and let you know I care)

Divide into smaller groups and discuss these questions.

1. Is conflict easy or difficult for you to handle? Why or why not?
2. How does conflict resolution apply to "Be of the same mind"?
3. Which of the five options do you most frequently use when there is conflict in your life?
4. What do the following verses mean to you? Romans 5:5; Ephesians 4:15, 25-27.

Stay in the small groups for a closing prayer time. Have each person share an area of conflict he or she is struggling with. Ask each group member to pray for the person on his or her left.

SESSION SIX: ACCEPT ONE ANOTHER

As everyone enters the room, divide into smaller groups. Allow time for each person to answer these questions:

- •What is one of your first memories?
- •What do you remember about the first house in which you lived?
- •What is an incident you remember from the fourth grade?
- •Who did you have a crush on, or who was your hero in grade school?[19]

Highlight the following information in lecture format.

The point at which the Gospel meets our personal needs, is when we realize that we are known and accepted as we are, without having to earn that acceptance. That's the free gift of God: *grace.*

How had Christ shown his acceptance?

1. In spite of (Luke 15:11-20,32).
2. Though there is no ability to repay (Luke 10:25-37).
3. In the midst of my rightful judgment (John 8).
4. To belong (Romans 1:6).
5. By one whose desire it is for me to grow (John 13:5-10).
6. For what I am meant to be (John 15:16).

Divide into smaller groups and ask these questions.

1. What does Christ's acceptance mean to you?

2. How can the above six areas be transferred in our relationships?

3. Which area of acceptance do you need to work on in specific relationships?

For this closing activity, ask the participants to sit in a circle in their small groups. Give each group a lighted candle, then turn off the lights. Ask one person in each group to hold the candle while the other members tell the candle-holder affirming comments. Pass the candle to the next person in the circle and continue the process. Make sure everyone has a turn holding the candle.[20]

SESSION SEVEN: ADMONISH ONE ANOTHER

Open this session by gathering in small groups. Have the person with the bluest eyes go first and answer this question: What was one of your first memories of church?

Highlight the following information in lecture format.

An element of Christ's love for us is that he does not leave us static, he continues to push us to growth. And that can't be done if we gloss over areas of inconsistency.

Here are some important steps for confrontation.

1. Examine yourself (Matthew 7:1-5). Are you seeing yourself in a mirror? What are your motives? What results do you desire?

2. Make sure your goal is in line with Ephesians 4:12-16. Is the unity in purpose? How will this affect the body?

3. Make "I" statements, not "you" statements. Are you attacking the person?

4. Provide creative alternatives. Are you just backing the person into a corner?

5. Pray for a spirit of love (Ephesians 4:15). Have you prayed for the person?

One final note: *If confronting someone makes you feel superior, then you are in the wrong.*

In small groups, discuss these questions.

1. When is it right—if ever—to admonish?

2. Which of the five steps were helpful to you?

3. Is there any relationship in your life currently where this principle applies? Explain.

Stay in the small groups for the closing. As a blessing and encouragement, personalize 2 Peter 3:18. Ask the members to say the next sentence to each person in their group, "(Name), continue to grow in the grace and knowledge of our Lord and Savior Jesus Christ." After everyone is finished, as a large group say, "To him be the glory now and forever. Amen."

SESSION EIGHT: GREET ONE ANOTHER

Open this session by asking the young adults to mingle for a few minutes and greet at least five people with handshakes or hugs.

Highlight the following information in lecture format.

Here, the scriptural principle of the "body" involved in the journey to maturity takes a very practical application.

The principle is one of *focus*. "Focusing in" on a daily basis. We do this by acknowledging the other person's presence. We don't look past or around him or her. We communicate in our greeting, "You are important to me." Listen to C.S. Lewis:

> It may be possible for each to think too much of his own potential glory hereafter; it is hardly possible for him to think too often or too deeply about that of his neighbor. The load, or weight, or burden of my neighbor's glory should be laid daily on my back, a load so heavy that only humility can carry it, and the backs of the proud will be broken. It is a serious thing to live in a society of possible gods and goddesses, to remember that the dullest and most uninteresting person you talk to may one day be a creature which, if you saw it now, you would be strongly tempted to worship, or else a horror and a corruption such as you now meet, if at all, only in a nightmare. All day long we are, in some degree, helping each other to one or other of these destinations. It is in the light of these overwhelming possibilities, it is with the awe and the circumspection proper to them, that we should conduct all our dealings with one another, all friendships, all loves, all play, all politics. There are no ordinary people ... Next to the Blessed Sacrament itself, your neighbor is the holiest object presented to your senses. If he is your Christian neighbor he is holy in almost the same way, for in him also Christ vere latitat—the glorifier and the glorified, Glory Himself, is truly hidden.[21]

Here are additional "one anothers" to study:
- Serve one another (Galatians 5:13)
- Bear one another's burdens (Galatians 6:2)
- Bear with one another (Ephesians 4:2)
- Be subject to one another (Ephesians 5:21)
- Encourage one another (1 Thessalonians 4:18)

Divide into smaller groups and answer these questions.

1. What are some behaviors we use that avoid focusing in on one another?

2. What are some specific ideas that help us focus?

3. How does Lewis' quote apply to your life today?

Ask one person to read aloud Philippians 2:3-4. Close with a time of silent prayer for friends.

LONELINESS: A GIFT OR A CURSE?

Begin this session on loneliness with this activity. Create a continuum by designating one side of the meeting room as "Agree" and the other side as "Disagree." Tell the young adults that you will read some statements. They are to move to the spot on the continuum that correlates with their opinion. Allow a few minutes for discussion after you read each of these statements.

•No one is exempt from loneliness.

•Loneliness is normal.

•It is possible to be lonely in a crowd.

•Loneliness is solvable.

•Loneliness is a gift.

Then, use the following information in lecture format. The material is from Christian Focus curriculum.[22]

There is an experience that continues to rear its unwanted "head." It happens to all of us. No one is exempt. The experience is loneliness.

The experience begins on a Friday night. You are alone and left to the task of entertaining yourself. You start with the TV. But news isn't exactly your idea of entertainment, so you move on to something else (leaving the TV on—the noise helps). What about something to eat? Please God, no more TV dinners! Rummaging through your refrigerator and cupboards—nothing seems to appeal to you, so you settle for a pint of ice cream. "Oh well," you say, "I deserve it." Let's try the stereo. That works fine—listening to music, eating your ice cream to the beat of the song—until you hear it ... it's "your song!" "That does it—no more stereo!" But now your mind is on him or her. Maybe TV will help again. You think, "No, not this time. Instead, I'll read a book." As the debate goes on in your mind, you sit almost motionless. That's when it begins—the walls seem to be moving in. You know it's not happening—but that doesn't seem to help. Needing to get out, you throw on a coat and start to drive. You end up seeing a movie, going for more ice cream, looking for a place to get a drink or all three. Loneliness ... it hits all of us. Married and single. Tall and short. Well-adjusted and the neurotic.

We seem to know plenty about loneliness. We know that loneliness is the most common experience of every human being. We know that loneliness is linked as the number-one cause of premature death. But our knowledge doesn't seem to help—when we are lonely.

Loneliness is not the same as aloneness. I know that because loneliness seizes me most acutely when I am with others—in a crowd. I fear that I will be ignored, or worse, upstaged by someone with a more charming personality. So I retreat.

I know about loneliness. Loneliness is:

•being single and aching to have someone share your life and love,

•assuming that those around you "have it all together" and look at you as being inferior,

•being married and unfulfilled,

•having a good day at work and only having four walls to share it with,

•saying "I love you" too late,

•feeling that no one would like you if you told them your secrets,

•taking an inventory of your life and feeling like you made the wrong choices,

•hurting inside and realizing that no one seems to understand or care about your pain.

I see loneliness happening in four stages.

The first stage is *awareness*. All of us, at one time or another, become aware of our sense of isolation and loneliness. Many of us attempt to postpone or even deny that awareness. We "keep busy," and are careful not to let on to those around us that deep inside we are crying from being lonely.

Our efforts are as futile as attempts to stop a flood with a bucket. The time comes when we are face to face with ourselves. And we are lonely. It is characterized by rejection, the feeling of separation from God and others. There is a need to wear a mask—"I can't let others know how I really feel!" And we find ourselves prone to competition—"Maybe I can earn some respect and admiration."

We need to remember what we said earlier in the book—"It's okay to be where you are." It's okay to be in the awareness stage. It's that time when we come face to face with ourselves. We may not like what we see, but we have not compounded any problems by hiding, repressing or denying.

AFFIRMATION EXERCISE: IT'S OKAY TO BE LONELY. LONELINESS IS NORMAL.

Give each participant a pencil and piece of paper. Have the young adults divide the paper in half, then write the word "loneliness" at the top. On one side of the paper, have them write possible causes for their loneliness. On the other side, have them write certain behaviors and activities they do when they're lonely.

Divide into groups of three and discuss the papers. At the end of the discussion, have the young adults write at the bottom of their paper "It's okay to be lonely." Continue with the session to let them know why this statement is true.

Although loneliness is normal, deep down inside of all of us there is longing to escape this loneliness. We long for love, caring, friendship. We want to be in a place where we can know and be known—that illusive thing called intimacy. We long for loneliness to magically disappear. That is the second stage of loneliness: *longing.*

Into the middle of this tension comes the father of lies, the Bible calls him the "deceiver," and he tells a lie about loneliness: "Loneliness," he says, "is a solvable problem." And we buy it. Then we move on to ...

The third stage: *playing games with our fantasies.* This game uses two special words: *when* and *if.* If loneliness is solvable, all I need to do is find that key which will take away my loneliness ... forever! So I look for that key in my fantasies ...

... when I get married,
... when I'm successful,
... if only my circumstances would change,
... when my sex life improves,

"Then," we say, "I will no longer be lonely!"

We find ourselves going from one thing to the next, discarding each thing (or person) that does not (or cannot) solve our problem.

Loneliness has caused us to "turn in." We think that when we "get our act together," we can relate to and care for others. In that process, we relentlessly pursue any offer for a "solution" to our pain. Our efforts are compounded by a society which thrives on exploiting our need for magic. Commenting on clubs and organizations which are built on appeals for friendship and/or a mate. Lee Steiner observes, "Most of the advertising sent off by the clubs are masterpieces of double-talk, creating the impression that this is a guaranteed method of solving one's loneliness."[23]

Our pursuit, in fact, does not take away our loneliness. It does, however, keep us occupied. And the motivational "carrot"—loneliness is solvable—encourages us to turn over any stone promising to give us the secret. In the end, we find ourselves at the fourth stage, *the breakdown of our fantasies.*

It does not take long before we realize that our games of "if only" and "when" do not remove our loneliness, as if by magic. Even so, many of us make such games a vocational hobby, afraid to acknowledge that loneliness is a part of us and that it is okay to experience that loneliness.

When our fantasies break down, anger is close behind. It begins with a spirit of discontent. It may not be verbalized (or even conscious), but the seed of "unthankfulness" has been planted. We become aware of an apathetic or even cynical attitude toward other people and life in general. We find ourselves easily angered at circumstances, "I never seem to get a fair deal!" At others, "If I had their circumstances, it would be easier." And at God, "He doesn't seem to answer, so I'm tired of asking." We become hurt and often bitter. Our problem of loneliness has not yet been solved—and we are left to pay the price ... a "punishment we know we do not deserve." Our anger only serves to cause us to withdraw into our shells even further, and we end up cursing the very life we long to enjoy.

"What would it be like," we wonder, "to have a world without loneliness?" Where do we turn?

If God were going to give you a gift, what would you hope for? happiness? money? a mate? Would it surprise you, if the gift he gave you was loneliness? That's right—loneliness.

I believe loneliness is a gift from God. It is not to be denied, not to run away from, not to be magically removed—but to be received and acknowledged as a gift, an opportunity for personal awareness and for growth.

As long as we see loneliness as a solvable problem, we cannot see it as a gift from God. When we see loneliness as it truly is—a gift from God—we can grow, we can learn, we can move on. How do we begin the process of seeing loneliness as a gift?

We begin by learning not to deny our loneliness—pretending it does not exist. Our loneliness is real. It is a normal part of life. We hear Clark Moustakas explain:

> Loneliness is as much organic to human existence as the blood is to the heart. It is a dimension of human life whether existential, sociological, or psychological, whatever its derivatives or forms,

whatever its history, it is a reality of life. Its fear, evasion, denial, and the accompanying attempts to escape the experience of being lonely will forever isolate the person from his own experience, will afflict and separate him from his own resources so that there is no development, no creative emergence, no growth in awareness, perceptiveness, sensitivity.[24]

I agree with that statement. So does the Bible. The Gospels ring with stories that hint to me that even Jesus felt loneliness. In the garden of Gethsemane, we sense his feeling of abandonment, by God and friends.

But there is a tendency in each of us to deny loneliness. We want to live life independently, not leaning on other people. We want to be "in control" and self-sufficient. We say "I can handle it!" But a nagging sense of loneliness keeps getting in the way. Sometimes it becomes so severe we can hardly think about anything else.

Loneliness, a gift? We wonder.

I believe God created us incomplete, not as a cruel trick to edge us toward self-pity, but as an opportunity to edge us toward others with similar needs; not as a solution to loneliness—but as the only context for growth! As we said earlier, if we relate to others simply because they can take away our loneliness, they become objects and are easily discarded.

Loneliness—that painful twinge inside—makes us reach out. We can be thankful for loneliness. Our temptation is to withdraw and become isolated. But growth comes when we choose to give a little of ourselves away. When we are forced to reach outside of our protective shell.

The mystery of God's love is that it manifests itself in community. And the irony is that community is born in loneliness. God's plan for us involves relationships. We understand his image in us as it is reflected in the way we relate to others. To understand relationships and God's plan that we be, we must come to terms with our loneliness.

If we do not, we are like the "many people in this life (who) suffer because they are anxiously searching for the man or woman, the event or encounter, which will take their loneliness away."[25]

Henri Nouwen goes on to give further definition to what we have been saying.

> The Christian way of life does not take away our loneliness; it protects and cherishes it as a precious gift. Sometimes it seems as if we do everything possible to avoid the painful confrontation with our basic

human loneliness, and allow ourselves to be trapped by false gods promising immediate satisfaction and quick relief. But perhaps the painful awareness of loneliness is an invitation to transcend our limitations and look beyond the boundaries of our existence. The awareness of loneliness might be a gift we must protect and guard, because our loneliness reveals to us an inner emptiness that can be destructive when misunderstood, but filled with promise for him who can tolerate its sweet pain."[26]

We may ask, "But where is that promise Nouwen speaks of? How can we respond to our own sense of loneliness?"

Are you thankful for your loneliness? Without a spirit of thankfulness, we will remain stuck in our need to run from and avoid any experience of being lonely. But it is loneliness which gives each of us a context for growth. Out of loneliness, there is our need for others. Out of loneliness, there is community. Out of loneliness, there is a family of brothers and sisters in Christ. If we didn't experience loneliness, we would feel self-sufficient and self-reliant—and ironically—that would be the loneliest place of all.

Thankfulness is difficult, because we most often don't feel thankful. That's when we need to recall Hebrews 4:14-16. Jesus knows our loneliness, because he's been there. And Jesus knows the temptation to have the loneliness taken away by a quick fix, because he's been there too. Because he's been there, we are given confidence. What does that mean? It means we can be thankful even when we don't *feel* thankful. Why? Because my confidence is based on what Jesus has done for me, not on what I feel.

AFFIRMATION EXERCISE: REACHING OUT

Distribute another piece of paper to the participants. On this paper, have them make a list of the reasons they can be thankful for the gift of loneliness. Then ask them, "How can you creatively treat others as if they are as lonely as you?" At the bottom of the paper, have the young adults list some of these ways to reach out to others.

Divide into the same small groups of three and discuss the papers. Then continue with the session.

When we focus on our need to remove our loneliness, we lose our ability to reach out and touch anyone else.

Remember that we said community is born in loneliness. That means loneliness:
•is not to be denied,

•is not to cause self-pity,

•is not solvable by a quick fix,

•is a magnet.

In this sense, loneliness is a beautiful gift, for without its pain, some of us would wall ourselves in and remain locked in our separateness. The gift of loneliness gives us the capacity to reach out. Hospitality is born in loneliness. Because my pain can become a resource that allows me to be truly empathetic and compassionate with another's pain.

We have heard the golden rule often: "Do unto others as you would like them to do to you." Applied to the subject of loneliness, it could be restated this way, "Assume that everyone else in the world is at least as lonely as you are, and then act toward them as you would want them to act toward you."

It is in reaching out that our pain of loneliness becomes "sweet pain." In reaching out and giving a little of ourselves away there is growth; there is hope; there is wholeness.

The good news is that we don't "go it alone." There is someone who stands with us. His name is Jesus. He lived, died and lives again. And he lives for you and me. Can we dare to reach out to him? He is reaching out to you!

THE TIMOTHY EXPERIENCE

Timothy was the son of a Greek man and a Jewish woman who had become a Christian. Owing to the training he received from his mother and his grandmother, Timothy already was a Christian when Paul took him away to be his helper in missionary work.[27] After the death of Paul, Timothy continued to teach the truth that Paul taught. As Timothy continued to teach, so others would teach also.

"Timothy" is a Greek word that means "God-honoring." Thus, "Timothys" are men and women who are seeking to honor God with their lives, gifts, talents and time.[28]

THE PURPOSES OF THE EXPERIENCE ARE TO:

•create one-on-one discipleship ties. The partners complete the 12-week discipleship series, then move on to "disciple" others.

•observe the command of our Lord. The Lord Jesus Christ commanded his disciples to make disciples by baptizing and teaching them all that he had taught them (Matthew 28:16-20).

•follow the process of our Lord. Using Jesus' relationship with his disciples as a model, I desire to select certain men and women and put them through a "discipling process," in order that I might fulfill my responsibility as a pastor/teacher, which is to "equip the believer" to do the work of the ministery (Ephesians 4:11-13).

•be involved in the desire of our Lord. As we are being equipped for growth and ministry, we will be growing in our desire to create for one another an environment for growth (Ephesians 4:14-16).

THE GOALS OF THE TIMOTHY EXPERIENCE ARE TO:

•provide a context for the "rubbing together" of two or more lives (Ephesians 4:16).

•allow a context where the experience of Jesus and the experience of one another can intersect (Acts 2:42-47).

•guide men and women to maturity by admonishing and teaching them. Mature men and women are those who are dependent on the Lord, rooted in the Bible, and able to discern between good and evil (Colossians 1:28-29; Hebrews 5:14).

•finish the 12-week experience, then pass on what was learned to others—develop more "Timothys."

THE ELEMENTS OF THE TIMOTHY EXPERIENCE ARE TO:

•experience quality time (Hebrews 10:25).

•experience a time of mutual prayer (1 Thessalonians 5:17,25).

•experience a mutual teaching ministry (Matthew 28:18-20).

•spend time building a mutual relationship of love (1 Thessalonians 2:7-9).

•experience a time of mutual evaluation (Luke 22:31-32).

•take advantage of opportunities to pass on our experience (2 Timothy 2:12).

TIMOTHY EXPERIENCE INFORMATION SHEET:

1. What is needed to start a discipleship experience? A deep, spiritual hunger.

2. What kind of relationship will we have? A relationship of brothers and sisters, as well as each other's servant (Matthew 23:8-12). Another way of saying it would be: "We are beggars simply telling other beggars where to find bread."

3. How often do we meet? We will meet once per week at a time mutually agreed upon. Our time together will begin at _____ and end at _____. Following the time together we may, at times, go out to coffee or dinner.

4. How long will we be together? We will study together for

12 weeks. From _____ to _____.

5. What books will each person need? A Bible and three-ring notebook. A Bible dictionary and Bible concordance are optional.

6. What happens after 12 sessions? After you complete the Timothy Experience, you can start another discipleship dyad. Start early during the time together to develop relationships with people you think are faithful to our Lord and to each other. Pray about them becoming "Timothys." Make sure that they don't confuse the Timothy discipleship experience with a Bible study class. After our time is complete, you're on your way.

7. What is the long-range dream? A church group built around small caring communities, strong one-on-one discipleship ties—where people can belong, stretch, grow, study and share—where the Holy Spirit is alive in healing, equipping and building up the body of Christ.

8. If I say "yes," what am I promising?

•Commit to this experience for a minimum of 12 weeks (or sessions).

•Share the story of your spiritual journey with each other.

•Support one another in prayer.

•Keep anything that is shared together in confidence.

•Call upon one another (in the middle of the night if necessary) for support and encouragement.

•Seek to call forth the spiritual gifts of one another.

•Share in the common discipline of Bible study and prayer.

•Look to your local church for further help and assistance.

Signed:_____

Date:_____

Each person is given a "Basic Bible Study Guide" which is one aspect of the Timothy Experience. The following objectives of the Bible study are general in nature. They allow each participant the opportunity to be creative in personalizing the scriptures. The objectives should be reviewed often permitting the Spirit of God to make known specific personal needs. The objectives should be shared and amplified in discipleship dyad meetings.

1. To learn to use one Bible study technique.

2. To come to a deeper personal commitment to Jesus Christ.

3. To live a more disciplined Christian life.

4. To develop sensitivity to the needs of others.

5. To develop right relationships with oneself, other Christians, the world and the Savior.

6. To discern and deal with personal weaknesses.

7. To learn to disciple others.

BASIC BIBLE STUDY GUIDE:

1. What does it say? (Understanding the *content* of the passage.)

•Read the passage several times.

•Ask the fundamental journalistic questions: Who? What? When? Where? Why? How?

•Make sure you understand every word in the passage by looking up those words you do not know in a dictionary.

2. What does it mean? (Discerning the *message*.)

•Study the important terms in the passage—those words or ideas around which the message is built.

•Look at the relationships of the parts of the passage. Are words or ideas repeated or contrasted or expanded?

•Formulate the basic concepts of the teaching by paraphrasing, restating or illustrating their truth.

•Discover parallel passages. It has been well said that the best commentary on scripture is scripture itself. Therefore, it is important to read other passages that may be developing similar teaching.

3. What does it mean to me? (Integrating the Word into *life*.)

•Honest introspection. Ask yourself, "How does this passage speak to me? How can I use it to build my faith?"

•Formulate specific courses of action in response to God's Word to you.

•Respond in faith giving glory to God for his faithfulness to you.

THE THREE MONTHS OF THE TIMOTHY EXPERIENCE INCLUDE:

•a minimum of 15 minutes per day in study of the assigned passage;

•the memorization of each assigned passage;

•a written record of individual study; and

•an hour together weekly for the purpose of sharing the fruit of your labors.

The weekly sessions have four parts: review, report, personalization, assignment.

The *review* time is designed to give the opportunity of evaluating progress, either through the successful completion of projects which emerge from one's study, or through new insights gained by meditating on a previously assigned passage.

The *report* time is given for the "disciples" to report the results of their study in the Word.

Personalization is the entire purpose of Bible study. We must take personally what God is trying to tell us. Honesty is important. This is a painful process and makes one exceedingly vulnerable, but is the only door to true spirituality. Sample projects may emerge such as asking someone's forgiveness, making restitution, helping out at home, volunteering at church, creating a personal discipline for Bible study, etc. The completion of these projects needs to be included in the following week's review.

Assignment of the next week's passage for study is the last task to be accomplished in each session.

TIMOTHY EXPERIENCE

(discipleship dyad assignments)

WEEK ONE: Where I Stand in Christ
(2 Corinthians 5:17)
- Discuss the "Basic Bible Study Guide." This is the method of study for the next 12 weeks.
- Review and personalize the list of Bible study objectives.
- Set aside a certain time each day—a minimum of 15 minutes—and determine to spend that time studying scripture.
- Assignment: Study and/or memorize John 15 and Colossians 2.

WEEK TWO: Being Rooted
(Colossians 2)
- Review "Bible Study Guide."
- Report results of Bible study, memorization and notes.
- Personalize! Personalize! Personalize! Projects?
- Assignment: Study and memorize Galatians 5:16-26. Meditate on Colossians 2. Begin praying for someone to be discipled at the end of this "Timothy Experience "

WEEK THREE: The Inner Struggle
(Galatians 5:16-26)
- Review projects (if any) and the results of having meditated on Colossians 2. Have you received an answer to your prayer for a disciple yet?
- Report on Galatians 5:16-26. Affirm your partner; don't over-

whelm him or her. He or she doesn't need to learn everything in three weeks.

•Personalize. Are you being honest with each other? Establish projects as necessary.

•Assignment: Study and memorize 2 Timothy 2:1-13. Meditate on previously assigned passages. Pray for your partner and for his or her prospective disciple.

WEEK FOUR: Discipline
(2 Timothy 2:1-13)

•Review projects and the results of having meditated on Galatians 5:16-26.

•Report on 2 Timothy 2:1-13.

•Personalize! Particular attention should be given to the personalization of verse 11. Promises you've received—you've not received.

•Assignment: Study and memorize 2 Peter 1:3-11. Meditate on previously assigned passages. Be alert. Seek God's guidance in the discernment of your spiritual gifts.

WEEK FIVE: Lifesigns
(2 Peter 1:3-11)

•Review. Have you continued to meditate on earlier passages?

•Report on 2 Peter 1:3-11. Is there progress in the use of the Bible study method? How can you or your partner improve?

•Personalize!

•Assignment: Study and memorize Romans 12:1-8. Meditate on 2 Peter 1:3-11.

WEEK SIX: Spiritual Gifts
(Romans 12:1-8)

•Review—lifesigns.

•Report on Romans 12:1-8.

•Personalize! Do you see any specific gifts in the life of your partner?

•Assignment: Study and memorize 1 Corinthians 13.

WEEK SEVEN: Love—a Way of Life
(1 Corinthians 13)

•Review gifts and discuss opportunities for their use that may have arisen during the past week. Projects?

•Report on 1 Corinthians 13.

•Personalize! How can these qualities become a part of your life? At which points are you most significantly lacking?

•Assignment: Study and memorize Matthew 6:5-15. Meditate on 1 Corinthians 13.

WEEK EIGHT: Constant Communication
(Matthew 6:5-15)
   •Review projects, etc.
   •Report on study and memorization of Matthew 6:5-15.
   •Personalize!
   •Assignment: Study and memorize 1 John 4:4-6. Meditate on previous passages. Review objectives.

WEEK NINE: Personal Power
(1 John 4:4-6)
   •Review your communication.
   •Report on your study of power in 1 John 4:4-6.
   •Personalize!
   •Assignment: Study Romans 8; 12; Ephesians 14. This will require a less thorough approach. Look for the many ministries of the Holy Spirit which benefit us. Memorize Romans 8:28-39. Your disciple and you will soon be moving toward others. It's time to begin planning for your next disciple! Pray!

WEEK 10: Overcomers/Building Up
(Romans 8:29-59)
   •Review the attitudes of prayer and any projects which resulted from last week's study. Are you meditating on previously memorized passages of scripture?
   •Report your discoveries about the Holy Spirit in Romans 8:29-59.
   •Personalize! What does all this mean for your life?
   •Assignment: Study Ephesians 6:10-20. Again we have a longer section for study. Note Jesus' strategy in dealing with a single individual. Find as many principles for working with individuals in this section as you can. Meditate on previously assigned passages. There is no memorization for this week. Are you ready for your next disciple?

WEEK 11: Prepare for Battle
(Ephesians 6:10-20)
   •Review the ministry of the Holy Spirit in your life.

•Report on your study of your armor. Where are your weak and strong areas?

•Personalize! How can you begin to employ these principles of ministry in your daily life?

•Assignment: You are on your own for study and memorization Review the past 11 weeks and this process toward Christian maturity. Review the objectives to assess your progress.

WEEK 12: Evaluation

At some time following the completion of these studies, it will be important to you and your partner to evaluate the process. How could it have been improved? Are there significant areas of Christian living that have been overlooked? What did you like or dislike? What substitutions, additions or deletions of scripture selections would you make? Has the labor been worth the reward? The answers to these questions will help both of you to make this experience more beneficial for those with whom you share it.

Now that you have completed the Timothy Experience, you are ready to "disciple" others.

IS REJECTION THE END?

Before the session, make copies of the following "Rejection" handout.

REJECTION

1. Most people my age react to rejection by:
2. I feel rejected when:
3. I reject others when I:
4. Feelings related to rejection are:

Distribute a pencil and copy of the handout to each person. Allow a few minutes to complete it, then divide into small groups for discussion.

Highlight the following information in lecture format. The material is from **Intimacy: Where Do I Go to Find Love?**[29]

Rejection hurts. We would rather not talk about it. But in the world where people have choices, rejection occurs. Rejection says, "What you are is no longer important to me." Rejection hurts because there is closure. A relationship ends.

Probably all of us have experienced the closure of a relationship against our choice. Parents leave children; friends change to acquaintances; boyfriends or girlfriends decide they would rather be "just friends"; husbands and wives leave marriages. Relationships end. Not necessarily for good reasons. Not necessarily by our choice. But some relationships do end. Can we learn from such closure?

1. Avoid seeing yourself as the "victim." Granted, you may have had little or nothing to do with the end of the relationship. It may have been "completely their fault." Even so, if you assume the role of being the victim, you forfeit responsibilities for your life and your choices and your growth. By choosing to be a victim you say, "I will wait for life to be done unto me. I am unable to take responsibility for me, and reluctantly hand it over to you."

I may have had no choice in the closure, but I do have choices and responsibility in the way I respond to that closure. By being a "victim," I sentence myself to the prison of a puppet's life, spending my days fantasizing about the time when someone will come into my life and "make me somebody." As a victim, I play games which begin with the sentence, "If only ...," hoping to convince myself that if my circumstances were only different, I wouldn't be in this mess.

2. Learn to forgive. If the relationship has closed against your choice, it is probably fair to say that you carry a legitimate hurt. Forgiveness does not deny that the hurt exists. In fact, forgiveness recognizes and affirms the reality of the hurt. Forgiveness does not deny reality. Forgiveness does not "need to forget." I've spent most of my life feeling guilty because of my inability to forget, and therefore believing that I had not forgiven. Forgetting is the "amputation method" of healing. We hope that by cutting off our arm we get rid of the pain in our hand. But in fact, the pain only moves to our head.

To forgive is to "set free." By choosing to forgive (and it *is* a choice, meaning that if I am a "victim," I will be unable to respond), I am saying to the person who hurt me, "I give up my right to hurt you back, to seek revenge, to get even, to make things fair."

Forgiveness is difficult, because it is easier to blame. I want everyone, including God to see how and where I was wronged.

"After all, he said he would call, and he didn't." "She told me I was the only one, but now I know I'm not." "Dad said he was going to take me on a trip, but he didn't have time."

Hurt. And we deserve some kind of revenge, or at least a special reward. My need for such fairness, or revenge, only serves to keep me tied to you and the past. And I soon discover that no amount of "undoing" or revenge will even the score.

Forgiveness sets me free. I am free from my need to settle the score, or to "prove my innocence," or to convince others how wrong you were.

In forgiveness, I give my identity back to God. I choose (there's that word again) not to be owned by you. In her book, **The Single Experience,** Andrea Miller affirms this fact:

> I had to go to God over and over again with my pride, my anger at being 'treated that way,' my need to control, my feeling of being misunderstood, my desire to be attractive to a man—my weaknesses one after another ... To seal myself off from this healing and refuse to get over a painful ending to a relationship was to keep myself from being the person he made me to be.[30]

Forgiveness is not governed by my emotions. My emotions may easily contradict the desire and choice to forgive. That's okay. That does not mean the forgiveness is invalid. Forgiveness, like intimacy, is an aerobic activity—requiring time, effort and practice. But I can begin that process today, by choosing to say, "I set you free."

3. Give up ownership. Forgiveness is difficult because we want to maintain some sense of "ownership" with that former relationship. I thought the person existed for me.

The irony of ownership is that the person we think "we own," in fact, ends up owning us. This person owns our time, our energy, our thoughts and our worries. Ownership is a form of pride that says, "I'm afraid to admit I'm not in control here!" Because the relationship so impacted and reflected my identity, I feel the need to maintain some control, so I'm afraid to give you up. Andrea Miller is helpful with this:

> When I was finally able to say out loud to God, 'I no longer exert any control over this man's behavior. He can do anything he wants to do without retribution or punishment or reward from me,' then part of the pain began to ease. 'Who am I,' I asked myself, 'to tell him he has to date me forever? He is free to do as he chooses. If he chooses not to be with me, that hurts, but it's his right. My responsibility is only to myself and to God. I'll just have to ask God how to get through the rest of the pain.'[31]

4. Avoid isolation. My temptation is to respond to a "hurt relationship" by saying, "That's it! That's the last time I'll be that vulnerable. That's the last time I'll give myself away so freely." We withdraw to our island or our fortress, and make bricks for the walls in our life.

Or I take the role of the martyr, "I must be incapable of loving. I must be unable to be intimate. I must be relationally inept!"

I am hoping that someone will take responsibility for me. It saves me from my need to grow, move on or try again.

We need to discard the myth that closure is always an enemy to my ability to be intimate again. To assume such is to create a situation where we will never risk again. In closure there is pain and there is loss, but that does not mean that hope is gone. That pain becomes our teacher, from which we learn and grow.

5. Don't assume responsibility for the other person's acceptance or rejection. Risk is frightening because there is no "money-back guarantee." And in our attempt to create such a guarantee, we easily fall into the trap of assuming responsibility for the other person's response. If the person accepts me, it was because of the way I performed, so I must continue that performance in order to continue receiving favorable responses. If the person rejects me, it was because of my inability to perform, so I must live with the guilt of my seeming incompetence. The obvious difficulty is that we find ourselves immediately back in the "dependence stage" of relational development. Ironically, there is a guarantee to this stage: stagnant and unhealthy relationships.

We need healing. We need to be set free from our self-imposed prisons of the past. If we have failed in a particular area, or have been rejected or hurt, our tendency is to hang on to that failure or pain or hurt so that it becomes our identity. And we find ourselves relating to people from that identity. We react to our past by perpetuating it. To "react" is to determine that it controls us. "Therefore, I am destined, because I was hurt yesterday, to be hurt today." Self-imposed prisons. Emotional baggage, bruises and hurts.

To love, to be intimate, I must learn the art of giving up. Giving up begins with the willingness to be healed. Does this mean that we deny the pain and hurt from the past? Do we pretend it does not exist? No. We do not deny the reality of pain, failure or hurt. But neither do we allow it to control our identity or our future. Our pain, failure, hurt or emotional baggage does not have to tell us who we are. If my identity is determined by my failures and pain, I will relate to you from the framework of self-pity.

Failure is never the final word. Rejection is never the final word. Grace is available to all. Grace dares to say that I am whole and loved, regardless of my circumstances, my emotions or the obstacles of my life. God is still in control.

Close this session with an affirming activity. Divide into small groups again, and give each person enough pieces of paper for each group member. Instruct the young adults to write a "telegram" (a short note) to each person in the group telling what they appreciate about him or her. Encourage the participants to sign their names. If they don't know one another, affirming comments such as these could be written: "I enjoy your smile." "You seem to be a happy person." "Love that dimple." Instruct the participants to deliver the telegrams.[32]

UNDER NEW MANAGEMENT: MY IDENTITY

Before this session on identity, play a couple get-acquainted games. For the first one, divide into small groups and give each person a paper and pencil. Each person in the group writes answers to four questions. Three of the answers are to be true and one is to be a lie. Some suggested questions:
- What is the farthest place you've been on a vacation?
- What is the dumbest thing you've ever done?
- What was something you were told not to do as a child but did it anyway?
- What is your favorite song?

Each person reads his or her answers to the group. The others guess which one is the lie. After all have guessed, the person tells which answer was the lie.[33]

For another get-acquainted activity, pair off into partners facing each other. Ask the partners to observe each other's appearance. Then, have the players turn back-to-back and make three changes. For example, switch watch to other wrist, take off glasses, etc. After a few minutes, ask them to face each other and try to guess what changes each one made.[34]

Begin the session. Highlight the following information in lecture format. The material is from Christian Focus curriculum. [35]

The level to which each of us can experience a whole life is related to the way in which we answer the question "Who am I?" We may say, "That question is as old as the stars!" Or, "I know, but why don't our answers get any better!"

It has been said that when you lose your identity you lose your soul! To understand our identity we begin with the question, "Who owns us?''

1. Sources of our identity checklist. There are many things that give input or "messages" as to who we are. We store up these messages and form an "identity checklist." We carry this checklist around in our minds assuming it will give us a clear picture of who we are. Here are some sources:

•**Society**. Says you're a number, a commodity. Involved in the buying-and-selling game. And we believe it. We want to be "10s" (but we're sevens looking for a relationship with an eight!) TV counts on it! You will buy certain things and have certain values.

•**School**. Says you're a grade. You are what you can produce.

•**Job**. Says you are what your skills are.

•**Marriage**. Says you are defined by who is your partner.

•**Parents**. Say you are what they couldn't be. They push you toward it. You can love your parents if they don't tell you who you are because they don't know.

•**Labels**. Single, divorced, never married, etc. We strive for labels which are *superior!*

•**Sins**. The accuser, the father of lies, says you are "worthless." Judas believed it and hanged himself.

•**Friends**. You wonder what they will think.

2. Identity cycle—the making of an unstable identity. We take our checklist and move into the four-stage identity cycle which looks something like this:

Stage One: We buy the identity checklist and we chase it relentlessly. For example:

•Divorcees are failures.

•Successful people are 10s.

•Accumulate enough things and pleasure, and life will be yours.

•Impressing enough people earns worth.

Stage Two: We become enslaved! It's the same thing that happened in Eden. Man wasn't content to have part of the garden; he wanted all or nothing. We talk of freedom but live in a society of complainers and addicts.

Unstable identities. So intently do we practice who we think we are, we prefer the act to being who we really are. When we build a wall we need to look at what we are walling in.

Stage Three: It tyrannizes us! We engage in a lifestyle which the "together" people engage in—and we drown ourselves in illusion.

By struggling to continually carry our checklist, we have a legalistic focus. This focus has several drawbacks.

•Oppression. We can never do enough to make it—to become a 10. Our checklist is not the truth about who we are. We are continually chasing after the illusive dream to complete us, to make us adequate humans.

Continual focus on need to make "the mark." My life becomes *legalistic.* Defining and redefining the line of achievement . . "that will give significance!" We push ourselves in order to attain When, in reality, we've fallen short. No amount of zeal or perfection will get us there. It requires the need for false righteousness, so that I can fool myself and others. It sets up the illusion of control.

•Self-fulfilling prophecy. Our checklist becomes a self-fulfilling prophecy; for example, divorcees are failures.

•Relationship sabotage. Our checklists and unstable identities lead to hiding and hurling. (See Genesis 3.) Some of us take hostages.

Stage Four: We have a discontent spirit. A spirit that is not thankful for who they are. A spirit characterized by hurt, bitterness, anxiety and relentless search.

We stay here because we want control! All identity checklists are built on the lie that there is something within us that gives us the potential to become completed beings.

Gather in twos or threes and discuss these questions.
• What are you chasing to make you feel adequate, loved and whole?
• What things give you a sense of identity?
Continue with the session.

3. The call to a redeemed identity. Read Galatians 5:1, 4-6. We need to break the cycle. We need to move to our identity center. A Christian is a person who recognizes that the real problem is not in achieving freedom, *but in learning service under a better master!* To come under new management!

This is scary because we need to give up control in saying who we are. And we want to be in control, but we fail to see that we are controlled by an oppressive master. Staying on the merry-go-round of needing to earn and prove.

The person who has final say in your identity is the person who made you—that person is God. He put flesh on that statement in the form of Jesus Christ.

Divide again into pairs or trios. Read Genesis 1:26-27 and John 13. Have them answer these questions.

1. What does the Creator say about us?
2. Did Jesus know where he came from? Explain.

Continue with the session.

You and I were created in the image of God!

Our relationship to God determines the strength of our identity. We need to confess. We need to hear God—be willing to change—take responsibility.

God says three things about my identity:

•**I am unique.** Read Psalms 8; 139. To see yourself as unique is the beginning. I am created by God. A creation of his personal touch. God formed me and he's not finished yet.

•**I am (potentially) related to God in Jesus.** Read John 1:12. To see yourself in relation to God, is to say "God, I am your child because of what your son Jesus did for me. You are in control of my life. You give me identity, and you have beautiful plans!" Anything less, and we stay in control. I am redeemed, bought back and pardoned, free from my need to earn worth and love! My identity is not dependent on what I make of it!

•**I have been given worth!** Read Peter 1:18-20.

•**I have the capacity to accept whatever state I'm in.** Read Philippians 3:13-14; Psalm 40:1-2. A firm place. To accept the state you're in is the beginning of life in all its fullness! It's a place from which you can grow. If you don't know where you're beginning, how can you go anywhere? We don't need to be someone else or somewhere else for joy to be our lot in life. We don't need to gain or gather.

We need to come back to the center—God. God is reflected to us through Jesus' life and love. We know who we are by keeping our sight set on him.

Close the session by telling the following story about the lion cub and the goats:

> Once there was a lion cub who ran away from home. He eventually came upon a village of goats and decided to make his home with them.
>
> Time slowly passed and the lion cub grew up thinking he was a goat: He ate like a goat; walked like a goat; talked like a goat. He even smelled like a goat.
>
> Papa lion had spent all this time looking for his long-lost son. Each day passed and no sign came of the lion cub's whereabouts. Still, the papa lion didn't give up his search.

One day, the papa lion came upon the village of goats, and he saw his son.

"Son," he cried. "What are you doing with the goats? You're a lion. You can roar! You are the king of beasts!"

"No, sir," replied the cub. "Don't you see? I'm a goat, not a lion. I eat like a goat; I walk like a goat; I talk like a goat. I even smell like a goat."

Papa lion knew he wasn't getting anywhere with his son, so he gently picked him up by the nape of the neck and took him over to the pond to show their reflections.

The little lion cub was struck by what he saw.

He saw their eyes.

He saw their faces.

He saw their likenesses.

He knew he was not a goat.

He knew he was a lion—the king of beasts.

He knew he could roar.

FORGIVENESS—IS IT POSSIBLE?

Before the session, make a wooden cross and bring a nail and 3x5 card for each person. You also will need a hammer. Make copies of the following handout:

FORGIVENESS

Choose three people you are most willing to forgive. Then choose three you are least willing to forgive.

_____Mrs. Jones steals your food for her hungry family.

_____Your friend steals $20 from your wallet.

_____15-year-old Rita shoplifts with a group of friends for kicks and blames you.

_____Your boyfriend or girlfriend tells you that he or she doesn't love you anymore and never did.

_____Once again, Perry steals your time—promises to meet you for lunch and doesn't show up.

_____A friend gossips about you behind your back.

Open the session with this activity which is designed to help participants examine their attitudes about forgiveness in relation to the behavior of others.[36] Distribute the handouts and pencils to the young adults. Allow a few minutes for them to complete it. Divide into small groups and discuss the answers. Why did the participants make the decisions they did? How might God see some of these situations?

Highlight the following information in lecture format.[37]

> Dear Terry: I had a two-and-a-half-year dating relationship that ended with a lot of misunderstanding and hurt. It's been six months since our breakup, and I'm still angry at him for all he did to me. Is that normal? I've tried to forgive him, but it doesn't seem to work. I don't feel like I've forgiven him. What should I do?

I've heard it said that "To err is human, to forgive is out of the question!" Any way you look at it, forgiveness is not easy. We stay tied into our past, we remain dependent on relationships that no longer exist, we spend our energy hoping to make things "fair." All the while we attempt to be Christian by smiling to all who ask, and saying, "Yes, I've forgiven them and forgotten all about it!" Our stomach betrays the fact that we're not telling the truth!

How do we break the cycle? Is forgiveness possible? Where do we begin the process? Is it necessary to forgive and forget?

To answer such questions we need to dispel some of the myths about forgiveness. One of the most common is the notion that we are to forgive *and forget*. It's accompanied by the idea that it's non-Christian to try and forgive someone when you're angry. In listening to such myths it is no wonder you feel "abnormal" for continuing to experience anger. Is forgiveness really forgetting? Is it done in a spirit where we deny that there was a legitimate hurt? I don't think so. And I don't believe the Bible thinks so. Forgetting is the amputation method of healing. To avoid the pain in our wrist, we cut off our arm—only to find that the pain moves to our head! And why is it that those persons who claim to have forgotten past hurts need to continually remind you that they have forgotten?! In fact, if we've really forgotten, there is no need to forgive.

But assuming that forgetting is spiritual, we attempt to repress any feelings of hurt, anger and guilt, only to find that we're more tied to the past and hurt than ever before.

Forgiveness does not deny real feelings. It does not ignore real hurts. It acknowledges them, and then dares to say that there is something bigger and more real. How do we find true forgiveness? Try these steps.

1. Understand that forgiveness is a choice. Forgiveness is not an emotion or feeling. We often feel guilty about our attempts at forgiveness because we don't *feel* like we've forgiven them. We've misunderstood forgiveness. It is a choice to let go. I appreciate Dr. Arch Hart's definition, "In forgiving you, I set you free from my need to hurt you back, to seek revenge, or to hold you solely responsible." Forgiveness is a choice that allows you to change. Not by denying reality. Not by overlooking the hurt. But by realizing that "not to forgive" keeps us chained to the past, to self-pity and to others. Forgiveness does not free the other person, it frees you.

It is not based on a feeling, but on the realization that I can give up my right to hurt you back, because the alternative is an emotional prison. If we continue to see forgiveness as an emotion, we will remain frustrated by our "inability" to forgive, and wonder whether it is ever possible.

2. Avoid seeing yourself as a victim. Yes, the hurt was real. But we remain stuck to the past if we continue to see "the other person" as solely responsible for the problem. If I continue to see myself as the victim ("It was his fault," "It was her behavior"), I am unable to move on, for I spend my energy fantasizing about "If only I would have said" Or, "When they apologize ...," etc.

"But what if it was their fault?" someone is sure to ask. Okay, let's assume it was 99 percent their fault. But until we take 100 percent responsibility for our fault, we are stuck at blaming and trying to make things "fair."

Forgiveness takes responsibility because it dares to say, "This hurts. I'm angry. But my letting go of my right to balance the score is bigger than my need to hang on."

3. Forgiveness is an aerobic sport. By definition, it is impossible to do aerobics for one day. Aerobics is a lifestyle. It takes time, practice and consistency. Forgiveness is the same. It takes time and practice. Making the choice to forgive today doesn't mean that you may not need to make it tomorrow. Your feelings may contradict that choice. But that's where we as Christians have an advantage. Our strength for practicing the aerobics of forgiveness is based on Jesus Christ's consistent forgiveness of us. "Be kind to one another, tenderhearted, forgiving one another, as God in Christ forgave you" (Ephesians 4:32).

As he continues to set us free, so we can continue to live free—

regardless of what our feelings tell us.

Close the meeting by distributing a 3x5 card to each person. Have the participants write down a problem they are having with forgiveness at this time. It may be they're having difficulty forgiving a family member or friend, or maybe they're having difficulty forgiving themselves.

After everyone has finished, allow a time of silence and invite everyone to come to the front and nail their problem to the cross.

Read Acts 10:43, "To him all the prophets bear witness that every one who believes in him receives forgiveness of sins through his name." Close with the Lord's Prayer.

THE ART OF CATCHING TEARS

Purpose: To learn that the "healing community" is not reserved for the few (the professionals), but that all of us as Christians are involved in the process of catching tears. At the conclusion of the session the group leaders should know:
- the nine elements of tearcatching,
- the areas of tearcatching where they are strong, and
- how they can become more effective tearcatchers.

Content: If the church is functioning properly, we will experience a healing presence. We are the bearers of one another's burdens (Galatians 6:2). We are told to rejoice with those who rejoice and to weep with those who weep (Romans 12:15). No Christian is exempt from the above verses, so we will need to take seriously our responsibility to be a part of that healing presence—"tearcatchers."[38]

Session: Go over the following nine characteristics of tearcatchers. After each element, lead the participants in the activity.

1. A tearcatcher knows his or her identity. Jesus was able to have compassion on people because his identity was not dependent upon his ministry. In other words, because Jesus knew who he was (or who he belonged to—"You are my beloved Son in whom I am well pleased"), he was free to concentrate on loving others. If we are not sure of our identity we will use our relationships to build up our self-image and will not be free to care for someone who needs an encouraging touch.
- Have the participants complete the following handout. Then discuss why we should have positive self-images according to the verses.

Bible Verses	What It Means for Me
Genesis 5:1	
Matthew 10:29-31	
John 15:16	
Romans 5:8	
1 Corinthians 3:16-17	

2. A tearcatcher has experienced brokenness, forgiveness and renewal. A tearcatcher knows what its like to experience the complete forgiveness of God after his or her pride has been broken. Why is this so important? Because our growth is based upon a common bond: Jesus loved us in spite of ourselves. Until we have personally acknowledged a need—brokenness—and experienced the forgiveness of Jesus, we will not be free to be a healing presence for anyone around us.

•Divide into small groups and have each person complete this sentence, "I experienced forgiveness when ..."

3. A tearcatcher is sensitive to the needs of others. If the church is the kingdom of "right relationships" it means relationships where there is that desire to rejoice with those who rejoice and weep with those who weep. If we are not in a place where we can be vulnerable and allow others that sense of vulnerability we will find ourselves unable to be sensitive.

Growing Christians are "real" Christians, with real needs, real concerns, real tears, real joys and real laughter. Those experiences produce most growth when they are shared by another person. That process of sharing is a healing process, and requires sensitivity.

•In the same small groups, have each person complete these sentences: "A real concern of mine is ..." And, "A real joy of mine is ..."

4. A tearcatcher shares the problem. It has been said that "pity wants to solve the problem; compassion wants to share the problem." And whenever we see people only as needing answers to their problems we have missed the biblical emphasis. Before they need answers, people need to know someone understands them. Though we may have never experienced what they have experienced, we can still demonstrate a heart that is willing to "walk a mile in their shoes." When we share the problem it becomes "our problem," not your problem or their problem. For, in fact, that is an outgrowth of koinonia (community).

•Write the following situation on 3x5 cards. Give one of the cards to each small group. They are to give ideas on how they could "share the problems."

Situation One: You have a friend who is a Christian. He is in love with a non-Christian woman and has come to you for advice. He wants to marry her, but has fears about it. What should he do? How could you help?

Situation Two: Your brother is feeling very, very low. He has just been laid off from his job and feels like a complete failure. He comes to you wanting to talk. What do you do? What do you say? How can you help?

Situation Three: A friend's parents are bugging her to get married. They think that she's getting too old to be single. Besides, they want grandchildren someday. She comes to you with this problem. How can you help?

Situation Four: A member of your young adult group has been coming less and less to church activities. You see her at a restaurant one day and begin to talk. She says the church is full of false people with false ideas and false religion. She doesn't need them. Besides she can get a more spiritual feeling from going on a solitary hike rather than going to church. "What do you say? How do you react? What do you do? How can you "share" the problem?

5. A tearcatcher is refreshing to be around. As the saying goes, "You are the dill pickle on the hamburger of life." Tearcatchers bring a sense of zest and life to a relationship. There is a freshness which is contagious. They bring a sense of encouragement by their presence.

Often in the New Testament, Paul talks about "encouraging one another." A tearcatcher makes sure that is a part of his or her life-style.

•Give the participants each a pencil and piece of paper. Have them write names of people and ways they can encourage them this week. For example, "Mike—call him on the telephone." "Sara—take her out for a Monday lunch."

6. A tearcatcher sees beyond the immediate to the

potential. In his relationships with the disciples Jesus always related to them as if they were "more" than they were. He was looking at their potential ... at what they could become. In this way, he was letting his relationship with them give them the freedom to grow. In the same way, a tearcatcher sees people as God sees them—and he always sees us beyond where we are now. A tearcatcher goes one step further: He or she actively works to encourage that potential growth. It is a picture of people who take each other's growth seriously.

•On the other side of their papers, ask the participants to write the name of one person they can call this week to encourage for further growth. For example, "Bill—ask him to come with me to a Bible study." Review the section on accountability relationships (see Chapter 6).

7. A tearcatcher is patient. Our old nature finds it difficult to be patient. We want answers "NOW"; problems solved "NOW"; growth "NOW." But that is not the real world. Growth takes time; it takes struggles; it takes pain and requires that one be stretched. As Christians we need to be willing to be patient with one another in this process. That means relationships where we continue to say, "I care enough to hang in there with you." It is easier to give a lecture. It is more difficult to form a relationship where we are willing to spend energy in concern for growth.

•Ask a volunteer to read 1 Corinthians 13. Have the young adults explain what the verses mean to them. How can we find patience in trying situations?

8. A tearcatcher takes his or her own growth seriously. On the other side of the coin, the picture of Jesus isn't all giving. There is a very simple reason why he was able to continually give: He made sure he was replenished. "Jesus withdrew to be with his Father" the Gospels repeat again and again. He took his own growth seriously. And because of it, he was able to give to others, to be a tearcatcher. He was refreshing because he was refreshed. Without this dimension there can be discouragement, loss of concern, and even burnout. Because of the consequences, this is a priority we cannot neglect.

•Distribute a 3x5 card to each person. Have the participants each set a goal for a daily quiet time with God. To begin, they only need to schedule three to five minutes a day. Have them set the goals, and keep the cards as reminders for their need to be spiritually replenished and refreshed everyday.

9. A tearcatcher has a servant's heart. "For the Son of man came to serve, not to be served." That statement sums up the profile of a tearcatcher: a servant—someone who is willing to give something of himself or herself for the growth of another. Servants do not seek personal comfort. They do not demand their own way. They serve.

By being available.

By listening.

By understanding.

By reaching out.

By showing love.

By "catching tears."

•Discuss these questions in small groups.

1. Have you ever thought of yourself as a "tearcatcher"? Explain.

2. As an adult, who do you seek out for advice or help? Why that person?

3. Of the nine principles mentioned, which one do you think is your greatest strength? Which one will you have to concentrate on the most to improve?

Close the session by dividing into small groups. One at a time, ask everyone give an "If I Could" present to the person sitting next to him or her.[39] Have the presents deal with tearcatching. For example, "If I could give any gift in the world to Mark, I would give him the gift of patience in trying times." Or, "If I could give any gift in the world to Cathy, I would give her a jar of dill pickles to remind her that she brings zest and life to any relationship."

CHAPTER 17

Questions Most Commonly Asked

Regardless of its thoroughness, no book can cover all the issues. So this chapter is dedicated to the bits and pieces, the odds and ends. It looks at some of the "difficult areas" and the questions that seem unanswerable. While not promising cure-all answers, it is important to bring these questions to a place of dialogue in order that we can be more effective in our approach to young adult ministry.

QUESTION: **Our program seems to attract "losers." Is there anything we can do about this?**

That's a valid concern. I assume that by "loser," this person is referring to primarily single young adults who are socially out-of-place, unkempt, uneducated or socially inept. What should our response be?

On the one hand, we don't want to advocate a "no losers allowed" policy, because we're sure that such a policy would not be in line with our Christian faith. On the other hand, we're afraid that the presence of "losers" will be a deterrent to newcomers. Is there an answer?

One thing I am sure of, the more you focus on the issue the more difficult it is to overcome. Some leaders feel the need to apologize for the presence of "undesirables." Some attempt to arrange certain events where "undesirables" would not be invited. That's too much energy for what is ultimately irrelevant. The more attention you give an issue, the more significance it assumes—and consequently, all the more power.

The only way to address the issue is to conveniently ignore it (thereby not giving it undue significance) and refocus on the important issue: building a healthy core group of leaders. I soon discovered that if I wanted a strong healthy core group to appear suddenly out of the blue, I would have to wait a long time. And I found myself blaming the "losers" in our group, claiming that they were the reason such a strong core didn't reveal itself. I learned that strong groups are built; they do not appear. And if I wanted to attract healthy people, I had to build a healthy core group. So instead of focusing on my liability—the presence of "losers"—I intentionally focused on the assets and began to build a strong, healthy core group.

A strong core is essential. Without it, undesirable elements can be cancerous to a group. With a strong core, the energy is redirected on what we as a group are building, and not on what we need to overcome. The stronger the group, the easier it is to diffuse negative elements. Such negative elements do not require our undivided attention.

And surprise, some of the "losers" in my group turned out to be "gems in the rough." They only needed the right job, appropriate responsibility or the right kind of encouragement.

Above all else, persevere. Rebuilding is not an easy task. But it is possible.

QUESTION: **Many of my sharp, strong leaders stay with me for six months to one year. Then they get married, and move away from the group. What can I do?**

Institute a no-marriage policy! Well, maybe that wouldn't work.

There are a few reasons that married people feel uncomfortable in a young adult group. One is their desire to "start a new life for themselves." Many newlyweds feel that it is necessary to begin establishing friendships with other couples. Unfortunately, this break is often at the expense of their old friendships. The second reason is simply a factor of time. Newlyweds—for good reasons—can tend to remove themselves from a variety of commitments and involvements, for the sake of having more time for their new mate. The third reason is a reaction to an unwritten policy in the young adult group. When I've asked some young couples why they've left the young adult group, their response has surprised me, "The group is for single people only, isn't it?" I also discovered that many of the couples were not attending any young couples fellowship, or the church didn't offer a young couples group and they were in limbo. In between, with nowhere to turn. What should our response be? My answer has several steps.

1. Resolve the issue of the makeup of your young adult group. Is it entirely for single young adults? Is it integrated? Does it matter? Is it printed in your purpose statement? Is it public knowledge? When persons marry are they required to leave?

2. Prepare for transition. If your young adult group is entirely for single persons, then the fact that married persons leave is only logical. What is important is the transition for that departure. How are couples being prepared for that transition? An idea to ease transition is to plan an ongoing growth group for couples contemplating marriage. The purpose of the group is to develop communication skills, understand conflict resolution, and do the groundwork for a possible marriage. Such a group communicates loud and clear to your young adults, that the ministry is committed to addressing the key needs during that transitional time. Too often, when a couple emerges in the group, we immediately write them off, "Oh, they'll be gone soon." Instead, we need to direct them into appropriate support structures.

The second idea to insure smooth transitions is to establish a solid fellowship for young couples. If it is necessary for them to leave the group, where will they transition to? Leaving them in limbo only encourages a departure from the church. It is my belief that the young couples fellowship also be under the authority of the young adult minister or director. In this way you maintain continuity, and provide a framework for future joint-group sponsored events.

3. Know the reasons why people leave. If it is your intention to maintain an integrated young adult group, then the fact that couples automatically leave would be a concern. It would be helpful to know the reasons why. Have you asked any who have left the reasons for their departure? Maybe it is discomfort, maybe it's the need to develop new friendships, or maybe they feel that the young adult group will no longer be addressing their needs. Such concerns are understandable. It is unrealistic to assume that a young adult ministry will meet the full range of needs for young adults—single and married, younger and older. Again, the growth groups will be essential. Plan specific programs that target unique needs. It is important to have intact structures which address the issues that couples face.

Sometimes, couples leave a young adult group because the single persons feel uncomfortable or threatened by their presence. The issue at stake here is the stereotypes we propagate. Such stereotypes should be an issue of teaching and dialogue in your young adult group.

4. Don't create an either/or situation. "Either you stay in our group or you leave the church." The healthiest churches I know provide an option. Couples are allowed to stay in the young adult group, or move to a group designed specifically for them. With such an option available, it helps diffuse the level of threat that a young adult director feels whenever people choose to leave the group. There is nothing positive gained by taking anyone's departure as permanent.

Departures come with the territory. And I have learned through my contacts with young adult programs, that the average percentage of married adults in a young adult group is around 10 to 15 percent maximum. It is generally true that couples move on shortly after their marriage. Departures are a part of transitions. It is important that we understand the nature of transitions, and provide places of support and refuge during such times.

QUESTION: **Why do women always seem to outnumber men in young adult groups?**

Good question. It is a rare group that has at least a 50-50 ratio of men and women. I can think of two reasons. The first is sociological. It's a fact that there are more single women in the United States then there are single men. Of course, you're probably wondering why they are all in your group!

The second reason is a result of Western values. Men have a more difficult time joining groups where there may be the implication of need. It is masculine to appear self-sufficient. For many men, joining a young adult group means coming face to face with the pressure of those ingrained values.

If you desire more men in your group, it is not enough to sit back and wait for them. Oddly enough, men are attracted by the presence of male leadership. I'm not referring to a leadership team that is solely comprised of males. I believe female leadership is essential. But there must be the presence of males in the leadership group to attract men. There's a sense, then, among the men that they are not coming to a "women's club." Again, male leadership needs to be developed; it doesn't just happen. There is a greater reluctance on the part of men to assume responsibility. Strong male leadership means finding quality time to nurture men whether it be one-on-one or in a leadership development group.

QUESTION: **We elect our leaders. Is that okay?**

I am still convinced that democracy is not the best way to select ministry leadership. Let me explain. In one group where I was a pastor, elections were part of the format I inherited. It was a majority vote and included nominations from the floor. I left it intact for the first six months. The problems with that system became readily apparent. There was no way to enforce prescribed qualifications; there was no way to encourage the role and necessity of spiritual giftedness; and there was no check and balance to insure against the election of someone who was either unprepared for leadership, or in an emotional state where a leadership position would be ill-advised.

With elections, we had treasurers who couldn't multiply. ("No one asked him, but he was such a nice guy.") Committee chairpersons who were not Christians. ("We just assumed.") Coordinators who were clear about the fact that they had an ax to grind. Elections can be reduced to popularity contests.

Selective leadership is still my recommendation. But selective does not need to be autocratic. It became our policy to have the existing leadership team be the selection committee for the next six-month term. Their purpose was to find one or two names for each position where a leader was needed. As a selection committee, they were introduced to the entire group, and were thereby made accessible to persons who had recommendations. The selection committee became the filter service. They knew the necessary qualifications, the recommended spiritual gifts and the red flags to avoid. As the minister, I was an ad hoc member of the committee and gave my input where necessary. I didn't feel it necessary to orchestrate any "power plays" around the committee. They needed to feel that it was their task to replace themselves.

Their recommendations were placed before the general body one month before the new leadership term. At that date, the body was allowed to vote on the name recommended for each leadership position. If the majority of the group felt uncomfortable and registered a "no" vote, the selection committee went back to work.

QUESTION: **I have a leader who volunteered for a position. I needed help, so I said okay. Now I realize this person**

is a negative influence, and very wrong for the job. How do I get rid of this volunteer?

There are no easy answers here. And it is very difficult to solve such a problem out of context. To understand the problem and any possible solution, we need to understand the circumstances that led to the problem. We make a mistake when we attempt to solve all leadership problems with a knee-jerk reaction. It's been called the fire-fighting approach to problems. Instead of preventative work, we frantically and clumsily try to eradicate obstacles so that we can "get on with the ministry." What we said earlier bears repeating, "Ministry and leadership development is not the absence of problems, ministry *is* your problems." What is important is a framework for dealing with the normal obstacles and problems that occur whenever people are involved.

Now back to the question. Let me respond by giving a series of observations.

1. Honestly face the consequences of leading out of desperation. The "warm body" theory of leadership brings with it a fistful of red flags. So part of this problem is the natural consequences of any lack of quality control. If I were in this situation my greater concern would be over the need for developing an adequate system for leadership development and selection. If there is no leadership development in place, I will continually deal with ineffective leaders, regardless of how I handle the immediate problem.

2. Communicate. Have you talked to this person? Do you spend time with him or her? Again, here is where the leadership development structure is essential. It establishes the fact that once a week, or at least twice monthly, I as a director or pastor am spending individual time with my leadership team. My need to be honest or confrontive with a negative leader will not appear to be a spontaneous knee-jerk reaction. It will occur in the context of a relationship that has been ongoing. Too often, we assign leadership roles to particular persons, and then depart the scene. That is a bad way to develop leadership, not to mention a good way to increase ulcers.

3. Never solve problems until all "assumptions" are clarified. There were times when I found myself being confrontive with some of my leaders, without even taking the time to ask their side of the story. I just assumed what I had heard was true.

4. Very often, negative behavior is a symptom of a

deeper issue. While it may be that the best course of action is to remove this individual from his or her responsibilities, let's not forget that this is a person who may be crying out for help, support, direction, healing or renewal. Perhaps, it would be the case that the individual simply needs a reassignment, or some relief in his or her responsibility. The primary issue here is that we are dealing with people, not just objects for program management. Remember, we're building big people. Big programs are the consequence of that foundational priority.

5. Be consistent with your own rules. Do we clearly communicate to our leaders what is expected of them? Will my confrontation with this negative leader come as a surprise to him or her? Will it be consistent with the way I have communicated all along?

With any "personal problems," context is vital. Problems are never solved in a vacuum. The best solution for this person's crisis, is to begin the process of insuring that there is a relational basis from which future problems can be addressed.

QUESTION: **We've tried the program planning arrow, and it doesn't work. So why spend the time on it?**

I'm never quite sure what "doesn't work" means, but it does imply the presence of frustration, unmet expectations or some sense of failure.

We need to be very clear that there is no planning system in existence that is capable of being a cure-all for everyone's ministry ailments. The program planning arrow (see Section Two) is not meant to guarantee program success. Its purpose is to keep us accountable to our ongoing need to ask the question "Why?" We need to regularly walk through the process of evaluating our programs. The programs we do must have reasons. Intentional programming is the issue.

While the arrow may not be for you, do not abandon the need or commitment to be involved in the planning process. Ministry based on spontaneous or haphazard programming is not effective ministry.

Why "waste" the time planning? The question comes from an inadequate view of the planning process. Planning does not take time away from you, it gives you a framework for being a good steward with your time. Planning helps eliminate wasteful or unnecessary efforts. Planning helps to focus our energy, and thereby increase the effective use of our time.

Of course, planning without follow-up is useless. But that is not the issue raised by this question. Like any book, you'll need to read and apply the parts that affect you and increase your effectiveness.

We must also understand that discouragement comes whenever we sense ourselves falling short of our predetermined goals. Failure is not the act of falling down. Failure is staying down and not trying again. Don't make your program goals a god. Be ready to learn from many of your plans that will fall short of pre-established goals. Learning takes place with continued questioning and planning. The question should not be, "Did we fail or succeed?" The question should be, "What are we learning as we journey together? And how can we apply that learning to create an environment of nurture and development?"

How often should we plan? I recommend reviewing your arrow (purpose statement, objectives, needs and programs) every six months minimum. Brainstorm and review in a retreat setting, incorporating as many young adults as is feasible.

QUESTION: **The senior pastor has authorized the institution of a program with young adults, but he doesn't seem to place a high priority on its development. He still sees young adults in terms of a payoff (money, attendance, etc.). What should I do?**

This question is all too common. That is unfortunate. But we must beware, lest we fall into the obvious trap: We hold back on our efforts, creativity, and enthusiasm because of the apathy or pessimism on the part of church leadership.

That is a difficult trap to avoid, there is a direct correlation between the health of the ministry components of a church and the health of the senior pastor and staff. That health is measured by interest, vision, the encouragement to dream, absence of self-righteousness, an absence of any need to dominate and control, and the desire that the church move forward with a unified heart.

If the attitudes reflected by your senior pastor or staff create a barrier to a healthy environment for young adult ministry, then programming cannot be conducted as if it were "business as usual." Those barriers must be addressed. The following may be helpful steps for your situations.

1. Examine your heart and motivations. If a confrontation (or at least an informative dialogue) is necessary, be aware that feelings of resentment, blame and anger will only intensify the barriers erected. There is nothing to be gained by attempting to bring about reform with an ax to grind.

2. Set up a meeting with your senior pastor (or staff person responsible for young adult ministry). Make it a lunch or breakfast if possible. Let him or her know your agenda—that you want to share your heart and dreams regarding young adult ministry. Don't use this first meeting to tell the pastor "everything the church is doing that is wrong and negative." Such an approach will only set a defensive posture for the meeting. Assume the best. It may be that the pastor's apathy is a result of unawareness or lack of proper information. Use the meeting as an opportunity to share your heart for young adult ministry, the potential impact the church can have on the community, and the environment necessary for a healthy young adult ministry. The purpose of your sharing is that it will give you the chance to tell the pastor that you are committed to your church, and to its potential in ministry with young adults. That's important. It is important that you not be seen as an instigator of discord. Your sharing also will begin to plant the seeds with the pastor that you are serious about young adult ministry, and you think the church should be as well.

If you assume a priority that such a meeting will have little effect, then you only lay the groundwork for a weak foundation that will make any attempts at young adult ministry almost impossible.

3. Take every opportunity to begin re-educating the church. Presentations or classes in adult Sunday school, inserts in the church newspaper or bulletin—all are to build support and initiative for your young adult ministry. Don't assume the church sees the need for an effective ministry with young adults. Take every opportunity to let the people dream.

4. Re-evaluate. If the first three steps fail, and the pastor still gives the air of condescension to young adult ministry, then it may be time for you to re-evaluate your role in building a ministry where there is no foundation. Leaving a church should be a last resort, and should be done with prayer and sound advice.

One final note, this whole process should not be done in isolation. If you are the only advocate, it only increases the possibility of defensiveness, frustration and knee-jerk decision-making. Make some alliances with persons in the church who will be your support structures as you walk this journey involving the strange bedfellows of church politics and ministry.

QUESTION: **Our young adult group has a Wednesday night program. It attracts a good number, but it has been referred to many times as a "meat market." What can we do to avoid this characterization? When people hear that description, it discourages them from attending.**

A bad image is not easy to overcome, especially if the image communicates that your young adult group is "just a pick-up place."

To begin, we cannot totally eliminate such an image. Whenever and wherever young adults gather (especially if the majority are single) there will be an evidence of expressed interest in the opposite sex. Whatever other reasons may bring them to the program, the hope of finding a friend—or date or mate—is somewhere on their list. There is nothing wrong with that reason. It would be foolish to pretend that the motive of meeting people of the opposite sex does not exist. Of course, if it is the only reason, then we have serious problems.

1. Discuss the issue with the group. How do we handle the situation if our group has been stereotyped, and it is starting to turn people off? I'm a believer in being up front. It will do no good to pretend the stereotype will go away if I ignore it or pray about it. My approach has been to stand before the group and tell it like it is. "A lot of people have complained to me that our group has become a pick-up joint. That's unfortunate. Because that's not why we're here. If you're here to 'hit' on someone, I'm sorry to hear that. Because this isn't the place to do that. We need this to be a place where relationships don't have to be threatening." My speech doesn't immediately solve the problem, but I do communicate that this is an issue we will not be afraid to talk about.

2. Make sure your leadership team is modeling appropriate behaviors. If members of the leadership team are using their position to take advantage of people, then change in the group as a whole will be difficult to initiate. Your leaders need to be consistent with the philosophy that a healthy young adult ministry is built on an environment where relationships are not influenced by intimidation and threat.

If there are individuals in the group who are visibly taking advantage of other persons, they should be confronted privately. Perhaps they are unaware of their behavior. If not, it needs to be clearly communicated that certain behaviors in a group context are not appropriate.

I also have learned not to take it personally when people criticize the group. I know that is easier said than done, but it is essential. An effective response to such a criticism or stereotype can only be a non-defensive response, one in which I am willing to own some of the weaknesses in the group. Because the issue for effective ministry is not whether we are perfect, but whether we're headed in the right direction.

Questions. I am sure there are many more, many that we have overlooked. Above all else, don't see you're unresolved questions as enemies to effective ministry. Effective ministry does not have all the answers, it is providing an environment where questions can be asked and discussed in openness and honesty.

Epilogue

Do you remember the first words the disciples heard after Jesus' Ascension? They were somewhat startling. "Men of Galilee, why do you stand there looking into heaven?" (Acts 1:11). In other words, "What are you waiting for? It's time to get about the business of ministry."

There's something of the disciples' "wait-and-see" attitude in all of us. I am reluctant to start anything new because of the risk factor. I am worried about rallying behind any cause because I might get "labeled." I am ambivalent about throwing all my energy into a particular ministry idea, because it might succeed and then, "What will I do?" Or, "What if my idea falls flat on its face?" I carve a comfortable road of mediocrity because I am afraid of both failure and success.

You may experience some of those emotions after reading this book. You may feel inadequate because your ministry with young adults is not as effective as it "should be." You may wish your situation and circumstances were different—more "ideal." You may feel unqualified or ill-prepared to minister with young adults. And you may wonder whether this is the right step for you. These feelings and doubts are normal. But Jesus gives you the same promise that he gave the disciples in the first chapter of Acts. They were told that they were free to risk and attempt great things for God because the Jesus who left them is faithful to his promise to live in them as they minister in his name.

Let us learn effective skills.

Let us learn to recognize ministry barriers.

Let us learn to adequately identify needs.

But let us never forget that Jesus is faithful to the end. He will not give up on us.

You may be wondering how you got to be one of "God's representatives" among young adults. Granted, young adult ministry is not easy. But now that we know that, we can get about the task.

It will not always be easy to measure success.

It will be frustrating to deal with transiency.

It will be tempting to play the numbers game.

It will be a challenge to give the ministry away.

But, in the end, it will be worth it. You may not see a harvest, but the important thing to remember is you are planting seeds. Keep planting with integrity and hope. And remember, Jesus is faithful. He will not quit.

Notes

CHAPTER 1

[1]1982-83 U.S. Census Bureau.
[2] Gail Sheehy, **Passages** (New York: Bantam Books, 1974), pp. 17-18.
[3]Ibid., p. 39.
[4]Ibid.
[5]Ibid., p. 40.
[6]Ibid., p. 41.
[7]Daniel Levinson, **The Seasons of a Man's Life** (New York: Ballantine Books, 1978), p. 139FF.
[8]1982-83 U.S. Census Bureau.
[9]Ibid.
[10]Suzanna McBei, "Here Come the Baby-Boomers," U.S. News and World Report (November 1984):68.
[11]Ibid., p. 71.
[12]"The Year of the Yuppy," Newsweek (December 1984):14.
[13]McBei, "Here Come the Baby-Boomers," p. 71.
[14]Orange County Register, 23 December 1984.
[15]Gallup Poll Data, **Emerging Trends,** February 1981, Princeton Religious Research Center.
[16]R.T. Gribbon, **When People Seek the Church** (Washington, D.C.: The Alban Institute, 1982), p. 3.
[17]Orange County Register, 31 December 1984.
[18]Gribbon, **When People Seek the Church,** p. 14.

CHAPTER 2

[1]Gail Sheehy, **Pathfinders** (New York: Morrow, 1981), p. 168.

[2]Ibid., pp. 114-115.

[3]Ibid.

[4]"The Year of the Yuppy," Newsweek (December 1984):29.

[5]Sheehy, **Pathfinders,** p. 115.

[6]Gail Sheehy, **Passages** (New York: Bantam Books, 1974), p. 84.

[7]Ibid., p. 85.

[8]"The Year of the Yuppy," p. 19.

[9]LA Times, 18 August 1985.

[10]Sheehy, **Pathfinders,** p. 168.

[11]Ibid., p. 128.

[12]Ibid., p. 109.

[13]"The Year of the Yuppy," p. 19.

[14]Suzanna McBei, "Here Come the Baby-Boomers," U.S. News and World Report (November 1984):71.

[15]R.T. Gribbon, **30-Year-Olds and the Church: Ministry With the Baby-Boom Generation** (Washington, D.C.: The Alban Institute, 1981), p. 3.

CHAPTER 3

[1]Heidi Yorkshire, "Esprit—Making Them All California Girls," Pacific Southwest Airlines (September 1985):14.

[2]"The Year of the Yuppy," Newsweek (December 1984):19.

[3]LA Times, 18 August 1985.

[4]"Marriage and Divorce Today" Leadership (May 1982):2.

[5]Keith Miller, **The Single Experience** (Waco, TX: Word, 1981), p. 228.

[6]Andrew Greeley, **Sexual Intimacy** (London: Thomas Moore, 1973), p. 161.

[7]Henri Nouwen, **The Wounded Healer** (New York: Image Books, 1979), p. 84.

[8]USA Today, 11 June 1985.

CHAPTER 4

[1]R.T. Gribbon, **Congregations, Students and Young Adults** (Washington, D.C.: The Alban Institute, 1978), p. 6.

[2]Ibid., p. 3.

[3]Ibid., p. 65.

[4]Gail Sheehy, **Passages** (New York: Bantam Books, 1974), p. 49.

[5]Gribbon, **Congregations, Students and Young Adults,** p. 15.

[6]Andrew Greeley, **Sexual Intimacy** (London: Thomas Moore, 1973), pp. 28-29.

[7]Gribbon, **Congregations, Students and Young Adults,** p. 14.
[8]Ibid.
[9]Ibid., p. 7.

CHAPTER 5

[1]R.T. Gribbon, **Congregations, Students and Young Adults** (Washington, D.C.: The Alban Institute, 1978), p. A9.
[2]James Fowler, **Stages of Faith: The Psychology of Human Development and the Quest for Meaning** (San Francisco: Harper and Row, 1981), p. 290.
[3]Gribbon, **Congregations, Students and Young Adults,** p. 17.
[4]Daniel Levinson, **The Seasons of a Man's Life** (New York: Ballantine Books, 1978), p. 91.
[5]Carol Weisner, "Why Young Adults Don't Pursue the Church," The Lutheran (June 1985):6.
[6]R.T. Gribbon, **When People Seek the Church** (Washington, D.C.: The Alban Institute, 1982), p. 18.

CHAPTER 6

[1]Morris West, **The Shoes of the Fisherman** (New York: Bantam Books, 1963), p. 112.
[2]Ibid., p. 67.
[3]Henri Nouwen, **The Wounded Healer: Ministry in Contemporary Society** (New York: Image Books, 1979), pp. 81-82.
[4]Ben Patterson, "Hanging on for the Eighth Year," Leadership 1 (Summer 1981):42.

CHAPTER 7

[1]1982-83 U.S. Census Bureau.
[2]"The View From Above: An Interview With Terry Fullum," Leadership 5 (Winter 1984):17.

CHAPTER 9

[1]C.S. Lewis, **Mere Christianity** (New York: Macmillan, 1964), p. 153.
[2]Rick Yohn, **Discover Your Spiritual Gift and Use It** (Wheaton, IL: Tyndale, 1982).

CHAPTER 10

[1]Modified Houts Questionnaire, Charles E. Fuller Institute of

Evangelism and Church Growth, P.O. Box 989, Pasadena, CA 91102, Copyright 1981, Fuller Evangelistic Association.

CHAPTER 13

[1]R.T. Gribbon, **Congregations, Students and Young Adults** (Washington, D.C.: The Alban Institute, 1978), pp. 49-52.

CHAPTER 14

[1]R.T. Gribbon, **The Problem of Faith Development in Young Adults** (Washington, D.C.: The Alban Institute, 1977), p. 11.
[2]Kenneth Leech, **Soul Friend: The Practice of Christian Spirituality** (San Francisco: Harper and Row, 1980).

CHAPTER 15

[1]Adapted with permission from SALT Newsletter Copyright © 1984, Vol. 1, #4, January. P.O. Box 1231, Sisters, OR 97759.
[2]Ibid., 1984, Vol. 1, #8, May.
[3]Ibid., 1984, Vol. 1, #9, June.
[4]Ibid., 1984, Vol. 2, #1, October.
[5]Ibid., 1985, Vol. 2, #9, June.
[6]Ibid.
[7]Ibid., 1985, Vol. 2, #10, July.
[8]Ibid., 1983, Vol. 1, #1, October
[9]Ibid., 1985, Vol. 2, #12, September.
[10]Ibid.
[11]Ibid., 1984, Vol. 1, #7, April.
[12]Questions adapted from Bobbie Reed, **Single on Sunday: A Manual for Successful Single Adult Ministries** (St. Louis, MO: Concordia, 1979).

CHAPTER 16

[1]From Terry Hershey, **Intimacy: Where Do I Go to Find Love?** Write to: Christian Focus, P.O. Box 17134, Irvine, CA 92714.
[2]James Carroll, **Prince of Peace** (Boston: Little, Brown and Co., 1984).
[3]Margery Williams, **Velveteen Rabbit** (New York: Doubleday, 1958).
[4]Lee Sparks, **Try This One ... Too** (Loveland, CO: Group Books, 1982), p. 31.
[5]Thom Schultz, **More ... Try This One** (Loveland, CO: Group

Books, 1980), p. 18.

[6]Cindy S. Hansen, **Try This One ... Strikes Again** (Loveland, CO: Group Books, 1984), p. 49.

[7]C.S. Lewis, **Four Loves** (San Diego: HarBraceJ, 1971), p. 169.

[8]Denny Rydberg, **Building Community in Youth Groups** (Loveland, CO: Group Books, 1985), p. 71.

[9]Andrew Greeley, **Sexual Intimacy** (Minneapolis: Winston Press, 1975), pp. 149-160.

[10]Rydberg, **Building Community in Youth Groups,** p. 75.

[11]Morris West, **The Shoes of the Fisherman** (New York: Bantam, 1982), p. 186.

[12]Rydberg, **Building Community in Youth Groups,** p. 87.

[13]For more information write to Christian Focus.

[14]Rydberg, **Building Community in Youth Groups,** pp. 61-62.

[15]Eugene Peterson, **A Long Obedience in the Same Direction** (Downers Grove, IL: InterVarsity, 1980), pp. 174-175.

[16]Ibid., pp. 175-176.

[17]Thom Schultz, **The Best of Try This One** (Loveland, CO: Group Books, 1977), pp. 40-41.

[18]David Augsburger, **Caring Enough to Confront** (Scottdale, PA: Herald Press, 1980).

[19]Rydberg, **Building Community in Youth Groups,** p. 61.

[20]Hansen, **Try This One ... Strikes Again,** p. 49.

[21]C.S. Lewis, **The Weight of Glory** (New York: Macmillan, 1980), pp. 14-15.

[22]For more information, write to Christian Focus.

[23]Lee R. Steiner, **Where Do People Take Their Troubles?** (Boston: Houghton Mifflin, 1945), p. 105.

[24]Clark Moustakas, **Loneliness** (Englewood Cliffs, NJ: Prentice Hall, 1961), pp. 34-35.

[25]Henry Nouwen, **The Wounded Healer** (New York: Doubleday, 1979), p. 92.

[26]Ibid., p. 84.

[27]**The New Oxford Annotated Bible With the Apocrypha** (New York: Oxford University Press, 1977), p. 1446.

[28]For more information, write to Christian Focus or Tim and Karen Jackson, Grace Community Church, 3201 South Terrace Road, Tempe, AZ 85282.

[29]Hershey, **Intimacy: Where Do I Go to Find Love?,** For more information, write to Christian Focus.

[30]Andrea Miller, **The Single Experience** (Waco, TX: Word,

1981), p. 194.

[31]Ibid., pp. 192-193.

[32]Rydberg, **Building Community in Youth Groups,** p. 89.

[33]Hansen, **Try This One ... Strikes Again,** p. 20.

[34]Schultz, **The Best of Try This One,** p. 14.

[35]For more information, write to Christian Focus.

[36]Ibid.

[37]Schultz, **More ... Try This One,** p. 49.

[38]For more information, write to Christian Focus. Idea adapted from Harold Ivan Smith.

[39]Sparks, **Try This One ... Too,** p. 50.

Resources

BOOKS FOR PERSONAL GROWTH

Passages, Gail Sheehy (Bantam)
 A helpful look at adult transition. From "Breaking Away" at age 18 through the "Trying Twenties" and the "Catch 30" crisis. How do those normal transitions affect who we are today?

Pathfinders, Gail Sheehy (Morrow)
 Not everyone finds life worthwhile. Why? What are the elements common to those who live life to the fullest? Sheehy's work makes good material for discussion groups and seminars.

The Road Less Traveled, Scott Peck (Touchstone)
 "Life is difficult," the book begins. And that's the thesis. A healthy life is one that develops the tools—discipline—to face the real—difficult—world.

Celebrating the Single Life, Susan Muto (Doubleday)
 The emphasis upon celebration is the key. It refocuses our attention on our ability to choose and not on the liability of our marital status.

When I Relax I Feel Guilty, Tim Hansel (Cook)
 We can't slow down. We can't say "no." But if we want to live "real life," those are two skills we need to learn. Tim is practical and very helpful.

The Single Experience, Keith and Andrea Wells Miller (Word)
 Being single can be rough sometimes, but it also can be rewarding.

It can be a tremendous time for evaluating priorities, discovering what really matters to you, and for honestly approaching God ... and yourself. This book faces the issues with the insight and personal honesty that will help make the single experience really count.

A Reason to Live! A Reason to Die! John Powell (Argus)
Discusses how coming to terms with everyday crises in life can open our eyes to a more meaningful life and faith. Faith is an I-Thou relationship between a person and his personal God, and as long as we accept life's situations, we will become more aware of both life and ourselves.

Healing for Damaged Emotions, David Seamands (Victor)
If you are hurting emotionally, this book will help you. Dr. Seamands is sensitive and has insight into today's emotional stresses, especially as they relate to spiritual growth and understanding. A book recommended for professionals, as well as lay people.

Freedom of Simplicity, Richard J. Foster (Harper & Row)
In this age of scarcity, in a society plagued by the unreasoning, self-destructive mania to achieve and accumulate, simplicity may be the only option left to us; but it is an option to be free and fulfilled, to live with grace, balance and joy.

Unconditional Love, John Powell (Argus)
The only love worthy of the name is unconditional love. It is genuine; it is the way God loves us; it is the way we should love others. There are no doubts in unconditional love, only total acceptance of another person.

Freedom From Guilt, Bruce Narramore/Bill Counts (Harvest House)
In this book, the authors combine their psychological and biblical insights to explore the dark caverns of human emotions and illuminate the path that leads through complete forgiveness to self-acceptance, spontaneous freedom and exhilarating growth. There is freedom from guilt.

Putting Away Childish Things, David A. Seamands (Victor)
David Seamands has written to help others identify their outdated childish patterns and then suggests ways of breaking them in order that they may grow to the Christian maturity God desires for them.

The Valiant Papers, Calvin Miller (Zondervan)
This book reveals the trials of being a guardian angel to a wayward

and difficult mortal who has yet to say yes to Christ. It speaks very pointedly to the undisciplined Christian and has an interesting section on sexuality and the single adult.

BOOKS FOR MINISTRY

Singles: The New Americans, Simenauer/Carroll (Simon and Schuster)

This book contains the results of a major national research effort (surveying 3,000 singles) to determine what they are thinking, feeling, wanting and doing. Research was completed in 1982. The book covers such topics as "How and Where Singles Get Together," "Dating Problems, Issues and Pleasures," "Sex and the Single Person," "The Single Parent," etc.

Reach Out to Singles, Raymond Kay Brown (Westminster)

Nearly one-half of our nation's adult population is single, yet singles comprise only a fraction of the church's membership. Why aren't single adults active in church? According to the author, the problem with singles ministry is the church itself. He presents a general assessment of the need for singles ministries as well as an overview of the pressures under which single adults live and the problems they face including a discussion of stereotypes many church people believe concerning single adults. Several options for ministry with singles are also explored.

BOOKS ON RELATIONSHIPS AND SEXUALITY

Intimacy: Where Do I Go To Find Love?, Terry Hershey

Intimacy. What is it? And why are we afraid of it? A practical look at the masks we wear, myths we carry and the necessary steps to develop this elusive thing called intimacy. For information, write Christian Focus, P.O. Box 17134, Irvine, CA 92714.

Eros Defiled: The Christian & Sexual Sin, John White (Inter-Varsity)

Premarital sex, extramarital sex, homosexuality and various forms of twisted sex. Dr. John White speaks with understanding and compassion about each of these sexual sins. He concludes with a telling chapter on how local churches can be communities for dealing with sexual sin in a context of love and forgiveness.

The Sexual Celibate, Donald Goergan (Image)

A look at celibacy from a Catholic perspective which ties in some good insights on the nature of friendship and the necessity of friends on our personal journey.

The End of Sex, George Leonard (Tarcher)

From a member of the "free sex movement" of the '60s, George Leonard's re-evaluation promises to give us a strong argument for a healthy context for sexuality. Well worth reading.

Sex for Christians, Lewis Smedes (Eerdmans)

Someone who's willing to openly address sacred cows. Smedes looks at masturbation, petting, premarital intercourse, adultery and homosexuality, not from a legalistic standpoint, but from a framework of responsibility and freedom.

The New Celibacy: Why More Men and Women are Abstaining from Sex and Enjoying It, Gabrielle Brown (McGraw Hill)

Those in single adult leadership will find this book particularly helpful with the notion, "I'm missing out on something ..." There are also some great practical helps for living a celibate life.

Caring Enough to Confront, David Augsburger (Regal)

Discussing trust, anger, change, prejudice, blame, guilt, loyalty and conscience, the author describes a lifestyle for Christians who care enough to risk confronting others when differences become important. Especially for the Christians who care deeply about relationships.

The Romance Factor, Alan Loy McGinnis (Harper & Row)

Warm, practical and inspiring ... truly romantic and Christian ... lends growth and insight into the marriage experience.

Living With Unfulfilled Desires, Walter Trobisch (InterVarsity)

This book relays the art of living a fulfilled life in spite of many unfulfilled desires. This is a compilation of letters written to answer the questions of teenagers and college students requesting counseling. Answers concerning areas of sex and romance such as daydreaming, petting, masturbation and homosexual affection are presented in a Christian perspective.

Why Am I Afraid to Love?, John Powell (Argus)

There is a capacity and a need to love and to be loved within each of us. Powell proposes how we might overcome our fear of rejection and realize our potential for a better, more meaningful life.

The Secret of Staying in Love, John Powell (Argus)
Explores the fundamental prerequisite to personal sharing: a joyful and genuine acceptance of self, the ability to say, "I'm really glad to be me!" Also shows how an awareness of our feelings can tell us a great deal about ourselves.

Why Am I Afraid to Tell You Who I Am?, John Powell (Argus)
Offers insights on self-awareness, growth and interpersonal communication. Discusses dealing with emotions, growing as a person and ego defenses. Concludes that the courage it takes for a person to reveal himself to others is based on a mature love.

A Love Story, Tim Stafford (Zondervan)
This is a good book for understanding what sex can do to a relationship and why it should be waited on. The letters in the book are written by people who are asking honest questions and Tim Stafford answers them well, using scripture and other real-life testimonies.

Dating & Relating, Cherie Scalf/Kenneth Walters (Word)
Brings refreshing candor to all aspects of Christian dating—from arranging that all-important first date to handling such sticky subjects as sex and going out with nonbelievers. In between there's a lot of practical help on communication, friendship and living the Christian life. A down-to-earth but eyes-to-the-skies approach to healthy single relationships.

Givers, Takers & Other Kinds of Lovers, Josh McDowell/Paul Lewis (Tyndale)
This book focuses on God's plan for marriage and sex and presents clear reasons why God's plan works best. God's plan is as complete and realistic as it is positive and happy. There is no reason to settle for less.

BOOKS ON MARRIAGE AND DIVORCE

Your Marriage Is God's Affair, Dwight Small (Revell)
A strong biblical basis for a healthy marriage, and a look at those things which are essential to keeping a marriage on the "right track."

Before Saying "I Do," James Christensen (Revell)
Have we done our homework before walking down the aisle? What are some of the questions we've missed?

More Than I Do, Harold Ivan Smith (Beacon Hill)
One of the three books which make up a premarital counseling set. This private devotional book for engaged couples invites heart-searching consideration of each other's spiritual as well as personal life.

Try Marriage Before Divorce, Dr. James Kilgore (Word)
Prescription for making a marriage work. Includes a collection of 30 self-disclosure or sharing exercises to be used for improving communication.

Letters to Karen, Charlie Shedd (Abingdon)
In this book, a loving father writes his engaged daughter a series of letters on the art of keeping love in a marriage. He gives examples from his own wonderful 25 years of marriage with her mother, on understanding, communication, remaining exciting and other important keys to a successful, happy marriage.

The Divorcing Christian, Lewis R. Rambo (Abingdon)
The author deals with possible adjustment problems faced by the newly divorced Christian. These adjustment measures are explored based on the author's own experiences.

Beginning Again: Life After a Relationship Ends, Terry Hershey (Thomas Nelson)
Effectively weaves practical suggestions and helpful discussions on coping with the loss of a love into the Gospel message of forgiveness and "beginning again." Comes with study guide, leader's guide, and cassette tapes. For information, write Christian Focus, P.O. Box 17134, Irvine, CA 92714.

BOOKS FOR CAREER

The Success Fantasy, Anthony Campolo (Victor)
How much success do you need to feel important? How much success can you take without being trapped? Is there a Christian way to succeed without greed? As society's false views of success invade our homes and churches, they erode Christian character. This book explains how this is happening, and why, and what we must do about

it. It is a penetrating analysis of the contemporary idolatry of success. But it is more than an analysis. It is a plea for the claims of Christ upon our value system.

The Pursuit of Excellence, Ted Engstrom (Zondervan)

Calls people to stretch themselves, to give up their small ambitions, and to pursue the path of excellence, using examples from scripture to show how God's people down through the ages have followed this mandate. Each chapter includes workable steps for a strategy for excellence in every area of life.

BOOKS TO ADAPT FOR YOUNG ADULT MINISTRY

The Group Retreat Book, Arlo Reichter (Group)

A one-stop retreat resource book. Offers dozens of tried-and-true retreat outlines by successful youth leaders. Excellent help for planning and conducting retreats. Big collection of topics that meets the needs of today's young people.

Spiritual Growth in Youth Ministry, J. David Stone (Group)

Practical approaches to building a young person's faith. This book has step-by-step instruction for an easy-to-follow program that really works with youth. Provides leaders with resources to meet young people's deep-rooted hunger for God.

Friend to Friend, J. David Stone/Larry Keefauver (Group)

Most people never turn to professional counselors with their struggles. They turn to friends. **Friend to Friend** shows you a simple step-by-step process that you can use to lead your friend through a problem. You'll be ready to respond in Christian love when your friends really need you.

Clown Ministry, Floyd Shaffer/Penne Sewall (Group)

Discuss the excitement of sharing the clown minister's childlike faith. Experience the warmth and joy of ministering to young and old alike. This book offers practical tips for every aspect of clown ministry. Plus, there are 30 detailed skits to use for Christian service and worship.

HANDBOOKS

"Transition and Support" Resource Handbook

Have you ever been in a situation where you needed to refer someone to a counselor? to a school? to a helpful book? Here's a good idea from Solana Beach Presbyterian Church. They have done their homework and put together a referral and resource pamphlet. It is an approach that says, "If there's help to be found, we can find it together." The pamphlet includes counseling services, colleges and continuing education programs, career opportunities, books and crisis intervention facilities.

They state their purpose on the inside page:

> This brochure was compiled by the Christian Singles Steering Committee of the United Presbyterian Church, Solana Beach. It is designed especially for those in transition and/or in need of personal support. The information included, however, is of value to everyone.
>
> Many of the groups and resources listed here are neither sponsored nor endorsed by the church. These are merely a few resources in the community that are available. The listings are not exhaustive but, rather, designed as a means of assisting you in your search. An additional list of referrals may be obtained at the church office.

For information, contact Christian Singles Steering Committee, United Presbyterian Church, 120 Stevens Ave., Solana Beach, CA 92075, (619) 755-9735.

MAGAZINES

YAM—Young Adult Ministries
The Young Adult Calvinist Federation
P.O. Box 7244
Grand Rapids, MI 49510
(616) 241-5616

Spirit Magazine
P.O. Box 1231
Sisters, OR 97759

ASSOCIATIONS

YAM—Young Calvinist Federation
Box 7244
Grand Rapids, MI 49510
(616) 241-5616

The Young Calvinist Armed Services Ministry
P.O. Box 7259
Grand Rapids, MI 49510

National Catholic Young Adult Ministry Association
4665 Willowbrook Ave.
Los Angeles, CA 90029

NEWSLETTERS

SALT Newsletter, P.O. Box 1231, Sisters, OR 97759, (503) 549-0442.

Small Group Letter, P.O. Box 1164, Dover, NJ 07801,
(201) 366-1654.

Action Information, Alban Institute, 4124 Nebraska Ave. NW,
Washington, D.C. 20016, (800) 457-2674.

Ministries With Young Adults, 2900 Queen Lane, Philadelphia, PA
19129, (215) 438-5600.

Trackings, 475 Riverside Dr., New York, NY 10115, (212) 870-2694.

Young Adult Ministry Packet, Reformed Church in America, 1790
Grand Blvd., Schenectady, NY 12309.

Apply It To Life™

Adult

BIBLE CURRICULUM
from Group

A PRACTICAL, EASY-TO-TEACH CURRICULUM FOR ADULTS

Think back on an important lesson you've learned in life. Did you learn it from reading about it? from hearing about it? from something you experienced? Chances are, the most important lessons you've learned came from something you experienced. That's active learning—a key element in Group's innovative curriculum for adults. Group's APPLY-IT-TO-LIFE ADULT BIBLE CURRICULUM™ encourages adults to...

- discover from each other's experiences how to grow closer to God,
- dig into the Scriptures and come away with a personal application of the passages,
- explore how God works through relationships, and
- learn what it means to be a Christian in a non-Christian world.

Each topic covers four lessons and includes everything needed for a class of any size: complete leaders guide, handout masters you can photocopy, publicity helps, and bonus ideas. Choose any or all of the eight titles now available...and turn your adult Bible studies in a new, active direction.

APPLYING THE BIBLE TO LIFE
ISBN 1-55945-504-7

THE CHURCH: WHAT AM I DOING HERE?
ISBN 1-55945-294-3

COMMUNICATION: ENHANCING YOUR RELATIONSHIPS
ISBN 1-55945-297-8

EVANGELISM FOR EVERY DAY
ISBN 1-55945-298-6

FAITH IN THE WORKPLACE
ISBN 1-55945-299-4

FREEDOM: SEEING YOURSELF AS GOD SEES YOU
ISBN 1-55945-502-0

JESUS
ISBN 1-55945-500-4

STRENGTHENING FAMILY RELATIONSHIPS
ISBN 1-55945-501-2

Order today from your local Christian bookstore, or write:
Group Publishing, Box 485, Loveland, CO 80539.

ANCIENT SECRETS of the BIBLE
COLLECTORS SERIES

PERFECT FOR CHURCH, CLASSROOM, AND HOME USE.

You'll see biblically accurate dramatizations. Expert testimony. Faith-building experiments. Thought-provoking debate. And you'll get a FREE 16-page Discussion Guide with each video. Perfect for Sunday school classes, home Bible studies, mid-week and youth group meetings, home schooling, adult courses, or whenever you want to explore Scripture.

WHICH OF THESE 13 VIDEOS WOULD YOU MOST LIKE TO ADD TO YOUR PERSONAL OR CHURCH COLLECTION?

Ark of the Covenant: Lost or Hidden Away?	ISBN 1-55945-733-3
Battle of David and Goliath: Truth or Myth?	ISBN 1-55945-729-5
The Fiery Furnace: Could Anyone Survive It?	ISBN 1-55945-736-8
Moses' Red Sea Miracle: Did It Happen?	ISBN 1-55945-731-7
Moses' Ten Commandments: Tablets From God?	ISBN 1-55945-732-5
Noah's Ark: Fact or Fable?	ISBN 1-55945-725-2
Noah's Ark: Was There a Worldwide Flood?	ISBN 1-55945-726-0
Noah's Ark: What Happened To It?	ISBN 1-55945-727-9
Samson: Strongman Hero or Legend?	ISBN 1-55945-735-X
Shroud of Turin: Fraud or Evidence of Christ's Resurrection?	ISBN 1-55945-737-6
Sodom and Gomorrah: Legend or Real Event?	ISBN 1-55945-730-9
Tower of Babel: Fact or Fiction?	ISBN 1-55945-728-7
Walls of Jericho: Did They Tumble Down?	ISBN 1-55945-734-1

GET IN ON THE SECRETS! EACH VIDEO IS GUARANTEED TO START DISCUSSIONS, TEACH BIBLICAL TRUTHS, AND SHED LIGHT ON BIBLE MYSTERIES! GET YOUR COPY TODAY!

From Group, the Innovator in Christian Education!

Order today from your local Christian bookstore, or write:
Group Publishing, Box 485, Loveland, CO 80539.